Andreas Roth

# Specification and Verification of Object-Oriented Software Components

# Specification and Verification of Object-Oriented Software Components

by
Andreas Roth

universitätsverlag karlsruhe

Dissertation, Universität Karlsruhe (TH)
Fakultät für Informatik, 2006

**Impressum**

Universitätsverlag Karlsruhe
c/o Universitätsbibliothek
Straße am Forum 2
D-76131 Karlsruhe
www.uvka.de



Universitätsverlag Karlsruhe 2006
Print on Demand

ISBN 3-86644-042-1

# Specification and Verification of Object-Oriented Software Components

Zur Erlangung des akademischen Grades eines

**Doktors der Naturwissenschaften**

von der Fakultät für Informatik

der Universität Karlsruhe (TH)

genehmigte

# Dissertation

von

**Andreas Roth**

aus Stuttgart

Tag der mündlichen Prüfung: 7. Februar 2006

Erster Gutachter: Prof. Dr. P. H. Schmitt, Universität Karlsruhe (TH)

Zweiter Gutachter: Prof. Dr. U. Aßmann, Technische Universität Dresden

# Acknowledgements

Many people contributed to this work in many ways, and I am grateful to all of them.

In first place, I would like to sincerely thank my supervisor, Prof. Dr. Peter H. Schmitt for giving me the opportunity to work on this project, for the freedom he gave me to pursue my ideas, for his careful support and guidance, and his valuable comments on earlier drafts of this thesis.

I am grateful to Prof. Dr. Uwe Aßmann for acting as second reviewer and for his positive response to my work.

I am deeply indebted to my colleagues Richard Bubel and Steffen Schlager for the many discussions we had, for the innumerable questions I got answered, for all joint work, for the excellent working atmosphere, and for your friendship. Thank you very much!

This work could not have been done without the inspiring background of the KeY project, for which I have worked for eight years, first as a student assistant then as a staff member. I would thus like to thank the project leaders and co-founders of KeY, Prof. Dr. Bernhard Beckert, Prof. Dr. Reiner Hähnle, Prof. Dr. Wolfram Menzel, and Prof. Schmitt, for creating this ambitious project and its motivating environment. Many thanks go to all (former) members of KeY, not already mentioned above, I had the pleasure to work with more closely during that time: to Prof. Dr. Wolfgang Ahrendt, Dr. Thomas Baar, Dr. Martin Giese, Vladimir Klebanov, Dr. Wojciech Mostowski, and Philipp Rümmer.

Thanks a lot to the students having assisted in the KeY project, who did their indispensable work with a lot of commitment. Especially, I would like to thank Christian Engel and Benjamin Weiß, whose work substantially supported my work on this thesis.

Finally a huge Thank You goes to my wife Melanie and my little son Jonas: Writing this thesis would have been so much harder without you!

Karlsruhe, May 2006
Andreas Roth

# Spezifikation und Verifikation objektorientierter Software-Komponenten

## (Deutsche Zusammenfassung)

In den letzten Jahren hat die *formale Spezifikation* und *deduktive Verifikation* objektorientierter Programme, die in kommerziell eingesetzten Sprachen geschrieben sind, wesentliche Fortschritte gemacht. Ein Beispiel für eine moderne Spezifikations- und Verifikationsumgebung ist das KeY System, das die Spezifikation mit Standard-Spezifikationssprachen unterstützt, und erlaubt, sequentielle Java-Programme gegen diese zu verifizieren.

Formale Spezifikation und Verifikation auf der Ebene einzelner Klassen und Methoden sind bei dem gegenwärtigen Stand der Wissenschaft recht gut verstanden. Der konsequente nächste und in dieser Arbeit verfolgte Schritt besteht heute darin, die erzielten Erfolge auf größere Programmeinheiten auszudehnen, das heißt ganze Komponenten komplett zu spezifizieren und zu verifizieren. Eine solche Vorgehensweise könnte das Vertrauen in von Dritten entwickelte Komponenten wesentlich erhöhen und damit die Wiederbenutzung fremdentwickelter Komponenten fördern.

Zwar ist es mit den bisherigen Ansätzen möglich, eine einzelne Komponente oder auch ein aus Komponenten aufgebautes Programm zu verifizieren. Darauf, dass eine verifizierte Komponente ihre Spezifikation in jedem beliebigen Wiederverwendungs-Kontext erfüllt, kann allerdings nicht unmittelbar geschlossen werden. Ein Hauptgrund ist die Anfälligkeit von Klassen-Invarianten, über *Aliasing*-Effekte unkontrolliert beeinflusst zu werden. Ein weiterer Grund ist, dass über den Wiederverwendungs-Kontext keine Annahmen getroffen werden können, z.B. dass Methoden nicht unbedingt konform überschrieben werden. Da eine erneute Verifikation einer Komponente in jedem neuen Kontext jedoch generell sehr aufwändig ist, und dieser Aufwand

Nutzern einer Komponente nicht zumutbar ist, ist *modulare Korrektheit*, d.h. die Erhaltung von Korrektheit unter Komposition, ein unverzichtbares Ziel. Ist dieses Ziel erreicht, ist es kein weiter Schritt mehr zu Komponenten, deren formale Spezifikation garantiert eingehalten wird.

Die Arbeit beschränkt sich auf sequentielle Programme der Sprache Java. Insbesondere leistet sie folgende Beiträge:

- Der Begriff der *Korrektheit* eines (möglicherweise in beliebigen Kontexten eingesetzten) Java-Programms bezüglich einer funktionalen Spezifikation auf der Basis getypter Prädikatenlogik wird formal gefasst. Das zentrale Modell hierbei ist das eines *Beobachters*, der Aufrufe auf dem Programm vornimmt, und die Ergebnisse nach Beendigung des Aufrufs beurteilt.

- Ein im Vergleich zu bisherigen Ansätzen, wie Besitz-basierten (*ownership*) Systemen [Müller, 2002] oder eindeutigen Zeigern (*unique pointers*) [Boyland, 2001] sehr ausdrucksstarkes Konzept, die für die modulare Korrektheit essentielle *Kapselung* von Daten in Programmen zu formalisieren, wird vorgeschlagen. Es lehnt sich stark an die Formalisierung von üblichen Klassen-Invarianten an und erweitert hierzu Spezifikationssprachen um Kapselungsprädikate.

- Da in den meisten Fällen der Kontext einer Komponente bestimmte Voraussetzungen erfüllen muss, damit die Komponente die gewünschte Leistung erbringt, wird der Begriff eines *generischen Erweiterungsvertrags* definiert, mit dem Einschränkungen an den Kontext spezifiziert werden können. Darauf aufbauend werden *Komponentenverträge* definiert: Wenn ein Kontext bestimmte Erweiterungsverträge erfüllt, sichert eine Komponente ihre Korrektheit bezüglich einer herkömmlichen Spezifikation zu.

- Der Kalkül für die Programmlogik *Java Dynamische Logik*, der sich in Beckert [2000] auf einen festen Programmkontext bezog, wird so verändert, dass man auch sich erweiternde Kontexte, wie sie im Zusammenhang mit Komponenten auftreten, betrachten kann. Besonderes Augenmerk gilt der Regel zum Abarbeiten des dynamischen Methodenbindens. Hier wird modulares Beweisen mit Hilfe von Methodenverträgen verlangt, die – durch Erweiterungsverträge sichergestellt – auch vom Wiederverwendungskontext erfüllt werden müssen.

- Den Kern der Arbeit bildet ein Ansatz zum Nachweis der modularen Korrektheit von einfädigen Java Programmen. Es werden *Beweisverpflichtungen* zum Nachweis von Methoden-Kontrakten, Klassen-Invarianten und *Assignable*-Klauseln (d.h. Angaben welche Lokationen eine Methode höchstens verändern darf) vorgestellt. Ferner werden Techniken zum Beweisen von Kapselungseigenschaften vorgestellt.

  Modulare (*dauerhafte*) Korrektheit von Invarianten in offenen komponentenbasierten Systemen basiert auf der Analyse von Invarianten über *Abhängigkeitsklauseln* und wird danach über zwei Techniken sichergestellt: *Selbst-Wächter* sind Klassen, die volle Kontrolle über eine für den Schutz der Invariante wichtigen Lokation haben. *Wächter* sind Klassen, die dafür sorgen, dass für diese Lokationen relevanten Objekte, nicht aus der Kontrolle der Wächter entkommen. Dies wird über eine spezielle Beweisverpflichtung auf der Basis von Kapselungsprädikaten sichergestellt. Außerdem müssen sowohl *Selbst-Wächter* als auch *Wächter* – und nur diese – die fragliche Invariante erhalten.

  Mit diesem Ansatz können Programme spezifiziert und verifiziert werden, die in unbekannten Kontexten oder in Kontexten mit bestimmten Eigenschaften (die durch Erweiterungsverträge beschrieben sind) eingesetzt werden.

- Die erarbeiteten Ansätze können mit dem KeY-System eingesetzt werden und sind an kleinen Fallbeispielen erprobt worden.

# Contents


**1 Introduction** **1**
- 1.1 State of the Art . . . . . 1
- 1.2 Problems . . . . . 3
- 1.3 Contributed Solutions . . . . . 10
- 1.4 Outline . . . . . 12

**2 Preliminaries** **13**
- 2.1 Closed and Open Programs and Components . . . . . 13
- 2.2 Java First Order Logic . . . . . 16
  - 2.2.1 Syntax . . . . . 16
  - 2.2.2 Semantics . . . . . 20
  - 2.2.3 Locations . . . . . 24
  - 2.2.4 Extended Terms . . . . . 24
- 2.3 Java Dynamic Logic . . . . . 28
  - 2.3.1 Updates . . . . . 29
  - 2.3.2 Syntax . . . . . 31
  - 2.3.3 Semantics . . . . . 32
  - 2.3.4 Additional Details . . . . . 33
  - 2.3.5 The JavaDL Calculus . . . . . 35
  - 2.3.6 Initialisation . . . . . 39
- 2.4 Proof Obligations . . . . . 41

**I Specifications for Extensibility** **43**

**3 Functional Specifications of Programs** **45**
- 3.1 Essentials of Formal Specifications of Programs . . . . . 46
  - 3.1.1 Operation Contracts . . . . . 47
  - 3.1.2 Invariants . . . . . 50
- 3.2 Observed-State Program Correctness . . . . . 51

3.2.1 Assumptions before Operation Calls . . . . . . . . . . . . 53
3.2.2 Operation Calls . . . . . . . . . . . . . . . . . . . . . . . . 58
3.2.3 Assertions of Operation Calls . . . . . . . . . . . . . . . 60
3.2.4 Treatment of Static Initialisation . . . . . . . . . . . . . 65
3.2.5 Assertions in the Initial State . . . . . . . . . . . . . . . 66
3.2.6 Naive Correctness . . . . . . . . . . . . . . . . . . . . . . 67
3.2.7 Observed-State Call Correctness . . . . . . . . . . . . . . 68
3.2.8 Observed-State Durable Correctness . . . . . . . . . . . 69
3.2.9 Relations between Durable and Call Correctness . . . . 70
3.2.10 Discussion of Observed-State Correctness . . . . . . . . 72
3.3 Specification Languages . . . . . . . . . . . . . . . . . . . . . . 74
3.3.1 UML/OCL . . . . . . . . . . . . . . . . . . . . . . . . . . 74
3.3.2 JML . . . . . . . . . . . . . . . . . . . . . . . . . . . . . . 76
3.4 Summary . . . . . . . . . . . . . . . . . . . . . . . . . . . . . . 78

**4 Specification of Encapsulation Properties** **79**
4.1 Requirements for Specifying Encapsulation . . . . . . . . . . . 80
4.1.1 Design Patterns . . . . . . . . . . . . . . . . . . . . . . . . 80
4.1.2 Alias Control: Related Work on Encapsulation . . . . . 83
4.1.3 Guidelines for Specifying Encapsulation . . . . . . . . . 84
4.2 Basic Encapsulation Predicates . . . . . . . . . . . . . . . . . . 85
4.2.1 The Acc Predicates . . . . . . . . . . . . . . . . . . . . . . 85
4.2.2 The Reach and Conn Predicates . . . . . . . . . . . . . . 88
4.3 Macro Encapsulation Predicates . . . . . . . . . . . . . . . . . 90
4.3.1 The Enc predicate . . . . . . . . . . . . . . . . . . . . . . 90
4.3.2 The GuardObj and UniqueAcc Predicates . . . . . . . . 92
4.3.3 The GuardReg and UniqueReg Predicates . . . . . . . . 95
4.3.4 Expressing Advanced Ownership Systems . . . . . . . . 98
4.4 Summary . . . . . . . . . . . . . . . . . . . . . . . . . . . . . . 100

**5 Component Specifications** **101**
5.1 Generic Extension Contracts . . . . . . . . . . . . . . . . . . . 102
5.1.1 Syntax . . . . . . . . . . . . . . . . . . . . . . . . . . . . . 103
5.1.2 Semantics . . . . . . . . . . . . . . . . . . . . . . . . . . . 106
5.1.3 Relative-Durable Correctness . . . . . . . . . . . . . . . 108
5.2 Component Contracts . . . . . . . . . . . . . . . . . . . . . . . 110
5.3 Summary . . . . . . . . . . . . . . . . . . . . . . . . . . . . . . 111

# II Modular Verification 113


**6 Modular Program Proofs 115**

6.1 Modular Validity and Modular Soundness . . . . . . . . . . . . 116
6.2 Modularity of the JavaDL Rules . . . . . . . . . . . . . . . . . . . 118
6.2.1 Method calls . . . . . . . . . . . . . . . . . . . . . . . . . . 118
6.2.2 Static Analysis for Valid Array Store . . . . . . . . . . . 124
6.2.3 Enumerating Dynamic Types . . . . . . . . . . . . . . . 125
6.2.4 The Other Rules . . . . . . . . . . . . . . . . . . . . . . . 126
6.3 Relative Modular Validity and Soundness . . . . . . . . . . . . . 127
6.4 Relative Modular Dynamic Logic for Java . . . . . . . . . . . . 129
6.4.1 Relative Modular Method Call Rule . . . . . . . . . . . 129
6.4.2 Other Non-modular Rules . . . . . . . . . . . . . . . . . 131
6.4.3 Modular Proofs with Generated Extension Contracts . 132
6.5 Summary . . . . . . . . . . . . . . . . . . . . . . . . . . . . . . . . 134

**7 Non-modular Verification of Call Correctness 135**

7.1 Towards Proof Obligations for Call Correctness . . . . . . . . 136
7.2 Lightweight Program Correctness Proof Obligations . . . . . . 137
7.2.1 The Basic Proof Obligation Template . . . . . . . . . . 137
7.2.2 Invariant Preservation . . . . . . . . . . . . . . . . . . . 138
7.2.3 Invariant Preservation Under Weaker Assumptions . . 139
7.2.4 Invariant Initialisation . . . . . . . . . . . . . . . . . . . 140
7.2.5 Postcondition Assurance . . . . . . . . . . . . . . . . . . 140
7.2.6 Postcondition Assurance Under Weaker Assumptions . 141
7.2.7 Assignable Clauses . . . . . . . . . . . . . . . . . . . . . 142
7.3 A System of Proof Obligations for Entire Call Correctness . . 146
7.4 Non-modular Optimisations . . . . . . . . . . . . . . . . . . . . 148
7.5 Pragmatics . . . . . . . . . . . . . . . . . . . . . . . . . . . . . . . 151
7.6 Summary . . . . . . . . . . . . . . . . . . . . . . . . . . . . . . . . 153

**8 Verification of Encapsulation 155**

8.1 Proof Obligations . . . . . . . . . . . . . . . . . . . . . . . . . . . 156
8.2 Naive Deductive Approach . . . . . . . . . . . . . . . . . . . . . 158
8.3 Modular Treatment of Accessibility . . . . . . . . . . . . . . . . 161
8.4 Static Analysis Techniques . . . . . . . . . . . . . . . . . . . . . 163
8.5 Summary . . . . . . . . . . . . . . . . . . . . . . . . . . . . . . . . 166

**9 Modular Verification of Call Correctness 167**
9.1 Analysis of Dependencies in Specifications . . . . . . . . . . . 168
9.1.1 Depends Clauses . . . . . . . . . . . . . . . . . . . . . 168
9.1.2 Syntactical Criteria for Depends Clauses . . . . . . . . 172
9.1.3 Proofs of Depends Clauses . . . . . . . . . . . . . . . . 174
9.1.4 Context-Independent Depends Clauses . . . . . . . . . 176
9.2 Self-Guards . . . . . . . . . . . . . . . . . . . . . . . . . . . 178
9.3 Guards . . . . . . . . . . . . . . . . . . . . . . . . . . . . . . 180
9.3.1 Motivation . . . . . . . . . . . . . . . . . . . . . . . . 181
9.3.2 Definitions . . . . . . . . . . . . . . . . . . . . . . . . 182
9.3.3 Proof Obligations for Guards . . . . . . . . . . . . . . 184
9.4 Modular Verification of Invariants . . . . . . . . . . . . . . . 190
9.5 Summary . . . . . . . . . . . . . . . . . . . . . . . . . . . . . 194

**10 Verification of Durable Correctness of Open Programs 195**
10.1 Strict Durable Correctness . . . . . . . . . . . . . . . . . . . 196
10.2 Durable Correctness with Extension Contracts . . . . . . . . . 199
10.3 Examples . . . . . . . . . . . . . . . . . . . . . . . . . . . . 203
10.3.1 Producer and Consumer with Shared Array . . . . . . 204
10.3.2 Linked List with Iterator . . . . . . . . . . . . . . . . . 212
10.4 Durable Correctness and Abstraction in Invariants . . . . . . . 216
10.5 Verification of Components . . . . . . . . . . . . . . . . . . . 221
10.6 Design Implications . . . . . . . . . . . . . . . . . . . . . . . 222
10.7 Summary . . . . . . . . . . . . . . . . . . . . . . . . . . . . . 223

**11 Conclusions 225**
11.1 Related Work . . . . . . . . . . . . . . . . . . . . . . . . . . 225
11.1.1 Program Specification and Verification . . . . . . . . . 225
11.1.2 Notions of Correctness of Programs . . . . . . . . . . . 227
11.1.3 Constraining Context . . . . . . . . . . . . . . . . . . . 228
11.1.4 Specification and Verification of Encapsulation . . . . . 229
11.1.5 Verification of Operation Contracts . . . . . . . . . . . 230
11.1.6 Analysis of Dependencies . . . . . . . . . . . . . . . . . 230
11.1.7 Modular Verification of Invariants . . . . . . . . . . . . 231
11.2 Future Work . . . . . . . . . . . . . . . . . . . . . . . . . . . 234
11.3 Summary of This Work . . . . . . . . . . . . . . . . . . . . . 235

**Bibliography 239**

# 1 Introduction

Causa latet, vis est notissima.

*(Ovid)*

Imagine object-oriented software components which are guaranteed to do what they promise to do. Imagine them to be used in an arbitrary context and they still do what they promise to do.

This work is about coming a step closer towards making this vision true. This work employs *formal* methods, which are the most rigid way of making guarantees about software. More precisely from the area of formal methods, we foster *formal specification* and *deductive verification*.

Using formal methods rigidly does not at all mean to be escapist; we are attacking software components written in the real-world widely spread object-oriented language *Java* [Gosling et al., 2000]. We are however *not* considering multi-threaded Java, nor effects of garbage collection. Both are completely different and on their own complex matters. On the specification side we are only considering *functional* specifications.

To see which concrete problems this work is attacking, this chapter provides an overview of the state of the art in specification and verification of object-oriented systems. Moreover it will present problems which make it—despite the successes in this area—problematic to have fully specified and verified, or short, trusted components.

## 1.1 State of the Art in Specification and Verification of Object-oriented Programs

In the last few years, formal specification and deductive program verification have made big steps forward towards being applied in commercial software development. Real-world programming languages have been approached. Especially *Java* has been in the focus of research because of its quite precise—though informal—foundations and its wide spread use in software development. Moreover, non-trivial applications could be verified [Mostowski, 2005]. Finally tools were built which made formal specification and verification accessible to people who are no ultimate experts in formal methods. An example is the KeY system [Ahrendt et al., 2005a], which quite well represents the state of the art in the specification and verification of object-oriented programs. Other systems are discussed in Sect. 11.1.

Verification is based on the existence of two artifacts: A program and a formal specification. While software engineers generally consider it quite easy to write code, writing formal specifications is usually considered much more difficult. The KeY system assists users with this task by supporting specification languages which accommodate the world of software engineering as well as that of formal methods—to the extend possible. The supported specification languages are the Object Constraint Language (OCL) [Warmer and Kleppe, 1999], which is part of the well accepted Unified Modeling Language (UML) [OMG] standard, and the Java Modeling Language (JML) [Leavens et al., 2005] which tries to syntactically resemble Java. Both, OCL and JML, are based on the idea of *design by contract* [Meyer, 1992] providing methods and classes with operation contracts and class invariants. Moreover tools are available within KeY which generate formal specifications from a pattern template mechanism and natural language input. Finally, the KeY system is integrated in the work bench of developers, as in a CASE tool or an integrated development environment. This allows for seamless integration of specification and verification in the software development process.

With a formal specification written in one of the specification languages, verification can start. Properties of specifications without relation to code can be verified (so called horizontal properties) [Roth, 2006]. When program code is there, its correctness with respect to the specification can be proven.

Indispensable ingredients of deductive verification are a logic and a calculus. KeY's deduction component is based on the dynamic logic JavaDL and the JavaDL calculus [Beckert, 2000]. In order to establish a link between the specification languages and JavaDL, OCL and JML specifications are automatically translated into the first order fragment of the JavaDL logic [Beckert et al., 2002]. From these expressions proof obligations are generated and fed into the theorem prover of KeY [Ahrendt et al., 2005a]. The implied correctness assertion are currently only on a per-method basis, that is, all make statements about a single method call, such as: 'this method preserves that property'. Similar statements about a whole program, that is, a set of classes, like 'a program satisfies its specification entirely', have not been supported.

## 1.2 Problems

Program verification systems like KeY quite comfortably and efficiently—at least compared with the degree of guarantees that are made—deal with *single* and *local* properties of programs. We may imagine a moment where a developer has performed a number of such proofs successfully. Can he or she be sure that the given program is correct with respect to the considered specification? What exactly is correct? And under which circumstances will correctness be ensured? We illustrate these questions with the help of the following example.

**Example 1.1.** Figure 1.1 shows an example Java program similar to an example in Bloch [2001]. The program provides Java classes `Date` (which does not contain an attribute for a day, for brevity reasons) and `Period`, the latter composed of two instances of the first. The month of a date is represented by an instance of class `Month`. The start and end dates of a `Period` can be retrieved from `Period` instances by 'getter' methods and set by 'setter' methods. The fields in `Date` can be got and set the same way. The side-effect free (*pure*, *query*) method `earlierOrEqual(Date)` allows to check whether the stored date is considered earlier than or equal to a given one. Most importantly to the subject of this work, all getter and setter methods have one peculiarity: they create a new instance of the argument object before storing the copy and before returning an object. This follows the design patterns *Copy Mutable Parameters* and *Return New Objects from Accessor Method* (see Sect. 4.1.1), also known as *defensive copies* Bloch [2001]. $*$

Note that the implementation depicted in Figure 1.1 already contains a (highly incomplete) functional specification of the expected behaviour, that is it contains a *class invariant* attached to class `Period` and a *method specification* at the `earlierOrEqual(Date)` method of `Date`. As invariant we conceive—as made popular by the design by contract methodology [Meyer, 1992]—a property being true in all states of a program except from intermediate states reached during the invocation of a method or constructor; as method specifications we employ *contracts* promising a post-condition to hold after the method invocation if preconditions are met. As specification language we have chosen here the Java Modeling Language (JML) [Leavens et al., 2005], which should be quite intuitively conceivable for those who know Java. The invariant says that the start date of the period should be before or equal to the end date in the natural sense. And `earlierOrEqual(Date)`

```
class Period {
  /*@ instance invariant
    @      start.year<end.year ||
    @     (start.year==end.year
    @      && start.month.val
    @              <=end.month.val);
    @*/
  private Date start, end;
  /*@ requires start!=null
    @          && end!=null;
    @*/
  public Period(Date d1, Date d2){
    if (d1.earlierOrEqual(d2)){
      this.start=d1.copy();
      this.end=d2.copy();
    } else {
      this.start=d2.copy();
      this.end=d1.copy();
    }
  }
  public Date getEnd(){
    return end.copy();
  }
  public void setEnd(Date end){
    if (!start.earlierOrEqual(end))
      throw new RuntimeException();
    this.end=end;
  }
}
class Month {
  /*@ invariant val>0 and val<=12 @*/
  private /*@spec_public*/ int val;
  public Month(int val){
    setMonth(val);
  }
  public void setMonth(int v){
    val = (v>0 && v<=12) ? v : 1;
  }
  public Month copy(){
    return new Month(val);
  }
}
```

```
class Date {
  /*@ invariant month!=null; @*/
  private /*@spec_public@*/
                         Month month;
  private /*@spec_public@*/ int year;
  /*@ requires month!=null @*/
  public Date(Month month,int year){
    this.month=month;
    this.year=year;
  }
  public Month getMonth(){
    return month.copy();
  }
  public int getYear(){return year;}
  public void setYear(int y){year=y;}
  /*@ normal_behavior
    @ requires cmp != null;
    @ ensures
    @   \result==(year<cmp.year
    @            ||(year==cmp.year
    @              && month.val
    @                <=cmp.month.val));
    @*/
  public /*@ pure @*/
    boolean earlierOrEqual(Date cmp){
    return (getYear()<cmp.getYear())
    || (getYear()==cmp.getYear()
      && getMonth()<=cmp.getMonth());
  }
  /*@ normal_behavior
    @ ensures
    @   \result.month.val==month.val
    @         & \result.year==year
    @         & \fresh(\result)
    @         & \fresh(\result.month);
    @*/
  public Date copy(){
    return new Date(getYear(),
                     getMonth());
  }
}
```

**Figure 1.1:** A simple Java program modelling periods

is specified in the sense that the argument lies before or on the same date represented by the given object if and only if the method returns `true`.

Consider now first the invariant $\varphi_{\texttt{Period}}$ of `Period`. A verification system like KeY is able to prove, for instance, that a method `setEnd(Date)` in `Period` preserves $\varphi_{\texttt{Period}}$, that is, assumed the invariant holds before method invocation it will hold afterwards. It is important to note that the *context* in which this check is performed is fixed. That means that KeY guarantees the preservation of $\varphi_{\texttt{Period}}$ if there are no further classes besides `Period`, `Date`, and `Month`. All other methods of `Period` can be proven to preserve $\varphi_{\texttt{Period}}$ and the constructor provably establishes this invariant for the created instance. Are we done now? Will the class invariant hold in all system states as we have expected?

**Example 1.2.** Assume for a moment that the constructor of `Period` lacked the `copy` method references and was instead implemented as follows:

```
public Period(Date d1, Date d2) {
  if (d1.earlierOrEqual(d2)) {
    this.start=d1;
    this.end=d2;
  } else {
    this.start=d2;
    this.end=d1;
  }
}
```

As its unmodified counterpart, this constructor establishes the invariant of `Period`.

We can now add the following class:

```
class Main {
  public Period myPeriod() {
    Date sep=new Date(new Month(9), 2002);
    Date feb=new Date(new Month(2), 2006);
    Period p=new Period(sep, feb);
    sep.setYear(2006);
    return p;
  }
}
```

When a call to `myPeriod()` terminates, an instance of `Period` exists which does *not* satisfy $\varphi_{\texttt{Period}}$: It represents a period which starts in September of 2006 and ends in February of 2006. *

Interestingly, it is not so obvious, whether we should consider this program behaviour as a bug or not. On the one hand, one could have the opinion that we were in fact not finished with verification of our program, because (at least) one method, namely `setYear()` did *not* preserve the invariant of `Period`. On the other hand, it is unrealistic that methods of `Date`, which is (at least by its name) a pretty general class and not only thought to be used as part of `Period`, should necessarily preserve an invariant of another class. Moreover if the `start` and `end` fields of a `Period` were sufficiently hidden from access from other classes than `Period`, as in the original implementation, we could not have provoked the faulty behaviour. We can observe two facts:

(i) It is not so obvious which conditions must be satisfied for a system to be classified as *correct*. For instance: in general *all* methods of a system can violate invariants.

(ii) It can be a matter of *encapsulation* whether a program is correct.

Our first observation says that naive verification of invariants is highly non-modular, since we need to consider verification conditions for every pair of invariant and operation. Only good enough, and sufficiently specified and verified encapsulation properties can help.

If we assumed that our program consisted of components, we could make even more observations. For instance we can assume that the classes `Date` and `Month` come from a library and our intend is to develop a component consisting of the `Period` class on top of these. Now, code for `Date` and `Month` would not necessarily be available and it would be even more unrealistic that these classes preserve the invariant of our new component `Period`. Even if we verify all methods and constructors of all the code that we have, that is, that of the new component, we cannot be sure that invariants hold in an arbitrary context; for instance they do not hold in a context which involves the `Main` class. We can draw the conclusion that,

(iii) with components it is even more crucial to have a sufficient degree of encapsulation, since it is no more possible to check that all methods cannot possibly violate invariants.

```
public interface Set {
  /*@ model Object[] elems;
    @ public instance invariant
    @  \forall(int i,j;
    @          i>=0 && i<elems.length && j>=0 && j<elems.length;
    @          elems[i].equals(elems[j]) ==> i==j) */
}
```

**Figure 1.2:** JML invariant for `java.util.Set`

Another way how we could consider the modified example to be correct, is that the *context* in which `Period` is used satisfies certain requirements. As a trivial example, if every method in the context would be obliged to preserve the invariant of `Period`, it would be forbidden to implement `Main` as above and thus we had no invariant violation. We observe that

(iv) it may depend on the behaviour of the context in which a component is used whether the component is considered correct.

For a more realistic example for this phenomenon, we have a look at the interface `Set` from the Java Collections Framework, here specified with JML:

**Example 1.3.** Consider the extract from the `Set` interface in Fig. 1.2. It is specified with a *model field* `elems` representing the entries in the set and an invariant requiring the elements to be all different w.r.t. the `equals` method.

This invariant is prone to be violated if clients of a `java.util.Set` instance modify elements of the set in a way that two elements which were not equal before are becoming equal. This danger is also reflected in the informal description of the `Set` interface [Sun Microsystems, Inc., a]:

> Note: Great care must be exercised if mutable objects are used as set elements. The behavior of a set is not specified if the value of an object is changed in a manner that affects equals comparisons while the object is an element in the set.

From the viewpoint of formal methods, it would be desirable to formalise this informal and vague warning. *

*Good encapsulation* and a *restricted context* are two instruments to support the functional correctness of programs in an open world. They are complementary concepts which can be combined *ad libitum*. They are however not equally desirable. Encapsulation is clearly the best choice, since we want to have as little obligations to the user of a component. Only if encapsulation is not possible we have to switch to restrictions of the context.

So far we have discussed what Meyer [1997] calls the *indirect invariant effect*. There is another problem with specifications in open programs, which we illustrate now. Programs using our `Period` component could make use of it by subclassing `Date`, quite a common way of re-using object-oriented programs. The subclass could be defined as follows:

```
class Date2 extends Date {
  public boolean earlierOrEqual(Date cmp) {
    return getYear()<=cmp.getYear();
  }
}
```

Clearly this implementation violates the specification of `earlierOrEqual` in `Date`. Even worse, overriding this method makes it possible to violate the invariant of `Period`. Assume the user of our component writes the following class:

```
class Main2 {
  public Period myPeriod2() {
    Date sep=new Date2(new Month(9), 2006);
    Date feb=new Date(new Month(2), 2006);
    Period p=new Period(sep, feb);
    return p;
  }
}
```

Then again a `Period` instance exists which does not satisfy its invariant, although we did not exploit the effect that we changed a date object 'through the back-door'. Even worse, a local judgement like 'a constructor call to `Period` establishes the invariant' provable by KeY in the required fixed program context is invalidated if the context is extended by a subclass of `Date`. We note that

(v) context extensions can invalidate judgements on programs (like the preservation of invariants or the fulfilment of operation contracts).

Here again we have two choices: We could either restrict the context, by requiring that `earlierOrEqual(Date)` may only be overridden in a way conforming to the original implementation. The alternative is to disallow the overriding of this method at all by declaring it final, which corresponds roughly to the encapsulating solution from above.

It can be argued that the observed phenomena are deficiencies of the used programming language or object-oriented programming in general. This is probably right and many complaints, with similar arguments as above, about object-orientation have been raised (see for example Broy and Siedersleben [2002]). So we could design our own fancy programming language which would evoke the mentioned problems. Or we could at least extend an existing language with new features. We will not do this. First of all, *some* of the above problems are also popular features of object-orientation, for instance, code inheritance *is* in practice used to adapt behaviour. Second, we have to face reality: Object-orientation and Java are currently used in practical software development and programming languages tend to have a comparably long life. Moreover we, and this is also the philosophy of the KeY project, do not want to develop techniques for unused toy languages as in the early years of formal methods. Instead, we rely on the abilities of developers to make for enough encapsulation with existing programming languages and to impose appropriate constraints on allowed contexts.

What would an experienced Java programmer do if he knew that his classes (as `Period`) were reused in an unpredictable way (as by `Main` or `Main2`)? There are some patterns that address these problems: Bloch [2001], for instance, recommends 'defensive copies' before storing the `start` and `end` fields. This recipe has been obeyed in the initial implementation of Ex. 1.1. In general it is enough to ensure that writable references to the objects stored in `start` and `end` objects are not exposed to the 'outside' of `Period`. And for the second problem concerning non-conforming overriding methods a programmer would declare his methods final as mentioned above or would at least write a comment that subclasses should be careful when overriding this method.

Already today, with current languages, programmers *can* write programs which are modularly sound. They do not necessarily need additional programming language features that support them, like they do not need additional languages features to write functionally correct software. What is missing however are means to specify and verify encapsulation required for modular correctness of a program. What is moreover missing is a clear notion of correctness of components. And what is finally missing is a system of proof obligations that allows to prove a program modularly correct. This work aims at providing these missing instruments.

## 1.3 Contributed Solutions

The two main contribution of this work are

- a definition of formal requirements on the correctness of object-oriented programs which run in an unknown context and
- a system of proof obligations to prove in a theorem prover that these requirements are satisfied.

On a more detailed level, the following solutions are provided:

- The essentials of a *functional specification* for sequential object-oriented programming languages are defined at the example of sequential Java and on the basis of typed first order logic.
- We elaborate on the notion of *correctness* of a program with respect to a specification. In particular a notion of correctness which can not be affected by program extensions is defined. More precisely we define two notions of correctness: observed-state call correctness and observed-state durable correctness. The first is simple to prove, but only useful in a closed context, and the second is more difficult to establish but desired in an open context.
- We provide a novel way of specifying and verifying *encapsulation* of object-oriented programs, suiting well to functional specifications in a design by contract style. Compared to competing approaches, our way to specify encapsulation is more general, does not require extensions of programming languages, and suits better to the way functional properties are specified. Static analysis techniques developed in other approaches can still be used, provided that the specified encapsulation property is that simple.
- The notion of a *component contract* is introduced, reflecting the fact that the context in which a component is used is often obliged to satisfy certain conditions. *Generic extension contracts* play the role of preconditions by imposing conditions on the context a component is used

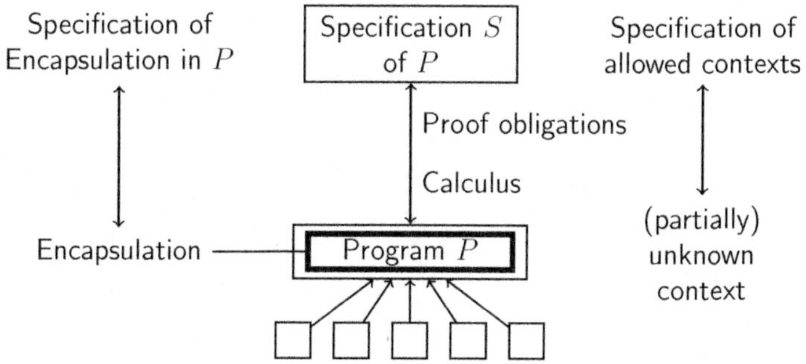


**Figure 1.3:** Overview on specification and verification of open object-oriented programs

in. Extension contracts make use of the concept of type parameters which allows to constrain the behaviour of types which are unavailable at the time of specification.

- An existing powerful, but non-modular program calculus for Java is investigated and lifted to the possible extend to a *modular program calculus*. Issues with the problem of dynamic binding, inherent to modularly proving Java programs, are solved by constraining the context with generic extension contracts.

- *Proof obligations* for program correctness in closed programs are presented and proven correct, among them a novel proof obligation for the correctness of the change information in *assignable clauses*. Starting from an analysis of specifications and the provably correct extraction of depends clauses, proof obligations for the correctness of *open programs* and components are provided. For complex invariants certain classes must be designated as a guard for which correctness and encapsulation properties must modularly be proven. If encapsulation is impossible, extension contracts are employed to at least ensure a relative notion of correctness. This solves the problems of indirect invariant effects.

These contributions have been placed in the schematic picture Fig. 1.3. Basically we are facing the classical situation of program verification, namely to relate a formal specification $S$ and a program $P$ with the goal to achieve a proof that the program is correct with respect to the specification. The new obstacles we are facing in this work is that $P$ is a component which is composed in an unknown or at most partially known way with other components. Two techniques, depicted by the two 'wings' of Fig. 1.3, are discussed in this work to cope with this: (a) to impose requirements on the *context* $P$ is used in and (b) to *encapsulate* data of $P$. Correctness is proven with the two ingredients of deductive verification: *proof obligations* and *calculus*. Both of them must be adapted to the new situation taking into account the unknown context.

## 1.4 Outline

Basic material of a more common nature is presented in *Chapter 2*. Most importantly, here, the program logic needed in specification and verification is introduced.

The rest of this work is divided into two main parts: one concerned with formal *specification* techniques for programs which are designed to be extended, the other with an approach for deductive *verification* in a modular fashion.

Part I is started with *Chapter 3*. It defines what program specifications are and defines two variants of correctness of programs. *Chapter 4* motivates and describes our approach to specify properties of encapsulation. Finally, *Chapter 5* introduces the notion of a component contract.

In Part II we discuss modular verification as an issue of a calculus and of proof obligations. *Chapter 6* covers the calculus, by modifying an existent non-modular program calculus to be more modular. *Chapter 7* is concerned with the simpler part of a system of proof obligations suited to programs not subject to be extended. *Chapter 8* provides means to prove encapsulation properties, which is a requirement to ensure correctness of programs modularly. This is done in *Chapter 9*, where we present a more sophisticated and modular system of proof obligations for closed programs. In *Chapter 10* the final step towards modular correctness of open programs and components is made, by again modifying the proof obligation systems developed before.

We conclude the work with an overview on related approaches in *Chapter 11*.

# 2 Preliminaries

Excludat iurgia finis.

*(Horace)*

This chapter defines basic concepts which are used throughout this work. We define open and closed programs, the used logics JavaFOL and JavaDL, as well as our notion of proof obligation. Mostly, these are common notions and notations developed in other contexts. In particular Sects. 2.2 and 2.3 present concepts elaborated in the KeY project. For a complete reference see Beckert et al. [2006a]. Nevertheless, some details are presented in a novel way or are generalised slightly, as for instance the notion of extended terms in Sect. 2.2.4.

## 2.1 Closed and Open Programs and Components

We are considering the programming language Java as described in Gosling et al. [2000]. The following limitations and conventions are to be followed:

- Only *sequential* programs are considered. Multi-threaded programs are outside of the scope of this work. A clearly defined sequential subset of Java is JavaCard [Sun Microsystems, Inc., b], which can be seen as target language of this work. However, we do not stick to all other strong limitations of JavaCard, concerning for instance a limited dimensionality of arrays and peculiarities with class initialisation.

- We consider only programs with private and protected fields. It is obvious that, with fields of default or public visibility, encapsulation needed for modularity is almost impossible to achieve. Such fields are thus disallowed. Note, that it is however possible to transform programs containing package private or public fields into programs having fields of allowed visibilities. For this, these fields are turned into protected fields and appropriate setter and getter methods are implemented and used.

When referring to Java programs, the standard terminology as described in [Gosling et al., 2000] is used. In addition, we use the word *operation* when referring to a method or constructor. We speak of an operation *in* a class or interface when this operation is declared in that class or interface and we classify an operation as *applicable* if there is an operation in that class or interface $T$ or in a supertype of $T$ which can be called by objects referencing a $T$-instance. Sometimes when referring to classes or interfaces we speak of a *(Java) type*.

In the next chapter we need to extract first order signatures from programs. We want to have available function symbols which correspond to certain operations in that program. More precisely, this narrows down to *side-effect free* operations. Since there is no syntactical criterion provided in Java (as opposed to UML, for instance, where *queries* can be tagged), if an operation belongs to this class of operations, the notion of a *pre-specified* program is introduced. This simply means that we are annotating operations with a keyword *pure*. Later side-effect freeness must be checked (see Sect. 7.2.7) for these operations.

**Definition 2.1.** A *pre-specified type* is a Java type which unlike normal Java classes allows to mark some of its non-void operations as *pure*. These operations are called *pure operations*.

Only rarely, programs are monolithic self-contained blocks of code. Usually programs make use of libraries and frameworks. In its extreme form and envisaged by software engineering pioneers, programs are composed of *components*. When a developer writes a new component $c_{new}$ he will often not be able to access internals of the components $c_1$ he uses. His component is *open* in the sense that it depends on components which he has only incomplete knowledge about. In particular he does not know if clients of $c_{new}$ do access $c_1$ separately and accidentally modify the state of $c_1$ though they only access $c_{new}$.

To reflect *incomplete* knowledge but maintaining a certain sort of compilability the notion of a class skeleton is introduced. Comparable to Java interfaces such skeletons just consist of operation declarations without implementation.

**Definition 2.2** (Class Skeleton)**.** A class skeleton is a pre-specified Java class except that it contains no method bodies.

A program $P$ of pre-specified Java classes *complies* with a set $Sk$ of skeletons if $P$ declares those classes, methods, and constructors which are declared in $Sk$.

With these two notions in mind, closed and open programs can be defined:

**Definition 2.3.** 1. A *closed (Java) program* is a set $P$ of pre-specified Java classes that can independently be compiled according to Gosling et al. [2000]. Any superset $P' \supseteq P$ of closed programs is a *closure* of $P$.

2. A set of pre-specified Java types is an *open (Java) program* if it is not a closed program.

3. A *program* is either an open program or a closed program.

For an open program $P$ there is a minimal set $Sk$ of class skeletons such that $P$ can be compiled together with a set $P'$ of classes which complies with $Sk$. $P'$ is called a *closure* of $P$. Often we refer to an open program as a set of classes and skeletons $P \cup Sk$.

A closed program $P$ always comprises a set of standard Java types, these are[1] `Object`, `Throwable`, `String`, `Cloneable`, `Serializable`. The set of these (pre-specified) classes is referred to as JCl.

By default we assume that open programs include JCl as skeletons.

The notion of a software *component* is controversial and often vaguely defined. One popular way to define component is to characterise obligatory properties, as for instance that it [Szyperski, 1998] (a) can be in multiple-use, (b) is not context-specific, (c) composable with other components, (d) encapsulated i.e., non-investigable through its interfaces, and (e) a unit of independent deployment and versioning.

In this work, we are going to use the quite general notion of a component as *a software item that is subject to software composition* [Aßmann, 2003] on the one hand and on the other hand a very precise instance of this definition as described in the following.

A *component* is, concerning the considered code, not much more than an open program. However with the term *component* it is emphasised that such open programs are made to be composed: *Components* are (in the sense of

[1]For the standard library classes from package `java.lang` we will omit the package prefix if no ambiguities can arise.

this work) open programs which are developed and deployed together and which are, according to Aßmann [2003], subject to composition. Composition means that components are put together in such a way that they make up a meaningful closed program.

Because of the deployment-as-a-whole and composition aspect, components have the characteristic that they are documented and specified in a way that makes composition with other components feasible. Since we are interested in a precise functional formal specification, components may have attached a special kind of specification, called *component contract*, which will be discussed in Chapter 5. Apart from this, the reader can most often simply associate the notions of *open program* and *component* as synonyms.

## 2.2 Java First Order Logic

Functional specifications of object-oriented programs are based on a typed first order logic, as will be described in Sect. 3. In the following, we describe a first-order fragment JavaFOL of JavaDL [Beckert, 2000]. The presentation mainly follows Giese [2006]. JavaFOL will be extended in Chapter 4.

### 2.2.1 Syntax

A *signature* $(\mathcal{T}, \mathcal{F}^{nr}, \mathcal{F}^{r}, \mathcal{P}^{nr}, \mathcal{P}^{r}, \preceq, \sigma, \tau)$ consists of

- a set $\mathcal{T}$ of type symbols,
- a set $\mathcal{F}^{nr}$ of non-rigid function symbols,
- a set $\mathcal{F}^{r}$ of rigid function symbols,
- a set $\mathcal{P}^{nr}$ of nonrigid predicate symbols,
- a set $\mathcal{P}^{r}$ of rigid predicate symbols,
- a function $\sigma$ which assigns an $n$-tuple of types, *the function or predicate symbol signature*, from $\mathcal{T}$ to each predicate or function symbol $p \in \mathcal{P}^{nr} \cup \mathcal{P}^{r} \cup \mathcal{F}^{nr} \cup \mathcal{F}^{r}$,
- a function $\tau$ which assigns a type, the *result type*, from $\mathcal{T}$ to each function symbol $f \in \mathcal{F}^{nr} \cup \mathcal{F}^{r}$,

- a transitive and reflexive binary relation $\preceq \subseteq \mathcal{T} \times \mathcal{T}$, the *subtype* relation; we say $t_1$ is a subtype of $t_2$ if $(t_1, t_2) \in \preceq$ and write alternatively $t_1 \preceq t_2$.

Sometimes, we write $\sigma_i(f)$ to denote $T_i$ if $\sigma(f) = (T_1, \ldots, T_n)$ $(n \geq 0, i = 1, \ldots, n)$. The arity of the $\sigma(f)$-tuple is denoted by $\alpha(f)$.

We require that all signatures contain the types $\text{INTEGER}, \text{BOOLEAN} \in \mathcal{T}$ as well as the usual rigid functions and predicates for these types. For INTEGER we have, for instance, the predicates: $\leq, \geq, <, >$ and the functions representing arithmetical operators $(+, -$, etc.), for the terms constructed with the usual 0 and succ functions we write $0, 1, 2, \ldots$. For BOOLEAN, we only define the functions TRUE and FALSE of arity 0.

Furthermore, `Null` $\in \mathcal{T}$. For `Null` we have only the 0-ary function `null`. Finally signatures must contain the type ANY, for which for all types $T \in \mathcal{T}$: $T \preceq \text{ANY}$.

Given a signature $\Sigma$, a program $P$ is a $\Sigma$-program if

- all types $\texttt{T} \in P$ are represented by some $r(\texttt{T}) \in \mathcal{T}$, in particular

  $$\text{JCl} \subseteq \mathcal{T}$$

  Furthermore `Null` $\in \mathcal{T}$. Finally for every type $T \in \mathcal{T}$ there is an array type $T\texttt{[]} \in \mathcal{T}$.

- the subtype relation of $P$ is reflected by $\preceq$, that is, for the types $T_1, T_2 \in \mathcal{T}$ induced by the program: $(T_1 \preceq T_2)$ iff $T_2$ is assignment compatible [Gosling et al., 2000, §5.2] to $T_1$.

- all local program variables of $P$ of type $T$ are represented by 0-ary non-rigid function symbols $f$ in $\Sigma$ with $\tau(f) = r(T)$ (these function symbols are called *program variable symbols*),

- all fields $a$ of $P$ of type $T$ declared in a class $D$ are represented by a unary non-rigid function symbol in $\Sigma$ with the name $a@(D)$ and $\sigma(a@(D)) = (r(D))$ and $\tau(a@(D)) = r(T)$ (these function symbols are called *instance field symbols*)

- all static fields $a$ of $P$ of type $T$ declared in a type $D$ are represented by a 0-ary non-rigid function symbol in $\Sigma$ with the name $a@(D)$ and $\tau(a@(D)) = r(T)$ (these function symbols are called *static field symbols*)

- in $\Sigma$ there is a binary non-rigid function symbol `[]`$_T$ for every array type $T$`[]` $\in \mathcal{T}$, called *array access symbols*, with $\sigma($`[]`$_T) = (T$`[]`, `integer`$)$ and $\tau($`[]`$_T) = T$,
- in $\Sigma$ there is further an $n+1$-ary ($n \geq 0$) non-rigid function $q_{T_0}$ with

$$\sigma(q_{T_0}) = (r(\mathtt{T}_0), \ldots, r(\mathtt{T}_n)) \text{ and } \tau(q_{T_0}) = r(\mathtt{S})$$

  for every pure $n$-ary instance method in $P$ declared in type $\mathtt{T}_0$ as `S q(`$\mathtt{T}_1$`, ..., `$\mathtt{T}_n$`)` (these function symbols are called *instance query symbols*),
- in $\Sigma$ there is an $n$-ary ($n \geq 0$) non-rigid function $q_{T_0}$ with

$$\sigma(q_{T_0}) = (r(\mathtt{T}_1), \ldots, r(\mathtt{T}_n)) \text{ and } \tau(q_{T_0}) = r(\mathtt{S})$$

  for every $n$-ary static method in $P$ declared as `S q(`$\mathtt{T}_1$`, ..., `$\mathtt{T}_n$`)` in type $\mathtt{T}_0$ (these function symbols are called *static query symbols*),
- in $\Sigma$ we have the unary rigid function symbol $\text{InstanceOf}_T$ for every $T \in \mathcal{T}$ with

$$\sigma(\text{InstanceOf}_T) = (\mathtt{Object}) \text{ and}$$
$$\tau(\text{InstanceOf}_T) = \text{BOOLEAN} \ ,$$

- there are *no further* non-rigid function symbols than those described above in $\Sigma$ (that is instance field symbols, static field symbols, array access symbols, instance query symbols, and static query symbols).

The last item is mainly to simplify our reasoning in later chapters.

We furthermore require from a signature $\Sigma$ and a $\Sigma$-program $P$ that $\Sigma$ contains an unbounded reservoir of function symbols which do not represent features of $P$. We will refer to these symbols as being *fresh*.

The following lemma will ensure that terms and formulae built over a signature $\Sigma$ for a $\Sigma$-program $P$ are also terms and formulae (resp.) if $P$ is extended with additional classes and interfaces.

**Lemma 2.1.** Let $\Sigma_1 = (F_1^{nr}, F_1^r, P_1^{nr}, P_1^r, \preceq_1, \sigma_1, \tau_1)$ be a signature and $P_1$ a $\Sigma_1$-program. Let $P_2$ be a program with $P_1 \subseteq P_2$. Then there is a signature $\Sigma_2$ for which $P_2$ is a $\Sigma_2$-program with $\Sigma_2 = (F_2^{nr}, F_2^r, P_2^{nr}, P_2^r, o_2, \tau_2)$ and

$$F_1^{nr} \subseteq F_2^{nr}, F_1^r \subseteq F_2^r, P_1^{nr} \subseteq P_2^{nr}, P_1^r \subseteq P_2^r, \preceq_1 \subseteq \preceq_2, \sigma_1 \subseteq \sigma_2, \sigma_{r,1} \subseteq \sigma_{r,2}$$

For the latter property we write simpler: $\Sigma_1 \subseteq \Sigma_2$.

For the relation $\preceq$ and a set of types $P \subseteq \mathcal{T}$ we define the set

$$P^{\preceq} := \{T' \mid T' \preceq T, T \in P\}$$

As usual, we need, in addition to the signature, a set $V$ of typed logical variables, which we assume to be present in the following without further notice. Logical variables have assigned a type $T$ from the signature. From time to time this is, for a logical variable $v$ denoted as $v : T$, if the type is relevant and not clear from additional explanations.

**Definition 2.4.** Let $\Sigma = (\mathcal{T}, \mathcal{F}^{nr}, \mathcal{F}^{r}, \mathcal{P}^{nr}, \mathcal{P}^{r}, \preceq, \sigma, \tau)$ be a signature. The set $\mathrm{Term}_T^\Sigma$ of terms of type $T$ is simultaneously for all types $T \in \mathcal{T}$ defined to be the smallest set with

- $v \in \mathrm{Term}_T^\Sigma$ if $v$ is a logical variable of type $T$.
- $f(t_1, \ldots, t_{\alpha(f)}) \in \mathrm{Term}_T^\Sigma$ if $f \in \mathcal{F}^{nr} \cup \mathcal{F}^{r}$, $t_i \in \mathrm{Term}_{T_i'}^\Sigma$, $T_i, T_i' \in \mathcal{T}$, $T_i' \preceq T_i$, $\sigma(f) = (T_1, \ldots, T_{\alpha(f)})$, and $\tau(f) = T$ for all $i = 1, \ldots, \alpha(f)$.

The set $\mathrm{Term}^\Sigma$ of all terms is $\mathrm{Term}^\Sigma := \bigcup_{T \in \mathcal{T}} \mathrm{Term}_T^\Sigma$

The set $\mathrm{Fma}^\Sigma$ of formulae of JavaFOL is the smallest set with

- $\mathrm{true}, \mathrm{false} \in \mathrm{Fma}^\Sigma$,
- $p(t_1, \ldots, t_{\alpha(p)}) \in \mathrm{Fma}^\Sigma$ if $p \in \mathcal{P}^{nr} \cup \mathcal{P}^{r}$, $t_i \in \mathrm{Term}_{T_i'}^\Sigma$, $T_i, T_i' \in \mathcal{T}$, $T_i' \preceq T_i$, $\sigma(p) = (T_1, \ldots, T_{\alpha(f)})$ for all $i = 1, \ldots, \alpha(p)$,
- $t_1 \doteq t_2 \in \mathrm{Fma}^\Sigma$ for $t_1, t_2 \in \mathrm{Term}^\Sigma$,
- $\neg\varphi_1 \in \mathrm{Fma}^\Sigma$, $(\varphi_1 \wedge \varphi_2) \in \mathrm{Fma}^\Sigma$, $(\varphi_1 \vee \varphi_2) \in \mathrm{Fma}^\Sigma$, $(\varphi_1 \rightarrow \varphi_2) \in \mathrm{Fma}^\Sigma$, $(\varphi_1 \leftrightarrow \varphi_2) \in \mathrm{Fma}^\Sigma$,
  $(\mathrm{if}\ \varphi_1\ \mathrm{then}\ \varphi_2\ \mathrm{else}\ \varphi_3) \in \mathrm{Fma}^\Sigma$
  if $\varphi_1, \varphi_2, \varphi_3 \in \mathrm{Fma}^\Sigma$; $\neg$, $\wedge$, $\vee$, $\rightarrow$, $\leftrightarrow$, if then else are *junctors*,
- $(\forall x{:}T.\ \varphi) \in \mathrm{Fma}^\Sigma$, $(\exists x{:}T.\ \varphi) \in \mathrm{Fma}^\Sigma$ if $\varphi \in \mathrm{Fma}^\Sigma$, $x$ is a logical variable (of type $T$), and $T \in \mathcal{T}$; $\forall$ and $\exists$ are *quantifiers*.

As a convention, terms $a(t)$ with instance attribute symbols $a$ as top-level operator are written as $t.a$, terms $\texttt{[]}_T(t_1, t_2)$ with the array access symbol $\texttt{[]}_T$ as top-level operator are written as $t_1[t_2]_T$ or just $t_1[t_2]$. If there are no ambiguities, that is, if no 'shadowing' occurs, field symbols $a@(D)$ are written just as $a$.

Often we will use notations like $\bigwedge_{\varphi \in \Phi}$ to denote a conjunction $\varphi_1 \wedge \ldots \wedge \varphi_n$ of all elements in a finite set $\Phi = \{\varphi_1, \ldots, \varphi_n\}$ $(n \geq 1)$ of formulae. If $\Phi = \emptyset$ then $\bigwedge_{\varphi \in \Phi}$ means the neutral element true. This is analogously stipulated for disjunctions.

As a further convention, we will use the abbreviating notation $t_0 \not\doteq t_1$ instead of $\neg(t_0 \doteq t_1)$. Furthermore, from time to time we use InstanceOf as a predicate. That is, if $\text{InstanceOf}_T$ is used as a predicate it is an abbreviation for $\text{InstanceOf}_T(\cdot) \doteq \text{TRUE}$.

As usual we define *closed* formulae: these are formulae where every occurrence of a logical variable is bound by a quantifier.

### 2.2.2 Semantics

The semantics of a first order logic is defined by a first order structure consisting of a universe and an interpretation of predicate and function symbols. Since we are later extending JavaFOL to a dynamic logic JavaDL, we identify *first order structure* and *state* with each other.

**Definition 2.5** (State). Let $\Sigma$ be a signature and $P$ a $\Sigma$-program. A *state* $s$ is a first order structure for $\Sigma$ and $P$. It thus consists of

- a universe $\mathcal{U}$ of Java objects, primitive values, and the natural numbers, partitioned into disjoint sets $\mathcal{U}_T$ for every $T \in P \cup \{\mathbb{N}, \texttt{boolean}\}$; for each type $T \in \mathcal{T}$ we define

$$\text{Dom}(T) := \bigcup_{\substack{T' \in \mathcal{T} \\ T' \preceq T}} \mathcal{U}_{T'}$$

- an interpretation $\cdot^{s,P}$ mapping $n$-ary $(n \geq 0)$ function symbols $f$ with $\sigma(f) = (T_1, \ldots, T_n)$ to functions

$$f^{s,P} : \text{Dom}(T_1) \times \cdots \times \text{Dom}(T_n) \longrightarrow \text{Dom}(\tau(f))$$

  and $n$-ary predicate symbols $p$ with $\sigma(p) = (T_1, \ldots, T_n)$ to relations

$$p^{s,P} : \text{Dom}(T_1) \times \cdots \times \text{Dom}(T_n)$$

Note that we have *disjoint* sub-universes, the type hierarchy is reflected in Dom. If an individual $e$ is an object and $e \in \mathcal{U}_T$ then $T$ is its unique dynamic type.

The subset of the universe of primitive values is called $\mathcal{U}^{\mathrm{prim}}$.

We particularly fix the interpretations of fields, arrays, and queries, as well as for InstanceOf. Since the first three are partial functions for some arguments, we employ a choice function $ch$ that delivers, for a function symbol and a sequence of objects, an unknown but fixed universe element. This handling of undefinedness follows Gries and Schneider [1995]. In the following cases the interpretations are fixed:

- for an instance field symbol $a$:

$$a^{s,P}(e) = \begin{cases} e.a & \text{if } a \text{ is defined for } e \\ & \text{and } e \text{ is created} \\ ch(a,e) & \text{otherwise} \end{cases}$$

- for a static field symbol $a@(C)$:

$$a@(C)^{s,P} = \begin{cases} C.a & \text{if } a \text{ is defined in class } C \\ & \text{and } C \text{ is initialised} \\ ch(a) & \text{otherwise} \end{cases}$$

- for an array access symbol $\texttt{[]}_T$:

$$\texttt{[]}_T^{s,P}(e_1, e_2) = \begin{cases} e_1[e_2] & \text{if } e_1 \text{ is a created array} \\ & \text{and } e_2 \text{ is a valid slot in } e_1 \\ ch(\texttt{[]}_T, e_1, e_2) & \text{otherwise} \end{cases}$$

- for an $n$-ary query symbol $q$:

$$q^{s,P}(e_1,\ldots,e_n) = \begin{cases} \text{the returned value of the method reference} \\ e_1.q(e_2,\ldots,e_n) \text{ called in } P \text{ in state } s \text{ if this is a} \\ \text{valid method reference to an instance method} \\[1em] \text{the returned value of the method reference} \\ q(e_1,\ldots,e_n) \text{ called in } P \text{ in state } s \text{ if this is a} \\ \text{method valid reference to a static method} \\[1em] \text{otherwise (also in the case of abrupt} \\ \text{termination): } ch(q,e_1,\ldots,e_n) \end{cases}$$

- for the function symbol $\text{InstanceOf}_T$:

$$\text{InstanceOf}_T^{s,P}(e) = \texttt{true} \quad \text{iff} \quad e \in dom(T)\backslash\{\texttt{null}\}$$

We further require that, if we fix the interpretations of field and array access symbols, then also the interpretations of all other non-rigid function symbols and the predicate symbols are fixed. That is, for all states $s_1$ and $s_2$, if $f^{s_1}(e_1,\ldots,e_n) = f^{s_2}(e_1,\ldots,e_n)$ for all $n$-ary field or array access symbols $f$, then also $g^{s_1}(e_1,\ldots,e_n) = g^{s_2}(e_1,\ldots,e_n)$ for all other non-rigid function and predicate symbols $g$.

Note that the interpretation of queries depends on programs. In all other cases from above this is however not the case, such that we may just write $\cdot^s$ instead of $\cdot^{s,P}$. The particularity of queries is due to dynamic binding of methods in Java, which we reflect in JavaFOL. Consider the following illustrating example.

**Example 2.1.** In the introductory example of Sect. 1.2 we had a pure method which occurs in a signature suiting to the example program as binary non-rigid function symbol `earlierOrEqual` with

$$\sigma(\texttt{earlierOrEqual}) = (\texttt{Date},\texttt{Date}) \text{ and } \tau(\texttt{earlierOrEqual}) = \text{BOOLEAN}$$

Let $d_1, d_2 \in \text{Dom}(\texttt{Date})$ represent the dates January 2006 and February 2006. In the program depicted in Fig. 1.1: $\texttt{earlierOrEqual}^{s,P}(d_1,d_2) = \texttt{true}$. However, if `earlierOrEqual(Date)` was implemented as in `Date2` then we yield the result $\texttt{earlierOrEqual}^{s,P}(d_1,d_2) = \texttt{false}$. *

Because of the dependency from programs the valuation function and the validity relation is, deviating from usual first order semantics definitions, parameterised w.r.t. a program $P$.

The valuation function is thus defined as follows:

**Definition 2.6.** Let $\Sigma$ be a signature, $P$ a $\Sigma$-program, $s$ be a state, and $\beta : V \to \mathcal{U}$ a variable assignment. Then we define inductively:

- $\text{val}_{s,P,\beta}(x) = \beta(x)$ for a logical variable $x$
- $\text{val}_{s,P,\beta}(f(t_1, \ldots, t_n)) = f^{s,P}(\text{val}_{s,P,\beta}(t_1), \ldots, \text{val}_{s,P,\beta}(t_n))$ if $t_1, \ldots, t_n \in \text{Term}^{\Sigma}$ are terms and $f$ is an $n$-ary function symbol of $\Sigma$.

The validity relation is defined as usual:

**Definition 2.7.** The validity $\models_P$ of formulae $\varphi \in \text{Fma}^{\Sigma}$ in a $\Sigma'$-program $P$ (with $\Sigma \subseteq \Sigma'$) is defined inductively as follows (for formulae $\varphi_1, \varphi_2, \varphi_3$, terms $t_1, t_2, \ldots \in \text{Term}^{\Sigma}$, logical variables $x$):

- $s, \beta \models_P t_1 \doteq t_2$ iff $\text{val}_{s,P,\beta}(t_1) = \text{val}_{s,P,\beta}(t_2)$
- $s, \beta \models_P p(t_1, \ldots, t_n)$ iff $(\text{val}_{s,P,\beta}(t_1), \ldots, \text{val}_{s,P,\beta}(t_n)) \in p^{s,P}$
- $s, \beta \models_P \neg\varphi_1$ iff not $s, \beta \models_P \varphi_1$
- $s, \beta \models_P \varphi_1 \wedge \varphi_2$ iff $s, \beta \models_P \varphi_1$ and $s, \beta \models_P \varphi_2$
- $s, \beta \models_P \varphi_1 \vee \varphi_2$ iff $s, \beta \models_P \varphi_1$ or $s, \beta \models_P \varphi_2$
- $s, \beta \models_P \varphi_1 \to \varphi_2$ iff not $s, \beta \models_P \varphi_1$ or $s, \beta \models_P \varphi_2$
- $s, \beta \models_P \varphi_1 \leftrightarrow \varphi_2$ iff $(s, \beta \models_P \varphi_1$ iff $s, \beta \models_P \varphi_2)$
- $s, \beta \models_P \text{if}\, \varphi_1 \,\text{then}\, \varphi_2 \,\text{else}\, \varphi_3$ iff $s, \beta \models_P (\varphi_1 \to \varphi_2) \wedge (\neg\varphi_1 \to \varphi_3)$
- $s, \beta \models_P \exists x{:}T.\ \varphi_1$ iff there is an object $d \in \text{Dom}(T)$ such that $s, \beta_x^d \models_P \varphi_1$
- $s, \beta \models_P \forall x{:}T.\ \varphi_1$ iff $s, \beta \models_P \neg\exists x{:}T.\ \neg\varphi_1$.

If $s, \beta \models_P \varphi$ holds for all $\beta$, we just write $s \models_P \varphi$. If $s \models_P \varphi$ for all $s$ we write: $\models_P \varphi$.

### 2.2.3 Locations

A concept used in several places throughout this work are *locations*. They are special in the sense that they are pairs, where one element is a syntactical symbol whereas the second part is from the semantical domain. Locations can be updated by a state change (see Sect. 2.3.1). They will also play a role in proofs of assignable clauses (Sect. 7.2.7) and depends clauses (Sect. 9.1) and are thus an important instrument in our work.

**Definition 2.8.** Let $\Sigma = (\mathcal{T}, \mathcal{F}^{nr}, \mathcal{F}^{r}, \mathcal{P}^{nr}, \mathcal{P}^{r}, \preceq, \sigma, \tau)$ be a signature. Let further be $\mathcal{U}$ a universe. A location is a pair $(f, (e_1, \ldots, e_{\alpha(f)}))$ with $f \in F^{nr}$, $e_i \in \text{Dom}(\sigma(f)_i)$ $(i = 1, \ldots, \alpha(f)))$. The set of all locations for a signature $\Sigma$ is $L_\Sigma$

The subset of locations which have as top level operator a field or an array symbol is called *concrete locations.*

Sometimes it will be convenient to denote with $(f, (E_1, \ldots, E_n))$ and $E_i \subseteq \mathcal{U}$ the set of locations

$$\{(f, (e_1, \ldots, e_n)) \mid e_i \in E_i,\ i = 1, \ldots, n\}$$

### 2.2.4 Extended Terms

With terms we can specify locations in our program. For instance let $s$ be a state, $t$ be a ground term and a a field defined in the static type of $t$. Then $t$.a describes the location of field a in object $\text{val}_s(t)$. Such descriptions can be used when we need to specify which locations may change during a method invocation. Unfortunately this is no sufficient means. We might want to say that all slots of an array described by the term $t$ may change by the method invocation. For this a more powerful construct than terms, called *extended terms*, is needed. Extended terms are evaluated to sets of individuals. In our example, we would write:

$$(\text{for } i : \textsc{Integer} \ ; 0 \leq i \land i < t.\texttt{length} \ ; t\texttt{[}i\texttt{]})$$

This follows closely the idea of Rümmer [2005] of quantified updates, which will be discussed in Sect. 2.3.1.

The set $\text{ExtTerm}_T^\Sigma$ of extended terms is the smallest set with

- $v \in \text{ExtTerm}_T^\Sigma$ if $v$ is a logical variable of type $T$.

- $f(t_1, \ldots, t_{\alpha(f)}) \in \text{ExtTerm}_T^\Sigma$ if $f \in \mathcal{F}^{nr} \cup \mathcal{F}^r$, $t_i \in \text{ExtTerm}_{T_i'}^\Sigma$, $T_i, T_i' \in \mathcal{T}$, $T_i' \preceq T_i$, $\sigma(f) = (T_1, \ldots, T_{\alpha(f)})$ and $\tau(f) = T$ for all $i = 1, \ldots, \alpha(f)$.
- $(\text{for } x \; ; \varphi \; ; t) \in \text{ExtTerm}_T^\Sigma$ if $t \in \text{ExtTerm}_T^\Sigma$, $\varphi \in \text{Fma}^\Sigma$, and $x$ a logical variable of some type. In $t$ and $\varphi$ at most the logical variables $x$ may occur free.

The set $\text{ExtTerm}^\Sigma$ of all extended terms is $\text{ExtTerm}^\Sigma := \bigcup_{T \in \mathcal{T}} \text{ExtTerm}_T^\Sigma$.

It is easy to see that $\text{Term}^\Sigma \subseteq \text{ExtTerm}^\Sigma$.

Extended terms are evaluated to subsets of the universe. Let us call the valuation function $\text{val}'_{s,P,\beta} : \text{ExtTerm}^\Sigma \to 2^\mathcal{U}$ for a moment. We will define it such that $\text{val}'_{s,P,\beta}(t) = \{\text{val}_{s,P,\beta}(t)\}$ for $t \in \text{Term}^\Sigma$. We identify an individual $e$ with the singleton set $\{e\}$. Then $\text{val}_{s,P,\beta}$ can be simply re-used for the valuation function of extended terms.

Let $s$ be a state, $P$ a program, and $\beta$ a variable assignment, then the valuation function $\text{val}_{s,P,\beta} : \text{ExtTerm}^\Sigma \to 2^\mathcal{U}$ is inductively (re-)defined as follows:

- $\text{val}_{s,P,\beta}(x) = \{\beta(x)\}$ for a logical variable $x$.
- $\text{val}_{s,P,\beta}(f(t_1, \ldots, t_n))$
  $= \{f^{s,P}(t_1', \ldots, t_n') \mid t_1' \in \text{val}_{s,P,\beta}(t_1), \ldots, t_n' \in \text{val}_{s,P,\beta}(t_n)\}$
  if $t_1, \ldots, t_n \in \text{ExtTerm}^\Sigma$.
- $\text{val}_{s,P,\beta}(\text{for } x \; ; \varphi \; ; t) = \bigcup_{*} \text{val}_{s,P,\beta'}(t)$ where $x$ is a variable of type $T$ and the union $*$ is over all $\beta'$ for which there exists an $e \in \text{Dom}(T)$ with $\beta' = \beta_x^e$ such that $s, \beta' \models_P \varphi$. Furthermore $t \in \text{ExtTerm}^\Sigma, \varphi \in \text{Fma}^\Sigma$.

### Top-Level operators

For extended terms we define the following function which delivers the top-level operator if this is a non-rigid function symbol and otherwise the symbol $\bot$:

- $\text{top}(v) = \bot$ for a logical variable $v$,
- $\text{top}(f(t_1, \ldots, t_n)) = f$ if $f \in F^{nr}$
- $\text{top}(f(t_1, \ldots, t_n)) = \bot$ if $f \in F^r$

- $\text{top}(\text{for } x \; ; \varphi \; ; t) = \text{top}(t)$

### Location Terms

**Definition 2.9.** The set of extended terms which have a field symbol or array access symbol as top level operator is called $\text{LocTerm}^{\Sigma}$, also called *(concrete) location terms*:

$$\text{LocTerm}^{\Sigma} := \left\{ t \in \text{ExtTerm}^{\Sigma} \;\middle|\; \begin{array}{l} \text{top}(t) \neq \bot \text{ and top}(t) \text{ is a field} \\ \text{or array access symbol} \end{array} \right\}$$

$\text{LocTerm}^{\Sigma}$ will be of particular importance later on since these extended terms are used to specify assignable clauses (see Sect. 3.1.1) and depends clauses (see Sect. 9.1).

Given a state, a term with a field as top operator may represent a location (see Sect. 2.2.3), and an extended term may represent a set of locations. The following definition clarifies the mapping between extended terms and locations.

**Definition 2.10.** Let $\beta$ be an arbitrary variable assignment. The function $\text{Loc}_{s,P,\beta}$ delivers a set of locations for a closed extended term $t \in \text{LocTerm}^{\Sigma}$, a state $s$, and a program $P$. $\text{Loc}_{s,P,\beta}(t)$ is inductively defined as follows:

- $\text{Loc}_{s,P,\beta}(f(t_1, \ldots, t_n)) = \left\{ (f, (e_1, \ldots, e_n)) \in L_{\Sigma} \;\middle|\; \begin{array}{l} \text{for all } i = 1, \ldots, n: \\ e_i \in \text{val}_{s,P,\beta}(t_i) \end{array} \right\}$
- $\text{Loc}_{s,P,\beta}(\text{for } x \; ; \varphi \; ; t') = \bigcup_{*} \text{Loc}_{s,P,\beta}(t')$ if $x$ is of type $T$
- $\text{Loc}_{s,P,\beta}(t) = \emptyset$ in all other cases for location terms $t \in \text{LocTerm}^{\Sigma}$

The condition $*$ of the union in the second line is: There exists $e \in \text{Dom}(T)$ and a variable assignment $\beta$ such that $s, \beta_x^e \models_P \varphi$

$\text{Loc}_{s,P,\beta}$ is canonically continued for sets of location terms. With $E \subseteq \text{LocTerm}^{\Sigma}$:

$$\text{Loc}_{s,P,\beta}(E) = \{\text{Loc}_{s,P,\beta}(t) \mid t \in E\}$$

In essence, $\text{Loc}_{s,P,\beta}$ picks the top-level operator of an extended term (as first argument of the returned location) and evaluates the arguments of the term (which it takes as further arguments of the returned location).

**Example 2.2.** Assume $t$ is the extended term

$$(\text{for } i \,;\, 0 \leq i \wedge i < \texttt{self.length} \,;\, \texttt{self.a}[i])$$

Then $\mathrm{Loc}_{s,P,\beta}(t)$ results in

$$\begin{aligned}\mathrm{Loc}_{s,P,\beta}(t) &= \mathrm{Loc}_{s,P,\beta}(\texttt{self.a}[i]);\ \beta'(i) = e_1 \in \{0, \ldots, \texttt{self}^s.\texttt{length}^s - 1\} \\ &= \{(\texttt{[]}, \texttt{self}^s.\mathrm{a}^s, 0), (\texttt{[]}, \texttt{self}^s.\mathrm{a}^s, 1), \ldots, \\ &\qquad (\texttt{[]}, \texttt{self}^s.\mathrm{a}^s, \texttt{self}^s.\texttt{length}^s - 1)\}\end{aligned}$$ *

### Prenex Normal Form of Extended Terms

As a shorthand notation we use

$$(\text{for } x_1, \ldots, x_n \,;\, \varphi_1, \ldots, \varphi_n \,;\, t)$$

in place of

$$(\text{for } x_1 \,;\, \varphi_1 \,;\, (\text{for } x_2 \,;\, \varphi_2 \,;\, \cdots (\text{for } x_n \,;\, \varphi_n \,;\, t) \cdots))$$

We further note that $(\text{for } x_1, \ldots, x_n \,;\, \varphi_1, \ldots, \varphi_n \,;\, t)$ is equivalent to

$$(\text{for } x_1, \ldots, x_n \,;\, \varphi_1 \wedge \ldots \wedge \varphi_n \,;\, t)$$

Each extended term can be translated into an extended term of the following shape:

$$(\text{for } x_1, \ldots, x_n \,;\, \varphi \,;\, t)$$

where $t \in \mathrm{Term}^{\Sigma}$. We assume that all variables bound by a (for ; ; ) in the following terms are distinct and are also distinct from occurring free variables. By applying the following equation (from left to right) this normal form is achieved:

$$f(t_1, \ldots, t_n) = (\text{for } x \,;\, \varphi \,;\, f(t'_1, \ldots, t'_n))$$

for one $t_i = (\text{for } x \,;\, \varphi \,;\, t'_i)$ and $t_j = t'_j$ for all $j \in \{1, \ldots, n\} \backslash \{i\}$. Applying the above equation preserves validity, that is for every extended term there is an equal one (w.r.t. the valuation function) which is in prenex normal form.

### Shorthands

Especially in Chapter 9 the following, very typical shape of extended terms appears quite often:

$$(\text{for } x : T \ ; \ \text{true} \ ; \ x.a_1.\dots.a_n)$$

We thus introduce the following shorthand notation:

$$*_T \quad := \quad (\text{for } x : T \ ; \ \text{true} \ ; \ x)$$

We can then simply write $*_T.a_1.\dots.a_n$ (for $x : T$ ; true ; $x).a_1.\dots.a_n$. For any even more convenient notation we write for a function symbol $f$: $f(*)$ instead of $f(*_{\sigma(f)})$.

## 2.3 Java Dynamic Logic

Java Dynamic Logic (JavaDL) is a multi-modal logic to reason about sequences of Java statements, described in detail in Beckert [2000] and Beckert et al. [2006b]. It extends JavaFOL, so every formula of JavaFOL is a JavaDL formula. Moreover the semantics of JavaFOL terms (and formulae) and JavaDL terms (and formulae, resp.) is the same on the common subset. For an intuitive understanding it may be sufficient to state roughly that sub-formulae can be of the shapes $\langle\alpha\rangle\,\varphi$ and $[\alpha]\varphi$, where $\alpha$ is a sequence of Java statements and $\varphi$ is again a formula. $\langle\alpha\rangle$ and $[\alpha]$ are the *modalities* of JavaDL. Since there are infinitely many sequences of Java statements the logic consists of infinitely many modalities. The intuitive meaning of $[\alpha]\varphi$ is that, if $\alpha$ terminates normally $\varphi$ holds in the final state; $\langle\alpha\rangle\,\varphi$ means that $\alpha$ must terminate and afterwards $\varphi$ must hold. The logic is closed under the usual first-order quantifiers and junctors, so the typical Hoare triple $\{\psi\}\alpha\{\varphi\}$ is formalised as $\psi \rightarrow [\alpha]\varphi$.

There is a third kind of modality in JavaDL, called *updates*. Updates are a concise notation of state changes, and in fact the JavaDL calculus (see Sect. 2.3.5) transforms the other modalities step by step into updates. With updates we start a more thorough introduction to JavaDL following in the rest of this section. Note however that we can only discuss certain aspects of the logic since this is not the primary focus of our work. The ultimate references for a more thorough discussion are Beckert [2000] and Beckert et al. [2006a].

### 2.3.1 Updates

The notion of updates was introduced by Beckert [2000] and was refined by Rümmer [2005]. The following presentation of syntax and semantics of updates follows these sources.

**Definition 2.11** (Syntax of Updates). If $\Sigma$ is a signature, the set of updates $\mathrm{Upd}_0^\Sigma$ over $\Sigma$ is defined to be the smallest set with

- $\mathrm{skip} \in \mathrm{Upd}_0^\Sigma$ (the *empty* update)
- $t_1 := t_2 \in \mathrm{Upd}_0^\Sigma$ if $t_1 \in \mathrm{LocTerm}^\Sigma$, $t_2 \in \mathrm{Term}^\Sigma$ (an *elementary* update)
- $u_1|u_2 \in \mathrm{Upd}_0^\Sigma$ if $u_1, u_2 \in \mathrm{Upd}_0^\Sigma$ (a *parallel* update)
- $(\mathrm{for}\ x\ ;\ \varphi\ ;\ u) \in \mathrm{Upd}_0^\Sigma$ if $\varphi \in \mathrm{Fma}^\Sigma$, $x$ a logical variable, $u \in \mathrm{Upd}_0^\Sigma$ (a *quantified* update)

We define the set $\mathrm{Upd}^\Sigma$ of updates as

$$\mathrm{Upd}^\Sigma := \mathrm{Upd}_0^\Sigma \cup \{*^0, *^1, *^2, \ldots\}$$

where $(*^0, *^1, *^2, \ldots)$ is an unbounded sequence of *anonymous* updates.

Updates modify locations of a program as defined in Def. 2.8. With the help of locations we define the semantics of updates as follows; explanations follow.

**Definition 2.12** (Semantics of Updates). A *semantic update* is a partial function $L_\Sigma \to \mathcal{U}$.

Let $u \in \mathrm{Upd}_0^\Sigma$ be an update. The semantic update $\mathrm{updval}_{s,P,\beta}(u)$ is defined for $u$ in a state $s$, a program $P$, and a variable assignment $\beta$ inductively as follows:

- $\mathrm{updval}_{s,P,\beta}(\mathrm{skip})(loc) = \bot$ for all $loc \in L_\Sigma$
- $\mathrm{updval}_{s,P,\beta}(f(t_1, \ldots, t_n) := t)$
$$= \{(f, (\mathrm{val}_{s,P,\beta}(t_1), \ldots, \mathrm{val}_{s,P,\beta}(t_n))) \mapsto \mathrm{val}_{s,P,\beta}(t)\}$$
- $$\mathrm{updval}_{s,P,\beta}(u_1|u_2)(loc) = \begin{cases} \mathrm{updval}_{s,P,\beta}(u_1)(loc) & \text{if } \mathrm{updval}_{s,P,\beta}(u_2)(loc) = \bot \\ \mathrm{updval}_{s,P,\beta}(u_2)(loc) & \text{otherwise} \end{cases}$$
  for all $loc \in L_\Sigma$

- $\text{updval}_{s,P,\beta}(\text{for } x \;;\; \varphi \;;\; u)(loc) = \begin{cases} \text{updval}_{s,P,\beta_x^e}(loc) & \text{where } e \text{ is the smallest element of } \mathrm{Dom}(T) \text{ such that } s, \beta_x^e \models_P \varphi \\ \perp & \text{if no such } e \text{ exists} \end{cases}$

  for all $loc \in L_\Sigma$ where $x$ is of type $T$

This definition requires some additional comments:

- We allow for updating several locations in parallel, which is intended by the symbol $|$. Parallel updates may cause clashes, which need to be resolved by the semantics. In our definition a *last-win* clash resolution is in place, that is the most right update decides. Note, that the operator $|$ is thus not commutative. It is however associative.

- For quantified updates it may be possible that several locations qualify to be updated. To resolve this clash, we choose one of them, namely the smallest. This requires a well-order on the universe. This can be achieved quite naturally, for instance, objects of each class can be ordered according to the order in which they are (to be) created.

- For the semantics of anonymous updates, we employ choice functions as above delivering an unknown but fixed universe element. We presume that there is one such choice function $ch^*$ for every anonymous update $*$ with a signature accepting a function symbol and a list of universe elements. Then: $\text{updval}_{s,P,\beta}(*)(f(e_1, \ldots, e_n)) := ch^*(f, e_1, \ldots, e_n)$ for all anonymous updates $*$ and all locations $(f, (e_1, \ldots, e_n))$. The range of $\text{updval}_{s,P,\beta}(*)$ is thus fixed for every anonymous update $*$ but not further specified.

#### Relation between Extended Terms and Quantified Updates

Extended terms have a close correspondence with updates. For each extended term $t$ with a non-rigid top operator and a set of names for rigid functions we can associate a special *anonymising* update $u(t)$ with $t$. This update assigns a rigid term to all locations $(f, (e_1, \ldots, e_n))$ described by $t$. This rigid term has the same appearance as the $f$ with the exception that it is rigid. Such an update is later (for instance in Sect. 7.2.7) used to override the effects of assignments to the locations described by $t$.

**Definition 2.13.** For extended terms $t \in \mathrm{LocTerm}^\Sigma$ with non-rigid top level operator an *anonymising update* $u(t)$ is inductively defined as follows. We assume that $\Sigma$ contains special reserved rigid function symbols $f^r$ for every non-rigid function symbol $f$ with the same signature and result type.

$$u(f(t_1, \ldots, t_n)) := (f(t_1, \ldots, t_n) := f^r(t_1, \ldots, t_n))$$
$$u(\mathrm{for}\ x\ ;\ \varphi\ ;\ t) := (\mathrm{for}\ x\ ;\ \varphi\ ;\ u(t))$$

For non-empty finite sets $E = \{t_1, \ldots, t_n\} \subseteq \mathrm{LocTerm}^\Sigma$, we make $u$ produce a parallel update. In the case of an empty set, the empty update is obtained:

$$u(E) = \begin{cases} u(t_1)| \cdots |u(t_n) & n > 0 \\ \mathrm{skip} & \text{otherwise} \end{cases}$$

## 2.3.2 Syntax

The definition of syntax and semantics of Java Dynamic Logic, JavaDL for short, relies on the notion of a *program context* [Beckert, 2000] (or just *context* for short, if not subject to be mixed up). The context is just a closed program in our sense, that is, a legal (e.g. compilable) set of JavaCard class and interface definitions.

**Definition 2.14.** A (program) context is a closed program.

**Definition 2.15.** The set $\mathrm{DLFma}^\Sigma$ of JavaDL formulae over signature $\Sigma$ is defined to be the smallest set with

- $\mathrm{Fma}^\Sigma \subseteq \mathrm{DLFma}^\Sigma$
- If $\varphi \in \mathrm{DLFma}^\Sigma$ and $\alpha$ is a sequence of statements [Gosling et al., 2000] then $\langle\alpha\rangle\,\varphi, [\alpha]\varphi \in \mathrm{DLFma}^\Sigma$
- If $u \in \mathrm{Upd}^\Sigma$ then $\{u\}\varphi \in \mathrm{DLFma}^\Sigma$

When we refer to modal formulae independent from their kind, we write $\langle\!|\,|\!\rangle$.

### 2.3.3 Semantics

The semantics of JavaDL is defined in terms of Kripke structures $(S, \rho)$ for a given signature $\Sigma$ and a $\Sigma$-program $P$, with a set $S$ of states over $\Sigma$ and $\rho$ is a family of relations $\rho_\alpha \subseteq S \times S$ for every sequence of Java statements or update $\alpha$. We require $\rho$ to have some additional properties:

**Definition 2.16.** A pair $(S, \rho)$ is a JavaDL-Kripke structure if

- all universes in all states in $S$ are the same set (*constant domain assumption*),
- rigid functions and predicates have the same interpretations in all states of $S$,
- $S$ consists of all possible states over $\Sigma$.
- if $\alpha$ is a sequence of Java statements then $\rho_\alpha$ is defined according to the Java semantics [Gosling et al., 2000]. Let $s_1$ be a state. It is required that there is a state $s_2$ with $(s_1, s_2) \in \rho_\alpha$ iff $\alpha$ terminates normally when started in $s_1$. In particular, if $\alpha$ terminates abruptly when started in $s_1$ then there is no $s_2$ with $(s_1, s_2) \in \rho_\alpha$.
- if $\alpha$ is an update we define $\rho$ with the help of semantic updates. Let $U$ be a semantic update. For a state $s$ we define the state $s^U$ as follows:

  $$f^{s^U,P}(d_1, \ldots, d_n) = \begin{cases} U(f, (d_1, \ldots, d_n)) & \text{if } U(f, (d_1, \ldots, d_n)) \neq \bot \\ f^{s,P}(d_1, \ldots, d_n) & \text{otherwise} \end{cases}$$

  Then we require from $(S, \rho)$ for all $s \in S$ and with $U' = \mathrm{updval}_{s,P,\beta}(u)$:

  $$(s, s^{U'}) \in \rho_u$$

Consequently $\rho_\alpha$ for some sequence of Java statements or update $\alpha$ is a partial function since it reflects the semantics of Java, which is deterministic. We can thus write $\rho_\alpha$ as a function. More precisely, for an update $u$, $\rho_u$ is always total by the definition of $\rho_u$.

Moreover for a given signature $\Sigma$, a $\Sigma$-program $P$, and a universe there is exactly one JavaDL-Kripke structure. We will associate $\rho$ with a program $P$.

We define validity of JavaDL formulae as follows:

**Definition 2.17.** Let $\varphi \in \mathrm{DLFma}^\Sigma$ and $P$ a program. The validity relation is defined as in Def. 2.7 if $\varphi \in \mathrm{Fma}^\Sigma$. For the other cases:

- $s, \beta \models_P \langle\alpha\rangle\, \varphi$ if there exists a state $s'$ with $s' = \rho_\alpha(s)$ and $s', \beta \models_P \varphi$
- $s, \beta \models_P [\alpha]\varphi$ for all states $s'$ with $s' = \rho_\alpha(s)$: $s', \beta \models_P \varphi$
- $s, \beta \models_P \{u\}\varphi$ if $s', \beta \models_P \varphi$ with $s' = \rho_u(s)$

Note, that as already for JavaFOL terms (because of the occurrences of queries), a JavaDL-Kripke structure, and thus the validity of formulae, depends on the context, that is in particular, if we extend the context by additional elements, the validity of formulae changes too. We may extend the context but build programs only over the *unextended* context; even then the meaning of JavaDL formulae differs between extended and unextended context.

**Definition 2.18.** A JavaDL formula $\varphi \in \mathrm{Fma}^\Sigma$ is valid *in a context* of a $\Sigma$-program $P$ if it is valid in all states of the JavaDL-Kripke structure for $P$. We write: $\models_P \varphi$.

A set of JavaDL formulae is valid in a context if all elements are valid in that context.

### 2.3.4 Additional Details

We cannot describe JavaDL in depth. Instead we emphasise properties which play a role in the rest of this work.

**Abrupt Termination.** It is obvious that we cannot completely explain the properties of the transition relations $\rho_\alpha$ of JavaDL-Kripke structures since it reflects the whole (officially only informally described [Gosling et al., 2000]) Java semantics. The state transitions are in most cases natural and described in Beckert [2000]. There is however an issue in how to model abrupt termination. JavaDL is designed to treat abrupt termination [Gosling et al., 2000] as non-termination [Beckert and Sasse, 2001]. That is if $\alpha$ terminates abruptly, $\rho_\alpha(s)$ is undefined for all $s$. Consequently $\models_P [\alpha]$ false.

**Method Body Statements.** So far we have just said that a program $\alpha$ contained in formulae $\langle\alpha\rangle\varphi$ are sequences of Java statements containing plain Java statements. This is not entirely true since we allow a bit more. Actually there are two extensions [Beckert, 2000] of which one is needed in the rest of this work. Whenever a statement is expected according to the original Java grammar, we allow a *method body statement*. If $\mathtt{p}_1,\ldots,\mathtt{p}_n$ are local variables of types $T_1,\ldots,T_n$, and `r` is a local variable of type $T$, further `self` a local variable of type $D$, then method body statements can have one of the following forms:

| | |
|---|---|
| $\mathtt{r=self.m(p_1,\ldots,p_n)@}D$ | if there is a non-void instance method `m` declared in $D$ as $\mathrm{T}_0$ $\mathtt{m(p_1,\ldots,p_n)}$ |
| $\mathtt{self.m(p_1,\ldots,p_n)@}D$ | if there is a void instance method `m` declared in $D$ as $\mathtt{void\ m(p_1,\ldots,p_n)}$ |

Method body statements are semantically equivalent to the implementation of the method in the indicated class. Return values are assigned to the variable called `r` above.

**Referring to Previous States** Sometimes a formula *behind* a modality aims to refer to the interpretation of a non-rigid function symbol $f$ in some state *before* execution of this modality. The approach of Baar et al. [2001] to solve this problem works by introducing rigid functions symbols $f^{@pre}$ for $f$. $f^{@pre}$ is appropriately defined in front of the modality and used behind the modality. This works since the interpretations of rigid functions remain constant by state changes. The following definition formalises this concept. It introduces a function pre which delivers for a term or formula a pair which consists of the corresponding term which refers to the pre-state and a mapping which defines which non-rigid function $f$ corresponds to which rigid function $f^{@pre}$.

**Definition 2.19.** Let $\Sigma = (\mathcal{T}, \mathcal{F}^{nr}, \mathcal{F}^{r}, \mathcal{P}^{nr}, \mathcal{P}^{r}, \preceq, \sigma, \tau)$ be a signature. For an extended term $t \in \mathrm{ExtTerm}^\Sigma$ or a formula $\varphi \in \mathrm{Fma}^\Sigma$, the function *pre* delivers a tuple $(t^{@pre}, F^{@pre})$ where $t^{@pre} \in \mathrm{ExtTerm}^\Sigma$ (or $t^{@pre} \in \mathrm{Fma}^\Sigma$, resp) and $F^{@pre}$ is a mapping from non-rigid function or predicate symbols $f$ to rigid function or predicate (resp.) symbols $f^{@pre}$. pre is inductively defined as follows:

- $\mathrm{pre}(v) = (v, \emptyset)$ if $v$ is a logical variable,

- $\text{pre}(f(t_1,\ldots,t_n)) = (f^{@pre}(t'_1,\ldots,t'_n), F_0^{@pre} \cup \{(f, f^{@pre})\})$
  if $f \in \mathcal{F}^{nr} \cup \mathcal{P}^{nr}$, $\text{pre}(t_i) = (t'_i, F_i^{@pre})$
  for $i = 1,\ldots,n$, $F_0^{@pre} = \bigcup_{i=1,\ldots,n} F_i^{@pre}$,

- $\text{pre}(f(t_1,\ldots,t_n)) = (f(t'_1,\ldots,t'_n), F_0^{@pre})$
  if $f \in \mathcal{F}^r \cup \mathcal{P}^r \cup \{\doteq\}$, $\text{pre}(t_i) = (t'_i, F_i^{@pre})$ for $i = 1,\ldots,n$,
  $F_0^{@pre} = \bigcup_{i=1,\ldots,n} F_i^{@pre}$,

- $\text{pre}((\text{for } x \,;\, \varphi \,;\, t)) = ((\text{for } x \,;\, \varphi' \,;\, t'), F_1^{@pre} \cup F_2^{@pre})$
  if $\text{pre}(\varphi) = (\varphi', F_1^{@pre})$, $\text{pre}(t) = (t', F_2^{@pre})$

- $\text{pre}(\neg\varphi) = (\neg\varphi', F_0^{@pre})$ if $\varphi \in \text{Fma}^\Sigma$, $\text{pre}(\varphi) = (\varphi', F_0^{@pre})$,

- $\text{pre}(\varphi_1 \wedge \varphi_2) = (\varphi'_1 \wedge \varphi'_2, F_1^{@pre} \cup F_2^{@pre})$
  if $\varphi_1, \varphi_2 \in \text{Fma}^\Sigma$, $\text{pre}(\varphi_i) = (\varphi'_i, F_i^{@pre})$ for $i = 1, 2$ (analogously for the other junctors),

- $\text{pre}(\forall x\!:\!T.\ \varphi) = (\forall x\!:\!T.\ \varphi', F_0^{@pre})$, $\text{pre}(\varphi) = (\varphi', F_0^{@pre})$,

- $\text{pre}(\exists x\!:\!T.\ \varphi) = (\exists x\!:\!T.\ \varphi', F_0^{@pre})$, $\text{pre}(\varphi) = (\varphi', F_0^{@pre})$.

For a map $F^{@pre}$ as defined in this definition, the following defining term $\text{Def}(F^{@pre})$ is created:

$$\text{Def}(F^{@pre}) := \bigwedge_{(f, f^{@pre}) \in F^{@pre}} \text{Def}(f, f^{@pre})$$

$$\text{Def}(f, f^{@pre}) := \begin{cases} \forall x_1\!:\!T_1.\ \cdots \forall x_n\!:\!T_n. & \text{if } f \in F^{nr}, \\ \quad f(x_1,\ldots,x_n) \doteq f^{@pre}(x_1,\ldots,x_n) & \sigma(f) = (T_1,\ldots,T_n) \\ \forall x_1\!:\!T_1.\ \cdots \forall x_n\!:\!T_n. & \text{if } f \in P^{nr}, \\ \quad (f(x_1,\ldots,x_n) \leftrightarrow f^{@pre}(x_1,\ldots,x_n)) & \sigma(f) = (T_1,\ldots,T_n) \end{cases}$$

### 2.3.5 The JavaDL Calculus

The JavaDL calculus is a sequent calculus for JavaDL. Main characteristics are symbolic execution of code and lazy evaluation of state changes through updates.

### Sequent Calculus

The set $\mathrm{Seq}^{\Sigma}$ of sequents over a signature $\Sigma$ is the smallest set containing all constructs of the form

$$\psi_1, \ldots, \psi_m \vdash \varphi_1, \ldots, \varphi_n \qquad (m, n \geq 0)$$

where $\psi_1, \ldots, \psi_m, \varphi_1, \ldots, \varphi_n \in \mathrm{DLFma}^{\Sigma}$. The formulae on the left-hand side of the sequent symbol $\vdash$ are called the antecedent and those on the right-hand side are called the succedent of the sequent. The validity of this sequent (in a state) is the same as the validity (in a state) of the formula

$$\psi_1 \wedge \ldots \wedge \psi_m \rightarrow \varphi_1 \vee \ldots \vee \varphi_n$$

The set $\mathrm{Rule}^{\Sigma}$ of rules of a sequent calculus over a signature $\Sigma$ is the smallest set of elements of the form ($k \geq 0$):

$$\frac{seq_1 \quad \cdots \quad seq_k}{seq_0}$$

with $seq_0, \ldots, seq_n \in \mathrm{Seq}^{\Sigma}$ We call $seq_0$ the *conclusion* and $seq_1, \ldots, seq_k$ the *premises* of this rule.

Usually $\mathrm{Rule}^{\Sigma}$ is described by means of *rule schemas*. These are schematical representations of rules. A typical rule schema of a sequent calculus for propositional logic is for instance the rule

$$\frac{\Gamma \vdash \psi \rightarrow \varphi, \Delta}{\Gamma, \psi \vdash \varphi, \Delta}$$

This construct is schematical because we say in addition that $\varphi$ and $\psi$ stand for arbitrary formulae and $\Gamma$ and $\Delta$ represent arbitrary sets of formulae. It thus represents infinitely many rules. Apart from this rather informal (we need to annotate side-conditions on legal instantiations in textual form!) traditional way, rule schemas can also be denoted in formal languages like the *taclet* language [Beckert et al., 2004].

With a set of rules we can construct a proof of an initial sequent:

**Definition 2.20.** A *(closed) proof* in $\mathrm{Rule}^{\Sigma}$ of a sequent *seq* is a tree with the following properties:

(a) each node is either marked with a sequent or is empty,

(b) for all nodes with sequent $seq_0$: if $seq_1, \dots, seq_n$ are the sequents of all the children nodes then

$$\frac{seq_1, \dots, seq_n}{seq_0} =: r \in \text{Rule}^\Sigma$$

(we say: $seq_1, \dots, seq_n$ are the result of an application of $r$ on (the node with) $seq_0$)

(c) the root is the sequent $seq$,

(d) all leaves are empty.

A *(closed) proof* in $\text{Rule}^\Sigma$ of a formula $\varphi$ is a (closed) proof of the sequent $\vdash \varphi$.

### JavaDL Rules

A unique set of rule schemas defines the JavaDL calculus. It is described in Beckert [2000]. The actual rule instances depend on a signature and a program. For a signature $\Sigma$ and a $\Sigma$-program $P$, we call the set of rules of the JavaDL calculus over a signature $\text{JavaDLRule}_P^\Sigma$.

Note, that rules and a proof using these rules refer to a program context $P$. Soundness of rules is thus defined relative to the context.

**Definition 2.21.** With $seq_0, seq_1, \dots, seq_k \in \text{Seq}^\Sigma$, a rule

$$\frac{seq_1 \quad \cdots \quad seq_k}{seq_0}$$

is sound in a context $P$ if the following implication holds: If $seq_1, \dots, seq_k$ are valid in $P$ then $seq_0$ is valid in $P$. A rule is sound if it is sound in all contexts.

### Overview of the Calculus

We continue with a short excursus to how the JavaDL calculus works. The JavaDL calculus rules that work on JavaDL sequents can be divided into the following categories [Ahrendt et al., 2005b]:

1. axiomatic program transformation rules,

2. axiomatic rules connecting program and first order logic,

3. axiomatic first-order or theory specific rules,

4. derived rules, i.e. rules whose application could be simulated by applying a series of axiomatic rules,

5. axiomatic rules that apply state changes (*updates*, see Sect. 2.3.1) on first order formulae.

The basic concept behind the JavaDL calculus is the paradigm of *symbolic execution*. In order to resolve a formula $\langle\alpha\rangle\ \varphi$ , the first active statement, i.e. the statement following an inactive prefix consisting of opening braces, `try`s, labels, etc., is taken into focus first. If it contains complex expressions, rules of group 1 transform it into less complex expressions. Otherwise the state change of the first statement is, by applying rules of group 2, memorised as an update written in front of the modality. When code in a modality is completely worked off, rules of group 5 make the formula pure first order, by simplifying and executing the accumulated updates.

### Soundness of JavaDL Rules

The soundness of calculus rules is, of course, crucial to the verification of programs. Unfortunately, the point of reference to rules capturing the Java semantics is the *informal* description of the Java language [Gosling et al., 2000], which makes it impossible to formally verify the rules against the official specification.

There are however a number of techniques which help to ensure the soundness of rules:

- Calculus rules, and also those covering the Java semantics, can be implemented in a simple declarative schematic way as *taclets* [Beckert et al., 2004]. Taclets are representations of traditional rule schemas, but have in addition an operational meaning, which makes them easy to compile into the graphical user interface of interactive theorem provers. Most importantly however they have a precise notion of schematic expressions which is the basis for all formal soundness considerations as described in the following items.

- Under the co-supervision of the author, a procedure has been implemented which ensures the soundness of derived rules, thcsc are rules which are justified by other axiomatic rules but which are useful to improve interactive and automatic proof construction [Bubel et al., 2004,

Rümmer, 2003]. The procedure generates proof obligations for non-axiomatic rules. The proof obligations are formulae of JavaDL, and can then be proven using the original set of taclets. Thus this technique can can also be referred to as *bootstrapping*. With this approach it is made impossible to introduce rules into the calculus which are unsound with respect to a set of core axiomatic taclets.

- Likewise under the co-supervision of the author a procedure has been implemented [Ahrendt et al., 2005b, Sasse, 2005] which cross-validates a special kind of axiomatic JavaDL taclets, namely the large set of taclets which perform a local program transformation (group 1 of the enumeration above), against a high-level Java language specification. This Java semantics is given in terms of a an existing SOS style Rewriting Logic semantics. With the help of the rewriting system Maude and a special lifting procedure (to cope with schematic programs) the program transformation encoded in the taclet is verified w.r.t. the rewriting logic semantics. Though this procedure does not ensure the soundness of the considered type of rules, it at least reinforces confidence in the soundness.
- For some Java specific taclets from group 2 in the enumeration from above, Trentelman [2005] has proven other taclets formally in the interactive proof system *Isabelle* w.r.t. the Java formalisation *Bali*.

Soundness of Java specific rules cannot, due to the informal language specification, be guaranteed. Nevertheless, the above enumeration showed that it is possible to come at least 'very close' to soundness. We thus postulate:

**Lemma 2.2.** Given a signature $\Sigma$ and a $\Sigma$-program $P$. All $r \in \text{JavaDLRule}_P^\Sigma$ are sound in $P$.

**Lemma 2.3** (Soundness). If there is a closed proof in $\text{JavaDLRule}_P^\Sigma$ of a formula $\varphi$ then $\models_P \varphi$.

### 2.3.6 Initialisation

The complete sophisticated class initialisation mechanism of Java is covered by the JavaDL calculus [Bubel, 2001]. We are giving a brief impression of this issue, just enough to understand the role of initialisation when defining

| Modifier | specification-only Field | Declared | Explanation | Initial Value |
|---|---|---|---|---|
| private static | T <first> | T | refers to the first object of the repository | |
| private static | T <nextToCreate> | T | the object to be used when the next instance creation expression is evaluated | |
| private | T <next> | T | instance field implementing the object repository as an acyclic infinitely long list | |
| protected | boolean <created> | Object | indicates whether the object has been created | FALSE |
| protected | boolean <initialised> | Object | indicates whether the object has been initialised | FALSE |
| private static | boolean <classPrepared> | T | indicates whether the class has been prepared | FALSE |
| private static | boolean <classInitInProgress> | T | indicates whether the class is currently being initialised | FALSE |
| private static | boolean <classInitialized> | T | indicates whether the class has been initialised successfully | FALSE |
| private static | boolean <classErroneous> | T | indicates whether an error has occurred during initialisation | FALSE |

**Table 2.1:** Specification-Only fields for class and instance initialisation (adopted from Bubel [2001])

admissible initial states for invoking an operation of a specified program. Object and class initialisation are symbolically simulated with the help of special *specification-only fields* (referred to in Bubel [2001] as *implicit* fields) which indicate the state of initialisation of classes and objects. The state of class initialisation is captured by specification-only static fields and the state of object initialisation by specification-only instance fields. Table 2.1 gives a brief overview on the present specification-only fields and their meaning.

Specification-only fields are assigned during the symbolic execution of the class initialisation routine and the constructor. These assignments take place at the positions which are required by the Java language specification [Gosling et al., 2000] and the descriptions in Table 2.1. Since for example the static initialisation routine can not be invoked directly, for proof purposes it is available as a *specification-only method* `<clinit>()`. With these specification-only fields and methods we have an *explicit*[2] representation of the state of class initialisation and object creation.

We can in particular specify the *initial state* of a program $P$ as indicated in the last column of Table 2.1. The initial state can also be characterised by means of a JavaFOL formula:

$$\varphi_{\text{init}} :\Leftrightarrow \bigwedge_{C \in P} C.\texttt{<classPrepared>} \doteq \text{FALSE}$$

The state of all other specification-only fields can be concluded from this property since `<classPrepared>` is set to TRUE when static initialisation starts. Thus if it is assigned FALSE all other variables are still set to their default values. This is thus a built-in property of JavaDL and axiomatised in the JavaDL calculus.

With the help of specification-only fields we can also formalise judgements in JavaFOL like 'all *created* objects of type $T$ satisfy property $\varphi$'. This is written down as follows:

$$\forall o{:}T.\ \big(o.\texttt{<created>} \doteq \text{TRUE} \rightarrow \varphi\big)$$

Often, when talking about programs and quantifying this is exactly what is intended; it occurs quite rarely that all, even not created objects, are to be qualified. Thus we introduce an abbreviating notation for all formulae $\varphi$ and all logical variables $o$ of type $T$:

$$\dot{\forall} o{:}T.\ \varphi \quad :\Leftrightarrow \quad \forall o{:}T.\ \big(o.\texttt{<created>} \doteq \text{TRUE} \rightarrow \varphi\big)$$

Similarly for the existential quantifier:

$$\dot{\exists} o{:}T.\ \varphi \quad :\Leftrightarrow \quad \exists o{:}T.\ (o.\texttt{<created>} \doteq \text{TRUE} \wedge \varphi)$$

## 2.4 Proof Obligations

The notion of proof obligation is quite central to the second main part of this work. We give a precise characterisation of *proof obligation* but do not define a further (unnecessary) formal language on top of JavaDL.

[2] This is why we do not use the original term *implicit* for specification-only fields. *Implicit* was introduced to state that these fields and methods are always implicitly be present.

A *proof obligation template* is a JavaDL formula schema with an attached name which (possibly) depends on *schema parameters*. Schema parameters may occur in the JavaDL formula at any node of the syntax tree. By replacing (*instantiating*) the schema parameters of a proof obligation with concrete elements, a concrete *instantiated* formula results. Attached (informal) description describes two aspects of an instantiation. It requires that

- the *instantiations* to the schema parameters are restricted to certain syntactical categories like formulae, operations, etc. This ensures that syntactically correct JavaDL formulae result.
- some parameters are instantiated a bounded number of times, for instance it may say that a schema parameter is instantiated *for all* operations of a certain class.

A *proof obligation* is a set of JavaDL formulae originating from an instantiation of a proof obligation template. Consequently a proof obligation is *valid* in a context if all elements are valid in that context. In the sequel we introduce two other flavours of validity. Validity on proof obligations is always interpreted in the sense of validity (in the respective flavour) of a set of formulae.

Proof obligations which relate programs and specifications are often called *vertical proof obligations* or *program correctness proof obligations* as opposed to *horizontal proof obligations* or *design validation proof obligations* which are properties of specifications only. In this work we only focus on *program correctness* proof obligations. See Roth [2006] for an account on horizontal proof obligations.

# Part I

# Specifications for Extensibility

# 3 Functional Specifications of Programs

Ignoranti quem portum petat
nullus suus ventus est.

*(Seneca)*

A specification is a description of the behaviour of a system. In this work we are merely concerned with *functional* behaviour, and not with temporal properties nor with performance guarantees.

The nature of specifications can be very different concerning the degree of formalisation. The range starts with informal descriptions which can be found in user handbooks and still informal though more precise description of Application Programming Interfaces (API) like those for the Java libraries. True *formal* specifications can be created with the help of formal specification languages which are backed by a precise semantics. This is the degree of formalisation we are focusing in the sequel. Yet the most precise and most formal kind of 'specification' is a concrete implementation of a system: All behaviour is (at least for sequential programs) clearly and unambiguously defined and even executable. So why should there be other kind of specifications at all?

Specifications that are different from implementations are important: They abstract away from *how* a behaviour is realised and just describe declaratively *what* is expected. They can be partial, that is, they may specify only certain aspects of a program and not the entire behaviour. Because they are (often) much clearer than algorithms, they are a better means to communicate to users of a system such as developers extending the system. This is particularly important with *open* programs which are designed to be extended. Finally formal specifications are besides implementations a second *formal* artifact which makes it possible to formally reason about the correctness of systems. Specifications are thus the necessary basis of formal methods like formal verification. Formal specifications are moreover a good compromise between the accessibility to human developers and the formality needed to do formal reasoning.

In the last decade one dominating concept of how object-oriented systems are specified has emerged: the methodology of *design by contract* [Meyer, 1992]. Specifications are designed according to the conceptual metaphor of legal contracts. As when a legal contract is entered, there are different parties, in object-oriented programming these are usually *objects*, which state certain promises to the respective other party and enter into a commitment to this party. On the other hand each party benefits from the reliable services the other party provides. Contracts for a program are thus a system of mutual obligations which *must* be fulfilled by the objects emerging from the program.

**Outline.** This chapter starts with the definition of what formal contracts are in the context of object-oriented programs, and more concretely Java programs. In Sect. 3.2 we are dealing with the question under which circumstances a program fulfils a contract-based specification. To continue the analogy to contracts, this section will constitute the law of contract for the formal contracts we are looking at. Finally, in Sect. 3.3 we briefly survey two specification languages which allow us to create formal contract-based specifications.

## 3.1 Essentials of Formal Specifications of Programs

In this section we define the syntax of formal contracts for operations and classes and give intuitive explanations of their meaning. A precise semantics of these contracts is discussed later (Sect. 3.2).

Contracts are always defined relative to a program $P$, which is, as defined in Sect. 2.1, a set of Java classes and interfaces. The parties which are involved in the contract are program elements of $P$. A contract is usually concerned with a specific program element, usually a method or class declaration, of the contract parties.

The nature of contracts is that they promise reliable services *and* hold obligations. Services and obligations of a contract must always be seen as an implication: If all obligations are fulfilled then all services can be provided.

Summarised, we can say all contracts have in common to consist of

- a set of parties, which are program elements from $P$,

- an object of contract which is (part of) a party,
- an obligation the parties have to establish such that
- a service, concerning the contracted element, is provided by the parties.

Note that this general notion of contract is a mere mental model and the above is, by far, no formal definition. In particular, when we now more precisely capture operation and invariant contracts, the involved parties do not all need to be explicitly given.

Technically we define two sets of contracts on a program $P$ in the following sub-sections: the set of operation contracts and the set of invariants. These two sets together form a *specification* of $P$.

**Definition 3.1.** Given a signature $\Sigma$ and a $\Sigma$-program $P$, a (JavaFOL) specification over $\Sigma$ of $P$ is a pair $(\mathrm{OpCt}, \mathrm{Inv})$ consisting of

- a set OpCt of operation contracts of $P$ over $\Sigma$ (Def. 3.2),
- a set Inv of invariants of $P$ over $\Sigma$ (Def. 3.8).

The *union* of two specifications $(\mathrm{OpCt}_1, \mathrm{Inv}_1)$ and $(\mathrm{OpCt}_2, \mathrm{Inv}_2)$ is defined component-wise:

$$(\mathrm{OpCt}_1 \cup \mathrm{OpCt}_2, \mathrm{Inv}_1 \cup \mathrm{Inv}_2)$$

### 3.1.1 Operation Contracts

The classical representative of a contract is an *operation contract.* In this case, the concerned program element is a declaration of an operation[1] *op*. The involved parties are the following two types:

- the unknown class which is the runtime type of an object which may call *op*,
- the type in which *op* is defined.

The latter can be derived from the description of the operation declaration *op*, which we assume to hold information on where it is declared, while the former is not specific to the contract; it can be just any type. The formal

[1]Remember that we denote methods and constructors as *operations*.

representation of an operation contract will thus only contain the operation declaration; there are no explicit entries for the involved parties.

According to Meyer [1992], the obligation in an operation contract is that the caller object ensures a condition $\varphi_{\text{pre}}$ (called *precondition*) before calling *op*. The service the contract guarantees is that the called method ensures the *postcondition* $\varphi_{\text{post}}$ to hold in the state when the method has terminated.

Beyond this classical form of an operation contract, there are a couple of more elements and details that must be available to cover the behaviour of programs sufficiently and to allow for modular reasoning.

First and foremost, as an additional obligation, *assignable clauses* (also known as *modifies* or *modifier clauses*) are part of a contract. An assignable clause indicates which locations are allowed to be modified by *op*. Modifications not visible to the outside, such as temporary modifications during the execution of *op*, are allowed though. Their precise semantics is discussed in Sect. 3.2.3.

Moreover a specifier may want to express the termination behaviour of *op*. It turns out that it is sufficient to specify whether the operation must terminate or if non-termination is allowed. From a practical point of view both options make sense: The first since almost never non-termination should be allowed, and the second since it can be quite difficult to *prove* termination. Skipping the obligation that *op* must terminate will thus facilitate formal verification. If operations are required to terminate and are correct in all other aspects, one refers to this assertion as *total correctness*, if termination is not required but assumed, this is referred to as *partial correctness*.

An operation may as well terminate *abruptly* by throwing an exception. We can however encode this in the postcondition $\varphi_{\text{post}}$ as follows: A special variable `exc` is used which can be specified to be equal to `null`, then no exception has been thrown by *op*, or contain an exception object, which is then specified to be the one thrown by *op*.

Preconditions and postconditions describe first order properties of a state. They are thus denoted as JavaFOL formulae as defined in the last chapter. Similarly, assignable clauses specify locations, which can be described by an extended term, so that an assignable clause is denoted as a set of extended terms.

**Definition 3.2.** Let $\Sigma$ be a signature and $P$ a $\Sigma$-program. An operation contract over $\Sigma$ for an operation of $P$ consists of

- the description *op* of an operation declaration in a class or interface declaration of $P$; according to Gosling et al. [2000] this is a triple consisting of:

- the identifier of the operation,
- the parameter types $T_1, \ldots T_n$, and
- the class or interface (or just skeleton) $T$ which declares the operation.

This suffices to identify an operation in a Java program; the return type $T^r$ can be uniquely derived from the above information.

- a precondition $\varphi_{\text{pre}}(\texttt{self}; \texttt{p}_1, \ldots, \texttt{p}_n) \in \text{Fma}^\Sigma$ containing program variables[2] `self` of type $T$ for the receiver object, and $\texttt{p}_1, \ldots, \texttt{p}_n$ of types $T_1, \ldots, T_n$ for the parameters,
- a postcondition $\varphi_{\text{post}}(\texttt{self}; \texttt{p}_1, \ldots, \texttt{p}_n; \texttt{r}; \texttt{exc}) \in \text{Fma}^\Sigma$ containing program variables `self` for the receiver object, $\texttt{p}_1, \ldots, \texttt{p}_n$ for the parameters (all of the same types as above), `r` of type $T^r$ for the returned value or object, and `exc` of the built-in type `java.lang.Throwable` for the thrown exception; `exc` and `r` are optional if the method's thrown exception or return type (resp.) is irrelevant or non-existent,
- a set $\mathit{Mod}(\texttt{self}; \texttt{p}_1, \ldots, \texttt{p}_n) \subseteq \text{LocTerm}^\Sigma$ of location terms, i.e. extended terms with field or array access symbol as top-level operator (Sect. 2.2.4), as assignable clause which may contain program variables `self` for the receiver object and $\texttt{p}_1, \ldots, \texttt{p}_n$ for the parameters (all of the same types as above); the set is missing in the contract or is equivalently replaced by the marker *everything* if no restrictions on modifications are required,
- a marker from $\{\mathit{partial}, \mathit{total}\}$; the marker *total* is set if and only if the operation contract requires the operation to terminate, otherwise *partial* is set.

**Definition 3.3.** An operation contract with operation description *op* is *for* an operation declaration *op'* if *op* describes *op'*.

[2] These program variables act as formal parameters, and are substituted on demand by other expressions, we could equally have chosen logical variables as formal parameters. `self` is skipped throughout the definition if the considered operation is a static method.

An operation contract *opct* is *applicable* to an operation $op'$ if *opct* is a contract for $op'$ or for a method which $op'$ (indirectly) overrides.

Note that the formulae and location terms being part of a specification are parameterised with variables $\texttt{self}, \texttt{p}_1, \ldots, \texttt{p}_n, \texttt{r}$, and `exc`. This is to make the expressions aware of the receiver object, the parameter objects or primitive values, the returned object or primitive value, and the exception object `exc` which was the reason for the abrupt termination of *op* and which is assigned `null` if no such abrupt termination happened.

Note further, that we, for a uniform treatment, assume that all operations have an operation contract; operations without contract have *true* as precondition, *true* as postcondition, the *partial* marker, and *everything* as assignable clause. The same defaults are set if a particular part of an operation contract is missing. For all operation contracts of an operation *op*, we write $\mathrm{OpCt}_{op}$.

### 3.1.2 Invariants

Invariants are properties that must hold in all states that can be observed. We will define this more closely in Sect. 3.2.

Following the Java Modeling Language [Leavens et al., 2006], two types of invariants can be distinguished:

**Instance invariants.** These invariants make statements about a specific (created) object $o$ of type $T$. In certain states, the specified property must hold for all created instances $o$ of $T$. We define these states precisely in Sect. 3.2. An instance invariant could be represented in JavaFOL as a formula with a free logical variable $o$; the free variable represents the object which the instance invariant must hold for.

**Static invariants.** These invariants do not refer to a specific object. Their representations as JavaFOL formulae are closed. The specified property must hold even if no object of the type a static invariant is attached to exists, and even if no object exists at all.

Looking more closely at these two kinds of invariants, there is in fact no need to further distinguish between static and instance invariants. The semantics of an instance invariant, represented in JavaFOL formula as $\varphi(\texttt{self})$ is equivalent to the meaning of the static invariant $\dot{\forall} o\!:\!T.\ \varphi(o)$. As required, and assured by quantifying over all created objects, if this formula is valid, the corresponding instance invariant holds for all created instances of $T$.

Later in Sect. 3.2.4 we will allow that our program adopts states where classes are not statically initialised. Note, that this is extending JavaCard where all classes are statically initialised beforehand, so that we would not have to cope with this case if we were not extending our focus to sequential Java. If such states are allowed however, say that in a state class `C` is not initialised, a formula like `a@(C)` $\doteq 0$ (`a` is a static field of `C`) would not hold. In the case of instance invariants we escape from this problem since we quantified over all *created* instances; here we cannot 'quantify' over all statically initialised classes, since we are only having a first order logic. The way out is that static invariants need to 'take care' themselves that they are valid in the initial state.

The example from above `a@(C)` $\doteq 0$ could be re-written as

$$\texttt{<classInitialized>@(C)} \doteq \text{TRUE} \rightarrow \texttt{a@(C)} \doteq 0$$

this is then trivially the case. When we imagine a scenario like in the KeY tool where invariants in FOL are created from a translation from a specification language like JML, then this translation needs to take care that such qualifications are introduced. Instance invariants in the normalised quantified form $\dot{\forall} o{:}T.\ \varphi(o)$ are trivially covered by the characterisation from above and are legal invariants for arbitrary $\varphi(o)$ with a single free variable $o$.

So we treat instance invariants and static invariants in a uniform manner. They are represented as closed JavaFOL formulae. One could say we only have *static* invariants.

We remark in conclusion, that though it cannot be seen as easily as with operation contracts, invariants can be considered as contracts, too. The role of the contract parties *and* the object of contract is played by *all* classes in $P$, the obligation of all classes in $P$ is that their methods establish the invariant, and the provided service is that invariants can be assumed when an operation is called.

## 3.2 Observed-State Program Correctness

In this section we define what we consider to be a correct program with respect to a JavaFOL specification. We define a new notion of correctness,

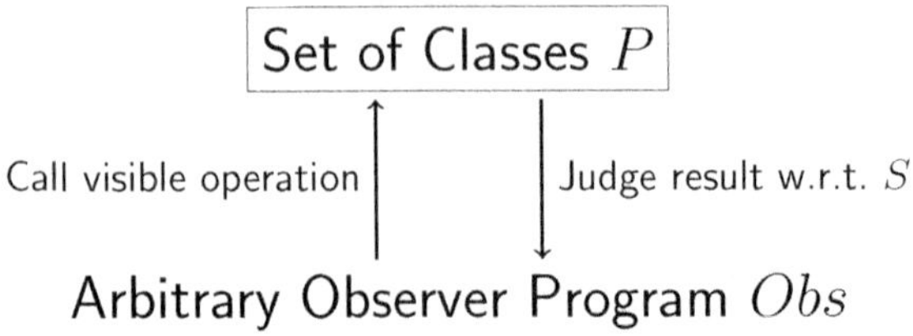


**Figure 3.1:** Illustration of the observer model

called *observed-state correctness*. This notion of correctness comes in two variants: *observed-state call correctness* and *observed-state durable correctness*. The first is valuable only in the context of closed programs, while the latter makes sense in the presence of open programs. However it is more difficult to show durable correctness. In Chapters 7 and 10 we present proof obligations which ensure the correctness criteria imposed here.

Let $P$ be a Java program and $S$ a specification for $P$. Under which conditions is $P$ correct with respect to $S$? To define correctness of a program we consider it most natural to take the view of an *observer* of $P$. We can think of the observer as an external program that calls a series of methods or constructors of $P$. By picking out an arbitrary one of these calls it is possible to judge whether the execution corresponded to the behaviour specified in $S$. Fig. 3.1 illustrates these settings.

The decision to take the view of an observer implies that we are *not* interested in *intermediate* states that are reached during the execution of the called method or constructor. The only states of interest are the state which the operation is invoked in (*pre-state*) and the state in which it terminates (*post-state*). Note, that this decision complies best with the *design by contract* methodology.

In the pre- and post-state, the observer may however inspect all internal details of the *whole* program $P$, that is he can see all locations of $P$ for the purpose of judging whether $P$ is correct.

The pre-state and the post-state of an operator call have to be characterised in more detail. It must be made clear which conditions can be *assumed* in the pre-state of the method or constructor and which must be *ensured* in its post-state. Furthermore, we should investigate which calls from the observer to the operation are allowed.

Apart from invoking a method or constructor, an observer of $P$ may trigger the static initialisation of classes in $P$. As sketched in Sect. 2.3.6, the JavaDL calculus simulates the static initialisation routine as a static *implicit method* $C$.`<clinit>()` of every class $C$. Like ordinary methods or constructors, `<clinit>()` can be invoked by the observer. Due to its special nature there are different assumptions and assertions to apply than for ordinary methods or constructors. This issue is discussed in Sect. 3.2.4. To make the approach manageable in practice, we require stronger conditions than actually necessary after static initialisation, and can thus make stronger assumptions on the state of static initialisation when calling ordinary methods and constructors (see Sect. 3.2.4).

Finally we remark that *observer* is a mere metaphor to justify our decisions concerning correctness. Since the observer is just a closure of the observed program, it becomes also manifest in the notion of a *program context* in which the observed program runs. There would even be no principal obstacle to identify these two notions. We however believe that it is a good mental model to think of an observer as an *actor* which calls a program and judges the results of the call.

### 3.2.1 Assumptions before Operation Calls

From an abstract point of view, both, the implementation and the specification of an operation describe a function that transfers a pre-state $s_{\text{pre}}$ to a post-state $s_{\text{post}}$. When we consider the specification of an operation, this function is however (most often) *partial*. This means, a specification may not define for *all* pre-states which post-state the operation establishes. This strategy strictly assigns the responsibility to check for conditions which are necessary for the operation to 'behave well' to the *caller*. With this clear division of labour, unnecessary checks (i.e. both in caller and receiver) are avoided [Meyer, 1992]. Moreover, working with assumptions allows for *partial* specifications that can at a later stage be completed to full functional specifications. Note, that the *implementation* of an operation is total if and only if the operation terminates; when it terminates but there is no precondition met, possibly unintuitive results may be the consequence for some inputs.

A not satisfied assumption does not mean that calling an operation is forbidden. It just means that with such a particular pre-state there is no behaviour *specified*. In such a case, anything can happen, be it non-termination, a thrown exception, or any other behaviour.

Two kinds of specifications and an implicit condition constrain the states $s_{\text{pre}}$ for which there is a specified behaviour of the method. They will be discussed in detail below:

- preconditions,
- invariants,
- state of initialisation and static initialisation.

Moreover we require that $s_{\text{pre}}$ is *reachable* from the start state of the system by calling operations on $P$ and performing statements in the observer. A reachable state can be any intermediate state in the observer. Without using the term *intermediate* we define:

**Definition 3.4.** A state $s$ is *reachable* by a program $P$ if there is an arbitrary closure $P^{cl}$ of $P$ such that at the end of a method execution of $P^{cl} \backslash P$ state $s$ is reached.

Obviously other states do not need to be considered as pre-states of an operation, since it will never be the case that, when an operation of $P$ is invoked, program execution is in another state.

In fact it would suffice to say that the only assumptions imposed on $s_{\text{pre}}$ are, that preconditions of the invoked operation hold (see below) and that $s_{\text{pre}}$ is reachable. When formalising proof obligations, such a requirement is unfortunately impossible to meet as our first order specification language is not capable of making statements about reachability of states. The way out is that we must *characterise* reachable states by properties which they must satisfy. And this is exactly what invariants do. Nevertheless for the theoretical definition of allowed pre-states we include the condition that these states must be reachable. When formalising proof obligations, we will weaken this assumption and allow even unreachable states as pre-states.

### Preconditions

Preconditions in operation contracts describe states for which the operation must establish the specific assertion in the operation contract. Since an operation may posses more than one operation contract, there is also more than one precondition available for this operation. *All* preconditions together define under which conditions calls to the operation yield a specified result. Or, in turn, if no precondition is valid, there is no result of the operation specified. So at least one of the preconditions or, in other words, the disjunction of all preconditions can be assumed to hold in the pre-state.

If $\Phi(\mathtt{self}; \mathtt{p}_1, \ldots, \mathtt{p}_n)$ is the set of preconditions of all operation contracts for an operation *op* then states $s_{\mathrm{pre}}$ satisfying

$$s_{\mathrm{pre}} \models_P \bigvee_{\varphi_{\mathrm{pre}}(\mathtt{self}; \mathtt{p}_1, \ldots, \mathtt{p}_n) \in \Phi} \varphi_{\mathrm{pre}}(\mathtt{self}; \mathtt{p}_1, \ldots, \mathtt{p}_n)$$

qualify as pre-states for a call to *op* with `self` as receiver and $\mathtt{p}_1, \ldots, \mathtt{p}_n$ as arguments.

When we are considering the correctness of an implementation w.r.t. one particular operation contract *opct*, this statement can of course be made more specific: we then require that the precondition of this particular operation contract *opct* must hold. The assumption stated above is obviously a consequence of such a stronger one.

### Invariants

Invariants describe conditions that are, for an observer, always present in the observed program. Though invariants are typically (and enforced by the specification languages UML/OCL and JML) defined in one class or interface, their effective scope is in fact global. In particular, a method called by the observer can rely on the fact that invariants hold which are defined in other types than that which the method is declared in. On the other hand, we will state below that an observed method must in turn establish the invariants of all other classes.

Assume that Inv is the set of all invariants in JavaFOL representation. Remember, that we have normalised instance invariants to closed formulae, so that we can treat instance invariants in the same manner as other static invariants.

An observer may now assume in the pre-state of a method or constructor, that the judgements formalised in Inv hold.

To validate this decision it is worthwhile to look at the assumptions in the following special cases:

- Consider a state where no classes are initialised and no objects created. According to our mental model, instance invariants do not need to hold in such a state. And in fact the instance invariant quantified over all created objects evaluates trivially to true. In Def. 3.8 we will, moreover, only allow static invariants which evaluate to true if all classes are not initialised.

- Before the invocation of a constructor, the instance invariant of the object to be created is not assumed to hold since we restrict our quantification to all created objects. This is as desired.

- When the constructor terminates normally an object is created and quantification includes it. Again this reflects our idea of what we expect from an invariant.

- When the constructor terminates abruptly the object is created but not initialised. We must however require that invariants hold for such objects, too. The reason is that during object initialisation references may have leaked and are then available to other objects. If this is really the case could be checked and in the case that it has not happened calculus rules would 'destroy' the unreachable object. This has however not been realised in JavaDL. The current solution makes it practically impossible to throw exceptions in constructors, invariants must be established before this can happen. This leads to unnatural code.

  An alternative would be to make invariants hold for all *initialised* objects only. This would however have the drawback that it would almost become impossible to *apply* invariants during verification, since it would be necessary to show that objects are initialised. This would however again require to specify in pre-conditions that all (reachable) objects are initialised, which would result in unreadable and impractical specifications.

As a summary, we have as additional requirement for a state $s_{\mathrm{pre}}$ which qualifies for a call to *op*:

$$s_{\mathrm{pre}} \models_P \bigwedge_{\varphi \in \mathrm{Inv}} \varphi$$

### Initialisation

It makes sense to have additional implicit assumptions to be present. For methods, we should require that the called object is already created, such that the following is always an implicit assumption at the method entry.

$$\texttt{self.<created>} \doteq \mathrm{TRUE}$$

This is however only true if there is a receiver object. In case of a constructor or a static method it does not make sense to add this assumption.

Note, that this requirement is stronger than just $\texttt{self} \not\doteq \texttt{null}$, since, as described in Sect. 2.3, we have a constant domain assumption, so all objects are assumed to exist before they are created. It is however not possible for an observer to call methods on such objects.

Moreover we have to require for all arguments $\texttt{p}_1, \ldots, \texttt{p}_n$ of the operation call to invoke that they are created or equal to `null`. Obviously an observer cannot use not created objects as arguments. So for all parameters $i = 1, \ldots, n$:

$$\texttt{p}_i\texttt{.<created>} \doteq \mathrm{TRUE} \quad \vee \quad \texttt{p}_i \doteq \texttt{null}$$

Furthermore some more assumptions are made due to static class initialisation in Sect. 3.2.4. Since these assumptions are also assertions we will treat them as additional invariants which are always present in our assumptions.

### The General Assumption

Altogether, this yields the following *general assumption* for a set $I$ of invariants and for the implicitly given set OpCt of operation contracts, an instance method *op*, and suitable variables $o$, $p_1, \ldots, p_n$ for the receiver object and the parameters of *op*:

$$\begin{aligned}\mathcal{A}_{op}(I; o; p_1, \ldots, p_n) := \bigwedge_{\varphi \in I} \varphi \wedge \Big( & \bigvee_{\substack{\varphi_{pre} \\ \text{precondition} \\ \text{of } \mathrm{OpCt}_{op}}} \varphi_{\mathrm{pre}}(o; p_1, \ldots, p_n)\Big) \\ & \wedge o\texttt{.<created>} \doteq \mathrm{TRUE} \\ & \wedge \bigwedge_{i=1,\ldots,n} (\texttt{p}_i\texttt{.<created>} \doteq \mathrm{TRUE} \vee \texttt{p}_i \doteq \texttt{null})\end{aligned}$$

for static methods and constructors *op*:

$$\mathcal{A}_{op}(I;;p_1,\ldots,p_n) := \bigwedge_{\varphi\in I}\varphi \wedge \Big(\bigvee_{\substack{\varphi_{pre}\\ \text{precondition}\\ \text{of } \mathrm{OpCt}_{op}}} \varphi_{pre}(p_1,\ldots,p_n)\Big)$$
$$\wedge \bigwedge_{i=1,\ldots,n} \big(\mathtt{p}_i.\mathtt{<created>} \doteq \mathrm{TRUE} \vee \mathtt{p}_i \doteq \mathtt{null}\big)$$

Most often, we use the general assumption for the case $I = \mathrm{Inv}$, where (as always) Inv are *all* invariants of the whole program. Thus we write

$$\begin{aligned}\mathcal{A}_{op}(o;p_1,\ldots,p_n) &:= \mathcal{A}_{op}(\mathrm{Inv};o;p_1,\ldots,p_n)\\ \mathcal{A}_{op}(;p_1,\ldots,p_n) &:= \mathcal{A}_{op}(\mathrm{Inv};;p_1,\ldots,p_n)\end{aligned}$$

This general assumption subsumes all the requirements stated above for states which qualify as pre-states for a call to *op* with *o* as receiver (if there is one) and $p_1,\ldots,p_n$ as parameters. It is thus generally sufficient to require from pre-states $s_{\mathrm{pre}}$:

$$\begin{aligned}&s_{\mathrm{pre}} \models_P \mathcal{A}_{op}(o;p_1,\ldots,p_n)\\ \text{and } &s_{\mathrm{pre}} \models_P \mathcal{A}_{op}(;p_1,\ldots,p_n) \quad \text{resp.}\end{aligned}$$

Only if we are focusing on a special operation contract, we may narrow down the set of allowed pre-states by requiring that the precondition of this operation contract holds in $s_{\mathrm{pre}}$.

In the sequel we use, for brevity, only the form $s_{\mathrm{pre}} \models_P \mathcal{A}_{op}(o;p_1,\ldots,p_n)$, and not the one lacking the $o$.

Note again, that we would, if it was possible to formalise in JavaFOL, require that $s_{\mathrm{pre}}$ is a reachable state.

### 3.2.2 Operation Calls

To compare implemented and specified behaviour, the observer must invoke the method or constructor. The call is arbitrary in the sense that we have arbitrary receiver and arguments for the call. We are thus using unknown but fixed objects which we assume to be stored in the suitably typed program variables `self` (for the receiver object, if one is needed) and as well suitably typed argument program variables $\mathtt{p}_1,\ldots,\mathtt{p}_n$. Depending on the signature,

| $\alpha_{op}(\texttt{self}; \texttt{p}_1, \ldots, \texttt{p}_n; \texttt{r})$ | |
|---|---|
| `r=self.`$m$`(`$\texttt{p}_1$`,...,`$\texttt{p}_n$`)@`$D$`;` | if *op* is a method implemented in type $D$ declared as $D_0$ $m(D_1, \ldots, D_n)$ |
| `self.`$m$`(`$\texttt{p}_1$`,...,`$\texttt{p}_n$`)@`$D$`;` | if *op* is a method implemented in type $D$ declared as `void` $m(D_1, \ldots, D_n)$ |
| `r=`$D$`.`$m$`(`$\texttt{p}_1$`,...,`$\texttt{p}_n$`);` | if *op* is a method implemented in type $D$ declared as `static` $D_0$ $m(D_1, \ldots, D_n)$ |
| $D$`.`$m$`(`$\texttt{p}_1$`,...,`$\texttt{p}_n$`);` | if *op* is a method implemented in type $D$ declared as `static void` $m(D_1, \ldots, D_n)$ |
| `r=new` $D$`(`$\texttt{p}_1$`,...,`$\texttt{p}_n$`);` | if *op* is a constructor declared as $D(D_1, \ldots, D_n)$ |

**Table 3.1:** Programs in Proof Obligations

a variable (usually called `r`) that captures the returned value of a non-void method call is needed.

The observer basically uses the statement $\alpha_{op}(\texttt{self}; \texttt{p}_1, \ldots, \texttt{p}_n; \texttt{r})$ listed in Table 3.1, depending on the program variables introduced above, as call to method or constructor *op*. Note, that we use *method body statements* as introduced in Sect. 2.3. This means, dynamic binding is not triggered by the observer call, instead a concrete method body is executed.

This is however not completely what is desired. Our observer should naturally not see the assignments made to the arguments of the operation call. Thus we assign the arguments $\texttt{p}_1, \ldots, \texttt{p}_n$ to fresh variables $\texttt{p}'_1, \ldots, \texttt{p}'_n$ before the method body statement. So if $\texttt{T}_1, \ldots, \texttt{T}_n$ are the static types of $\texttt{p}_1, \ldots, \texttt{p}_n$ we use instead of $\alpha_{op}$ the following statements:

$\texttt{T}_1\ \texttt{p}'_1 = \texttt{p}_1;$
$\vdots$
$\texttt{T}_n\ \texttt{p}'_n = \texttt{p}_n;$
$\alpha_{op}(\texttt{self}; \texttt{p}'_1, \ldots, \texttt{p}'_n; \texttt{r})$

Recall that JavaDL defined abrupt termination as non-termination. If the observer 'executes' $\alpha_{op}(\texttt{self}; \texttt{p}_1, \ldots, \texttt{p}_n; \texttt{r})$ this implies that no statement about the post-state of an abruptly terminated *op* can be made, at least with the standard modalities $\langle\cdot\rangle$ and $[\cdot]$. Thus, this Java sequence is not sufficient to make statements about exceptional behaviour of methods. Not too much is missing, though, to get information on thrown exceptions: Potentially thrown exceptions are caught and assigned to an additional program variable `exc` which is assigned `null` before invoking the method or constructor:

$$\widetilde{\alpha}_{op}(\texttt{self};\texttt{p}_1,\ldots,\texttt{p}_n;\texttt{r};\texttt{exc}) := \left\{\begin{array}{l}
\texttt{T}_1\ \texttt{p}'_1\ \texttt{=}\ \texttt{p}_1\texttt{;}\\
\vdots\\
\texttt{T}_n\ \texttt{p}'_n\ \texttt{=}\ \texttt{p}_n\texttt{;}\\
\texttt{exc=null;}\\
\texttt{try\{}\\
\quad \alpha_{op}(\texttt{self};\texttt{p}'_1,\ldots,\texttt{p}'_n;\texttt{r})\\
\texttt{\} catch (Throwable e) \{}\\
\quad \texttt{exc = e;}\\
\texttt{\}}
\end{array}\right.$$

In post conditions the value of `exc` may now be referred to. It is either `null`, then *op* terminated normally, or is assigned an exception which is the reason for the abrupt termination.

From time to time however, we are not interested in the actual thrown exception but would only like to know that a postcondition holds independently of the question whether the method terminated normally or abruptly. Then, the following Java sequence suffices:

$$\widetilde{\alpha}_{op}(\texttt{self};\texttt{p}_1,\ldots,\texttt{p}_n;\texttt{r}) := \left\{\begin{array}{l}
\texttt{T}_1\ \texttt{p}'_1\ \texttt{=}\ \texttt{p}_1\texttt{;}\\
\vdots\\
\texttt{T}_n\ \texttt{p}'_n\ \texttt{=}\ \texttt{p}_n\texttt{;}\\
\texttt{try\{}\\
\quad \alpha_{op}(\texttt{self};\texttt{p}'_1,\ldots,\texttt{p}'_n;\texttt{r})\\
\texttt{\} catch (Throwable e) \{\}}
\end{array}\right.$$

### 3.2.3 Assertions of Operation Calls

As stated above it must be ensured that an operation, called by an observer in an allowed pre-state, establishes the postcondition of an operation contract, preserves all invariants of the program, respects the modifies clause, and complies with the specified termination behaviour.

For now we ignore termination behaviour and assume that an operation *op* called by an observer in an allowed state $s_{\text{pre}}$ terminates in a state $s_{\text{post}}$.

While it is quite clear that the postcondition of the contract must be satisfied in $s_{\text{post}}$, we are now more closely looking at assignable clauses.

### Correctness of Assignable Clauses

An assignable clause should specify those locations which are allowed to change. The set may, though, be larger, that is an assignable clause describes a superset of those locations that actually change.

With the help of the $\text{Loc}_{s,P,\beta}$ evaluation, we can quite easily define the semantics of an assignable clause: If a location is modified between the pre-state and the post-state, then this location must be specified by the assignable clause.

**Definition 3.5** (Satisfaction of Assignable Clause [Beckert and Schmitt, 2003]). Let $\mathit{Mod}(\texttt{self}; \texttt{p}_1, \ldots, \texttt{p}_n)$ be an assignable clause over signature $\Sigma$. It is *satisfied* by a pre-state $s_{\text{pre}}$ and a post-state $s_{\text{post}}$ if for all $n$-ary instance field symbols and array access symbols $f$ of $\Sigma$, all $i = 1, \ldots, \alpha(f)$ and all $e_i \in \text{Dom}(\sigma_i(f))$ the following holds:

$$f^{s_{\text{pre}}}(e_1, \ldots, e_n) \neq f^{s_{\text{post}}}(e_1, \ldots, e_n)$$

implies that $(f, (e_1, \ldots, e_n)) \in \bigcup_{t \in \mathit{Mod}(\texttt{self}; \texttt{p}_1, \ldots, \texttt{p}_n)} \text{Loc}_{s_{\text{pre}},\beta}(t)$.
We write: $(s_{\text{pre}}, s_{\text{post}}) \models_P \mathit{Mod}(\texttt{self}; \texttt{p}_1, \ldots, \texttt{p}_n)$.

We conclude the investigation of the correctness of assignable clauses with the following property of assignable clauses [Beckert and Schmitt, 2003].

**Lemma 3.1.** Let $M = \mathit{Mod}(\texttt{self}; \texttt{p}_1, \ldots, \texttt{p}_n)$ be an assignable clause over $\Sigma$ and $\rho$ the family of state transition functions $\rho_\alpha$ from a JavaDL Kripke structure for a $\Sigma$-program $P$. If the following three conditions hold:

$$\begin{aligned} \text{there is } s_{\text{post}} \text{ with } (s_{\text{pre}}, s_{\text{post}}) &\in \rho_\alpha \\ (s_{\text{pre}}, \rho_\alpha(s_{\text{pre}})) &\models_P M \\ s_{\text{pre}} &\models_P u(M)\varphi \end{aligned}$$

then $s_{\text{pre}} \models_P \langle\alpha\rangle\, \varphi$

*Proof.* See Beckert and Schmitt [2003] for a proof with simple locations terms. □

Note that $u(M)$ denotes the anonymising update as defined in Def. 2.13. This update assigns each location in the assignable clause a fresh rigid constant (or function term).

### Obligations of an Operation

There are some properties a program must fulfil independently from specifications. Remember from Def. 2.1 that we are considering *pre-specified classes and interfaces*, that is, some operations are marked as being *pure*. Purity means that this particular operation *op* does not modify the state and terminates [Leavens et al., 2005] or in other words all operation contracts assigned to *op* have an empty assignable clause and the *total* marker.

**Example 3.1.** In Ex. 1.1, `earlierOrEqual(Date)` is pure. Its operation contract is thus implicitly complemented with

```
@ requires false;
@ assignable nothing;
```
*

Alternatively we could *add* an operation contract with empty assignable clause and the *total* marker, but this would also include an implicit precondition true in the added contract. Thus the operation would have an effective general assumption which is equivalent to true. It would hence be obliged to preserve invariants (as we will see soon) in *every* pre-state. This is clearly not the intend of making a method pure, so that we do not pursue this alternative.[3]

*Note:* From now on we assume that every specification of a program includes these operation contracts for all pure operations.

Suppose the conditions imposed in Sect. 3.2.1 hold in a reachable state $s_{\text{pre}}$. Then, the following is asserted for every call to *op* in such a state:

1. if the *total* marker of *opct* is set, the call must terminate in a post-state

2. if it terminates, then in the post-state $s_{\text{post}}$

   a) the postcondition $\varphi_{opct}(\mathtt{self}; \mathtt{p}_1, \ldots, \mathtt{p}_n; \mathtt{r}; \mathtt{exc})$ of *opct* is valid in $s_{\text{post}}$:

$$s_{\text{post}} \models_P \varphi_{opct}(\mathtt{self}; \mathtt{p}_1, \ldots, \mathtt{p}_n; \mathtt{r}; \mathtt{exc})$$

[3] See also discussion on JML mailing list [Jmlspecs-interest] from 2005-01-08.

b) the assignable clause $Mod(\texttt{self};\texttt{p}_1,\ldots,\texttt{p}_n)$ is satisfied by the pre-state $s_{\text{pre}}$ and the post-state $s_{\text{post}}$:

$$(s_{\text{pre}}, s_{\text{post}}) \models_P Mod(\texttt{self};\texttt{p}_1,\ldots,\texttt{p}_n)$$

c) all invariants are valid in $s_{\text{post}}$, that is: $s_{\text{post}} \models_P \text{Inv}$

A crucial question is that of abrupt termination, for which we need to refine the statements from above. In contrast to the terminology in JavaDL we define, on the level of specifications, that a method terminates if it terminates abruptly, since otherwise we could not make any statements about the conditions of abrupt termination. The postcondition, however, may contain expressions which control abrupt termination. As already pointed out above, these expression formalise properties about the variable `exc` which represents the exception thrown by the operation, or `null` if there was no abrupt termination. So for instance, by requiring $\texttt{exc} \doteq \texttt{null}$ as a top-level conjunct of the postcondition, a specifier can forbid abrupt termination.

For invariants, there are neither markers *total* or *partial* to indicate if termination is required nor is it possible to make statements about thrown exceptions. This is quite natural since, if the operation call does not terminate, there is no need to establish the invariant in any state. If it terminates however, in its post-state all invariants must be valid. This must even be the case if the operation terminates abruptly, since the caller might catch thrown exceptions and continue with the execution of other statements, for which the general assumption that *all* invariants hold would otherwise be violated.

We summarise the results of the discussions so far. It turns out, when we define proof obligations, that it makes sense to separate (a) the tasks of fulfilling operation contracts and (b) the task of establishing invariants after an operation call. We thus provide notions for both obligations of an operation.

In practice it is useful to have a *relativised* notion of fulfilling an operation contract and preserving invariants. When we make use of contracts in a proof then it will be useful that we make less assumptions than the complete general assumption. We thus provide variants of our two new notions with the addition *under the assumption* of a subset of all invariants.

**Definition 3.6.** Let *op* be an operation declared in type $T$ with parameter types $T_1,\ldots,T_n$ and return type $T^r$ in a program $P$. Let further be

$\mathtt{self}$ a program variable of type $T$, $\mathtt{p}_1, \ldots, \mathtt{p}_n$ be program variables of types $T_1, \ldots, T_n$, $\mathtt{r}$ be a program variable of type $T^r$, and $\mathtt{exc}$ a program variable of type `java.lang.Throwable`.

1. Let *opct* $= (\text{op}, \varphi_{\text{pre}}, \varphi_{\text{post}}, \mathit{Mod}, \tau)$ be an operation contract of a specification of $P$. Furthermore $I \subseteq \text{Inv}$. *op′ fulfils the operation contract opct under the assumption of I* if *opct* is applicable to *op′* and for all reachable states $s_{\text{pre}}$ and all $e_{\mathtt{self}} \in \text{Dom}(T)$, $e_i \in \text{Dom}(T_i)$ $(i = 1, \ldots, n)$ with $\mathtt{self}^{s_{\text{pre}}} = e_{\mathtt{self}}$ and $p_i^{s_{\text{pre}}} = e_i$ with

$$\begin{aligned} s_{\text{pre}} &\models_P \mathcal{A}_{op'}(I; \mathtt{self}; \mathtt{p}_1, \ldots, \mathtt{p}_n) \\ s_{\text{pre}} &\models_P \varphi_{\text{pre}}(\mathtt{self}; \mathtt{p}_1, \ldots, \mathtt{p}_n) \end{aligned}$$

   the following conditions hold:

   - if the *total* marker is set there is a state $s_{\text{post}}$ with

$$(s_{\text{pre}}, s_{\text{post}}) \in \rho_{\tilde{\alpha}_{op'}(\mathtt{self};\mathtt{p}_1,\ldots,\mathtt{p}_n;\mathtt{r};\mathtt{exc})}$$

   - if there is such a state $s_{\text{post}}$ then:

$$\begin{aligned} s_{\text{post}} &\models_P \varphi_{\text{post}}(\mathtt{self}; \mathtt{p}_1, \ldots, \mathtt{p}_n; \mathtt{r}; \mathtt{exc}) \\ (s_{\text{pre}}, s_{\text{post}}) &\models_P \mathit{Mod}(\mathtt{self}; \mathtt{p}_1, \ldots, \mathtt{p}_n) \end{aligned}$$

2. *op′ fulfils the operation contract opct* if it fulfils *opct* under the assumption of Inv.

3. *op preserves a set of invariants I* of a specification of $P$ *under the assumption* of a set of invariants $I' \subseteq \text{Inv}$ if for all reachable states $s_{\text{pre}}$ and all $e_{\mathtt{self}} \in \text{Dom}(T)$, $e_i \in \text{Dom}(T_i)$ $(i = 1, \ldots, n)$ with $\mathtt{self}^{s_{\text{pre}}} = e_{\mathtt{self}}$ and $p_i^{s_{\text{pre}}} = e_i$ with

$$\begin{aligned} s_{\text{pre}} &\models_P \mathcal{A}_{op}(I'; \mathtt{self}; \mathtt{p}_1, \ldots, \mathtt{p}_n) \\ (s_{\text{pre}}, s_{\text{post}}) &\in \rho_{\tilde{\alpha}_{op}(\mathtt{self};\mathtt{p}_1,\ldots,\mathtt{p}_n;\mathtt{r})} \end{aligned}$$

   the following condition holds for all $\varphi \in I$:

$$s_{\text{post}} \models_P \varphi$$

4. *op preserves a set of invariants I* of a specification of $P$ if it preserves $I$ under the assumption of Inv.

With this, the basic notions of observed-state correctness are fixed and will be completed by the definitions in Sections 3.2.7 and 3.2.8. Before, we have to consider the subtle issue of static class initialisation and the assertions for initial states.

### 3.2.4 Treatment of Static Initialisation

We must make rather strong but realistic assumptions on the state of static class initialisation in all states an observer can consider. We assume the following: All classes in $P$ have either already *successfully* processed static class initialisation or have not started with their static initialisation. In pathological cases, classes can be in an *erroneous state* after having processed class initialisation, though such classes and their instances may behave according to their specifications. Although the JavaDL calculus allows a correct treatment of these cases, we rule out that erroneous classes exist when a method or constructor is called, since in practice it is

- unlikely that a programmer ever *intends* to have erroneous classes during the execution of his program; if they occur something is likely to be wrong, and
- highly complicated to prove properties with more liberal assumptions than we are postulating.

Thus we forbid programs which produce erroneous classes. Such programs are defined not to be correct.

The static initialisation routine of a class $C$ is simulated in JavaDL by a static method `<clinit>()` implicitly declared in $C$. As for ordinary methods and constructors, an observer may invoke `<clinit>()`, that is—in reality—the observer triggers static initialisation.

The following assumptions are encoded and treated as implicitly present invariants, that is we include the following to the set of all invariants Inv:

$$\bigwedge_{\substack{C \in P \\ \text{and } C \text{ is} \\ \text{not abstract}}} \Big( \texttt{<classErroneous>@}(C) \doteq \text{FALSE} \\ \wedge \texttt{<classInitialisationInProgress>@}(C) \doteq \text{FALSE} \Big) \tag{3.1}$$

We require that assumptions and assertions for ordinary methods and constructors, which were postulated above, should hold for `<clinit>()`, too.

There is only a minor adjustment to be made which we express by means of an implicit operation contract for `<clinit>()`.

**Definition 3.7.** The *standard operation contract* of $C$.`<clinit>()` consists of the precondition

$$\begin{aligned} & \texttt{<classInitialised>@}(C) \doteq \text{FALSE} \\ \wedge\ & \texttt{<classPrepared>@}(C) \doteq \text{FALSE} \end{aligned}$$

and the termination marker *total*.

A JavaFOL specification *complies to the standard initialisation policy* if it contains the standard operation contract and has (3.1) as part of its invariants.

*Note:* From now on, in the rest of this work, we only consider specifications which comply to the standard initialisation policy.

To summarise: For static initialisation we *assume* the general assumption and the precondition from the standard operation contract to hold. As we included (3.1) to the invariants, the general assumption contains the condition that no class is erroneous and not being initialised as well as all invariants hold. It is *asserted* that static initialisation terminates, again no class is erroneous, and all invariants hold. Java by itself ensures that no class is currently being initialised after a static initialisation terminates, so that this part of the implicitly given invariant can never be made false.

### 3.2.5 Assertions in the Initial State

We have already defined the notion of *preserving* invariants. The obvious reasoning is then, roughly, as follows: All operations preserve all invariants, then they are valid in all reachable states. Obviously there is an element missing for such an *inductive* reasoning[4]: that is the base case. Invariants must hold in initial states too.

Most of our invariants are instance invariants, which are quantified over all created instances. Since in the initial state no classes are initialised and thus no instances created, these invariants are trivially true in these states.

Consider however our example static invariant in its original form from Sect. 3.1.2: $\texttt{a@(C)} \doteq 0$. In the initial state this formula is not true and thus

[4] We will explicitly see such an induction in Lemma 9.9.

this formula is not an invariant. The modified version

$$\texttt{<classInitialized>@(C)} \doteq \text{TRUE} \rightarrow \texttt{a@(C)} \doteq 0$$

is however true in the initial state characterised by the formula $\varphi_{\text{init}}$ as defined in Sect. 2.3.6 and could thus be an invariant.

**Definition 3.8.** An invariant over signature $\Sigma$ of a $\Sigma$-program $P$ must satisfy the following property:

$$\models_P \varphi_{\text{init}} \rightarrow \varphi$$

We say: The invariant is valid in the initial state of $P$.

The following property is important when dealing with extended contexts. Assume an invariant holds in the initial state. If we extend our program with further classes, the validity of the invariant in the initial state does not change.

**Lemma 3.2.** Suppose $P$ is a $\Sigma$-program and $P'$ a closure of $P$. If a formula $\varphi \in \text{Fma}^{\Sigma}$ is valid in the initial state of $P$ then it is valid in the initial state of $P'$.

*Proof.* Let $s$ be the initial state of $P$ and $s'$ the initial state of $P'$. All interpretations in $s$ are the same as in $s'$, $s'$ is just based on a larger signature, with one exception: The only dependency to programs in JavaFOL formulae comes from query terms which are dynamically bound. Such query terms are in an initial state evaluated to a fixed but unknown value since no object exists. They thus cannot play a role when evaluating $\varphi$. $s \models_P \varphi$ implies $s' \models_{P'} \varphi$ □

### 3.2.6 Naive Correctness

Naive correctness is the simplest definition of correctness we can imagine and it is probably the one which comes into ones mind without having carefully thought about the intricate issue. On the other hand it is quite easy to prove naive correctness. This semantics will not play a big role in the rest of this work, though we later, in Sect. 5.1.3, come back to it.

**Definition 3.9** (Naive Correctness)**.** Given a program $P$ and a specification $S$ for $P$. Let *op* be an operation and $C$ be the class in which *op* is declared. Let $I$ be all invariants declared for $C$, that is:

$$I := \{\varphi \mid \varphi = (\dot{\forall} o{:}T.\ \varphi') \in \text{Inv}\}$$

*op* is *naively correct* if it fulfils its operation contracts in $S$ under the assumption of $I$ and if it preserves $I$ under the assumption of $I$. $C$ is correct if all its operations are naively correct. A program $P$ is naively correct if all its classes are naively correct.

**Example 3.2.** In our introductory example from Sect. 1.2, `Period` is naively correct, since all operations of `Period` preserve `Period`'s invariant under the assumption of this invariant. That `Date` does not so in the modification, does not matter and explains why we call this semantics naive. *

### 3.2.7 Observed-State Call Correctness

We sum up the discussion from above in the following definition of observed-state call correctness:

**Definition 3.10** (Observed-State Call Correctness). A program $P$ is *observed-state call correct* w.r.t. a specification $S$, if

1. all operations *op* fulfil all operation contracts of $S$ for *op*,
2. all invariants Inv of $S$ are preserved by all operations of $P$, and
3. all invariants are valid in the initial state of $P$.

Our observer model does not directly occur in this definition. We can however imagine that the observer is a class with a static method in which it invokes the operations. Before doing that this static method establishes all invariants of $S$.

**Example 3.3.** Consider again Ex. 1.1. We observe that the closed program {`Period`, `Date`, `Month`} is call correct since no method call can violate $\varphi_{\texttt{Period}}$. In particular `setYear(int)` cannot invalidate `Period`'s invariant because an observer (like `Main` in Ex. 1.2) cannot produce a state where he can call `setYear(int)` on the start or end date of a period.

In the modified example Ex. 1.2 this is however the case as `Main` demonstrates. {`Period`, `Date`, `Month`} is here not call correct.

The open program {`Period`} is call correct in both versions as all operations of this class fulfil their obligations, that is fulfil operation contracts and preserve invariants. *

### 3.2.8 Observed-State Durable Correctness

Call correctness is insufficient if we think of the following situation. A program $P$ is finished and proven to be *call correct*. Then it is distributed and used by some clients. They may now trust in the specification possibly attached to $P$, *but* only under the assumption that they establish *all invariants* of $P$ before they call a method in $P$. Though one can expect from a client to establish a precondition of the operation it calls, it is unacceptable to demand the establishment of invariants; in particular since invariants are spread over the whole system and *every* invariant needs to be taken into account.

The notion of durable correctness re-orders responsibilities concerning invariants. Invariants only have the character of an obligation to those classes *inside* of $P$. For the *outside* (that is, the observer) they are guaranteed. As only proviso for the outside we demand that calls to $P$ satisfy one of the preconditions of the called operation. This remaining requirement is in fact so essential for the *design by contract* approach that it will be kept throughout this work.

**Definition 3.11** (Observed-State Durable Correctness)**.** Let $P^{cl}$ be a closure of a program $P$ and $S$ a specification for $P$. We call $\mathit{Obs} := P^{cl} \backslash P$ the observer of $P$. Furthermore we assume that every method or constructor *op* of $P$ with an operation contract in $S$ is called by *Obs* only in a state where the precondition of at least one fitting operation contract from $S$ is satisfied.

$P$ is *durable invariant correct* w.r.t. $S$ if for *all* choices of $P^{cl}$: all invariants Inv hold in all states in which no operation of $P$ is in progress (or on the stack) and all invariants are valid in the initial state of $P$.

$P$ is *(observed-state) durable correct* w.r.t. $S$ if

1. all operations *op* fulfil the operation contracts of $S$ which are for *op* and

2. $P$ is durable invariant correct.

**Lemma 3.3.** Let $S$ be a specification for an open program $P$. $P$ is durable correct (w.r.t. $S$) iff every closure of $P$ is durable correct (w.r.t. $S$).

*Proof.* '$\Leftarrow$': Let $P^{cl}$ be a closure of $P$, we assume that it is durable correct. Furthermore, we can assume that every call to an operation of $P$ from $\mathit{Obs} := P^{cl} \backslash P$ satisfies preconditions according to $S$ (otherwise the direction is trivially true). Because $P^{cl}$ is durable correct it preserves the operation contracts of $S$ and its operations terminate in states where the invariants of $S$ hold, $P$ is durable correct.

'$\Rightarrow$': Let $P^{cl}$ be a closure of $P$. And $Obs$ an observer of $P^{cl}$. That is $Obs' := Obs \cup P^{cl} \setminus P$ is an observer of $P$. In all intermediate states of $Obs'$ invariants hold because of the durable correctness of $P$, thus this is the case also in $Obs \subseteq Obs'$. Operation calls on $P$ fulfil contracts in $S$ likewise. □

**Example 3.4.** The closed program {`Period`, `Date`, `Month`} in Ex. 1.1 is not durable correct since an observer may subclass `Date2` as seen in the example. With it, the observer reaches an intermediate state in which `Period`'s invariant does not hold. If we however forbid overriding of `earlierOrEqual(Date)` by declaring it final (and do the same for the `copy()` method of `Date`) then {`Period`, `Date`, `Month`} would be durable correct.

In Ex. 1.2, {`Period`, `Date`, `Month`} is not durable correct, since it is not call correct and therefore not durable invariant correct: A method of the observer can simply terminate when the method `setYear(int)` has performed its malicious state change.

{`Period`} in Ex. 1.1 is not durable correct for the same reasons as for the already discussed program {`Period`, `Date`, `Month`}, but by making the called methods in `Date` final as above, {`Period`} is durable correct.

The variant of {`Period`} in Ex. 1.2 is, not durable correct for the same reasons, but even declaring operations final would not help, since there is anyway an observer which produces a state in which the invariant of `Period` does not hold. The set of classes {`Main`, `Period`, `Date`, `Month`} is such a corresponding closure. *

### 3.2.9 Relations between Durable and Call Correctness

It is quite easy to show the call correctness of a program as we will see later with the help of suitable proof obligations. Unfortunately, the following lemma uncovers that call correctness for *open* programs does not help much to achieve durable correctness.

**Lemma 3.4.** Let $S$ be a specification for an *open* program $P$.

1. $P$ is call correct (w.r.t. $S$) if every closure of $P$ is call correct (w.r.t. $S$). The other direction does not hold in general.

2. $P$ is call correct (w.r.t. $S$) if it is durable correct (w.r.t. $S$). The other direction does not hold in general.

*Proof.* 1. Let $P^{cl}$ be an arbitrary closure of $P$. We assume that $P^{cl}$ is call correct, that is all operations fulfil their operation contracts of $S$ and all invariants Inv of $S$ are preserved by all operations of $P^{cl}$. This applies in particular for all operations of $P$ since they are a subset of those of $P^{cl}$. Thus $P$ is call correct.
Example 1.1 in its modified version shows a counterexample for the other direction: `Period` and `Date` together, a closure of `Period`, are not call correct, since a call to `setYear(int)` would invalidate the invariant of `Period`, though `Period` is call correct.
2. Let $P$ be a durable correct program. Since all observer programs which stop after calling an operation of $P$ establish all invariants in that state, all invariants are preserved by all operations of $P$. Fulfilling operation contracts is a condition to both call correctness and durable correctness. Thus $P$ is call correct.
Again, Example 1.1 shows a counterexample for the other direction: `Period` is call correct, that is, all calls to `Period` preserve the invariants of $P$, but not durable correct, as the observer program in `Main` demonstrates. □

Also for closed programs call correctness follows from durable correctness.

**Lemma 3.5.** Let $S$ be a specification of a closed program $P$. $P$ is call correct (w.r.t. $S$) if it is durable correct (w.r.t. $S$). The other direction does not hold in general.

*Proof.* Proof as for open programs (Lemma 3.4(2)).
A counterexample for the other direction can be obtained when considering the closed program {`Period`, `Date`, `Month`}. It is call correct, but not durable correct as demonstrated before. □

Altogether the relation between call correctness and durable correctness of open and closed programs is depicted in Fig. 3.2.

Call correctness is a notion of correctness that is quite easy to ensure by deductive verification. Since it is not sufficient for open programs to ensure durable correctness we need to bridge the gap between call correctness and durable correctness. We will thus need to find ways to strengthen call correctness such that the other direction of Lemma 3.4(2) holds.

$$
\begin{array}{ccc}
\text{all closures of } P \text{ are call correct} & \Leftarrow & \text{all closures of } P \text{ are durable correct} \\
\Downarrow & & \Updownarrow \\
P \text{ is call correct} & \Leftarrow & P \text{ is durable correct}
\end{array}
$$

**Figure 3.2:** Durable and call correctness of open and closed programs

### 3.2.10 Discussion of Observed-State Correctness

Instead of an observed-state semantics, JML [Leavens et al., 2005] obeys in the tradition of Larch [Guttag and Horning, 1993] a visible state semantics [Poetzsch-Heffter, 1997]. We discuss this issue extensively in the following since it is important to motivate that observed-state correctness is really what is desired.

A state is *visible* [Leavens et al., 2005] for an object $o$ if it occurs at one of the following moments during the execution of a program[5]:

- at the end of a constructor invocation which is initialising $o$,
- at the beginning and end of a non-static method call with $o$ as receiver,
- at the beginning and end of a static method which is declared in the class of $o$ or a superclass.
- when no constructor, non-static method invocation with $o$ as receiver, or static method invocation for a method in $o$'s class or a superclass is in progress.

A state is visible for a type $T$ if it occurs after static initialisation for $T$ is complete and it is a visible state for some object that has type $T$.

A visible state semantics requires all instance invariants declared in type $T$ to hold for every object $o$ of type $T$ and for every visible state for $o$. All static invariants declared in $T$ must hold in every visible state for $T$.

Clearly this semantics is stronger than observed-state durable correctness. The example program in Fig. 3.3 is durable correct but not visible-state correct: With the visible-state semantics, the methods `m1()`, `m2()`, and `m3()` are disallowed:

[5] We leave out finalizers and JML's helper methods for simplicity.

```
public class A {
  private int i = 1;
  /*@ instance invariant i>0 */

  public int getI() { return i; }
  /*@ requires p>0;
    @ ensures i==p;
    @*/
  public void setI(int p) { i=p; }
  public void m1() {
    setI(0);
    i=1;
  }
  public void m2() {
    i=0;
    setI(1);
  }
  public int m3() {
    i=0;
    i=(new B()).m5(this);
  }
  /*@ ensures \result>0 @*/
  public int m4() {
    return 42/i;
  }
}

public class B {
  /*@ ensures \result>0 @*/
  public int m5(A a) {
    if (a.getI()<=0) a.setI(1);
    return a.m4();
  }
}
```

**Figure 3.3:** An example program demonstrating the differences between visible state semantics and observed-state semantics

- The invariant that field `a` is positive must be established when the call from method `m1()` to `setI(int)` terminates. This is not the case. With observed-state correctness, this state does not matter since it is not observed by an observer.
- In `m2()` the visible state semantics requires that the invariant holds before the call to `setI(int)` starts. This is not the case but again an observer does not notice such a state and when `m2()` terminates the invariant is valid again.
- `m3()` is disallowed for the same reason with the visible state semantics, but it is allowed in the observed-state semantics.

We believe that our view is more natural and liberal. Only states observed from the outside must be correct.

An often quoted reason for a visible state semantics (cf. Barnett and Naumann [2004], Huizing and Kuiper [2000]) is the danger of *reentrant calls* (another, equivalent, notion is *call-back*). Consider the classes `A` and `B` from our example. We make the assumption that an observer may only override methods if the same specifications as in the overridden methods are annotated. Moreover we require for `m5(A)` and all overridden versions the stricter contract that its postcondition is satisfied independently of any invariant. The mechanism for constraining other classes not present in the considered program are described in Chapter 5.

When an `A` instance $a$ executes `m3()` it calls method `m5(A)` on a `B` instance. By that time, $a$ does not satisfy its invariant. This is however a state which is not observable from outside the considered program {`A`, `B`}. The `B` instance calls back to $a$, namely the method `m4()`, but before it 'repairs' $a$ by making `A`'s invariant valid. Consequently the returned value, which is then assigned to $a$`.i` is admitted for the invariant.

Obviously the program {`A`, `B`} is durable correct: Which ever method we (the observer) invoke, after the method returns `A`'s invariant holds. We see no reason why it should not be classified as correct.

As anticipation of Chapter 6, we remark that with the help of our JavaDL calculus we *can* enforce visible state semantics. When we do modular proofs by symbolic execution (for instance of `m2()`) and want to use contracts (here: that of `setI(int)`) we need to show that the precondition of `setI(int)` and all invariants hold. This shows that the exclusive use of method contracts which include *all invariants* as part of their precondition establishes the visible-state semantics. The correctness of the above example could then not be shown. On the other hand, we could simply symbolically execute (or 'inline') `setI(int)`, and thus can prove the correctness of `A`. Please note however, that all these considerations are on the calculus level, not on the semantics level.

## 3.3 Specification Languages

JavaFOL specifications provide the very essentials of specifications. There are no syntactic convenience notations, it is not standardised. Recent standard specification languages for object-oriented systems are much more suitable for the practitioner. In this section we describe how two popular specification languages, UML/OCL and JML, can be mapped to JavaFOL specifications.

### 3.3.1 UML/OCL

The Unified Modeling Language (UML) is a graphical modelling and specification language for object-oriented systems. It consists of several diagram types which allow to model different aspects of a system. UML is standardised by the Object Management Group. As a sub-standard the Object Constraint Language (OCL) [Object Modeling Group] is part of UML. OCL provides a textual notation for requirements of the specified system which cannot be modelled by the graphical diagram types of UML. Specifications in OCL are mostly concerned with functional specification of the static structure of a system.

More precisely, if the types of a Java program $P$ are considered as UML classes, Java fields as UML attributes and Java methods and constructors as UML operations, and OCL constraints for such a UML structure diagram are given, the OCL constraints can be translated [Beckert et al., 2002] into a specification of $P$ using JavaFOL in the sense presented in Sect. 3.1. A translation following Beckert et al. [2002] has been implemented under the supervision of the author and is integrated in the KeY system.

OCL provides mere pre- and postcondition pairs for defining operation contracts. Abrupt termination cannot be modelled in the standard version, we showed however earlier how OCL can be conservatively enhanced to model such implementation details [Roth, 2002] by using an implicitly extended underlying UML model. Termination behaviour can neither be modelled with OCL: the standard requires constrained operations to terminate, which obviously makes sense, but complicates verification. Tools like KeY thus offer possibilities to show—if desired—only partial correctness of operations.

Assignable clauses are missing as well in standard OCL. A usual argument why they are not needed is that *only those* locations mentioned in a postcondition may change. But since this is a notion of change which is quite hairy and difficult to approach with formal methods, tools like KeY have developed their own assignable clauses following Beckert and Schmitt [2003], Katz [2003]. Assignable clauses are simply considered sets of ground terms of FOL, thus not taking into account that also extended terms can be allowed.

Operation contracts in OCL are, as in our FOL specifications, attached to an operation declaration, and are not inherited to subtypes.

The OCL standard [Object Modeling Group] specifies the validity of invariants as follows:

> An invariant [...] must be true for each instance of the classifier at any moment in time. Only when an instance is executing an operation, this does not need to evaluate to true.

The first sentence implies that OCL supports instance invariants only. Static invariants are not formalisable. The second sentence justifies that we use observed-state correctness, and that we use durable observed-state correctness when dealing with open programs.

Altogether, our approach, using our JavaFOL specifications with observed-state correctness, fits to the—in this respect, at least, quite imprecise—UML/OCL standard specification.

### 3.3.2 JML

The Java Modeling Language (JML) is characterised [Leavens et al., 2006] as a behavioural interface specification language that can be used to specify the behaviour of Java programs. Specifying with JML works by annotating comments to the Java source code or by providing an extra file containing annotations and a copy of the signature of the specified Java source.

Compared to OCL the abundance of language features is overwhelming. JML provides pre- and postcondition pairs, assignable clauses, possibilities to specify termination behaviour and abrupt termination behaviour, instance and static invariants. In addition it has a concept of visibilities of specifications, inheritance and overriding of contracts, and most importantly of 'specification-only' model elements, such as *model fields*, *model methods*, and *model classes*, which allow to specify even Java interfaces appropriately.

These JML features can all be represented in our notion of specification (Def. 3.1) using JavaFOL. A translation from JML to JavaFOL has been designed and implemented under the supervision of the author [Engel, 2005].

In the following we want to give a brief overview of features where the representation of JML features in the specification format of Def. 3.1 is not so obvious.

**Termination Behaviour.** JML specifies termination with a `diverges` clause in an operation contract. The keyword is followed by a boolean expression (corresponding to a JavaFOL formula) indicating the condition which holds in the pre-state if the operation does not terminate. Thus `diverges true` indicates that the operation is allowed not to terminate, and `diverges false` specifies that termination is required. These two cases are easy to translate into our specifications: for the former *partial* is set and for the latter *total*. For all other conditions $\varphi$, the operation contract is replaced by one with *partial* (or equivalently `diverges true`). And another contract is introduced having as precondition the original precondition conjunctively joined with $\varphi$ and *total* (or equivalently `diverges true`) as termination specification. Obviously these two contracts have the same meaning as the original one, but use only means equivalent to the *total* and *partial* markers.

**Abrupt Termination.** Abrupt termination is specified with the help of a special `signals` clause[6] with attached exception type $E$ and a condition $\varphi$, with the intended meaning that if an exception of type $E$ is raised $\varphi$ holds in the post-state. In our model, we assign the thrown exception to a variable which we access in the regular postcondition. Thus if `exc` is that variable, we can write equivalently to `signals(E)` $\varphi$:

$$\text{InstanceOf}_E(\texttt{exc}) \doteq \text{TRUE} \rightarrow \varphi$$

as a top level conjunct of the postcondition of a contract. Details can be found in Engel [2005].

**Assignable Clauses.** Assignable clauses in JML are expressions with field or array access as top-level operator. The semantics is defined by the statement that

> from the client's point of view, only the locations named [...] can be assigned to during the execution of the method. However, locations that are local to the method (or methods it calls) and locations that are created during the method's execution are not subject to this restriction.

Liberalising this definition, we allow for temporary violations during the run of the method. For most practical applications this specification does not make a big diference. Special constructs are allowed such as `a[*]` standing for an arbitrary access to an array slot, `a[`$i$`..`$j$`]` for an array access at indices between $i$ and $j$, and `a.*` as a substitute for an arbitrary field access. It is no problem to represent the former two constructs; we translate them to our extended terms as follows:

$$\begin{aligned} a\texttt{[*]} &\longrightarrow (\text{for } k \,;\, 0 \leq k \wedge k < a.\texttt{length} \,;\, a[k]) \\ a\texttt{[}i\texttt{..}j\texttt{]} &\longrightarrow (\text{for } k \,;\, i \leq k \wedge k \leq j \,;\, a[k]) \end{aligned}$$

[6]Note: `normal_behavior` and `exceptional_behavior` are just syntactic sugar for this.

> To translate `a.*` is not immediately possible, but the practical use of such an assignable element is questionable. An extension to regular expressions over field and array accesses seems more useful.

The semantics of JML specifications is, though not formally, but quite precisely described. To a large extend, the semantics of JML reflects our semantics, for instance, the handling of undefined expression is the same. There is one major difference: JML uses a *visible state semantics* for invariants, which we discussed in Sect. 3.2.10. We have decided to (slightly) *deviate* from the JML visible state semantics when we transfer JML specifications to our contract notion. However, we do this for good reasons: Our semantics is more oriented at the client view of a component, and is less interested in its internal states, which serves information hiding. Finally if someone wants to stick to the stricter notion of visible states, consequential use of method contracts including all invariants in preconditions establishes that goal, too.

## 3.4 Summary

In this chapter we have introduced our notion of specification of a Java program, which consists of operation contracts and static and instance invariant contracts, using first order formulae and extended first order terms. We have assigned an observed-state semantics to the contracts. Two variants were given: call correctness and durable correctness, and their relations were discussed. Most importantly we will use durable correctness for open programs. Finally we have investigated the source of specifications, which (usually) arise from specification language (such as UML/OCL and JML) expressions and observed that we may—with one minor and acceptable modification—have a faithful mapping from specification language constraints to our JavaFOL specifications.

In Chapter 5 we will weaken the notion of durable correctness to a notion of relative-durable correctness: The context will be obliged again to satisfy certain conditions. The whole Part II will be concerned with deductively treating the notions of observed-state correctness introduced in this chapter.

# 4 Specification of Encapsulation Properties

> Bene qui latuit bene vixit.
>
> *(Ovid)*

Durable correct open programs are in general impossible to write without a good degree of encapsulation. Developers may design such well encapsulated programs, but in state-of-the-art object-oriented specification languages, there are no or only insufficient means to *specify* properties of encapsulation. This lack of specification power means that it is also impossible to *verify* components to be durable correct. We thus need to enhance our languages of specification with capabilities to specify encapsulation. This is what is approached in this chapter. The developed concept has also been presented in Roth [2005]; the presentation here follows that paper in some parts.

Apart from the mere correctness and verification issue, encapsulation plays a major role in object-oriented software development: It reduces the complexity of inter-object relations, and thus makes the division of tasks into subtasks, indispensable to master complex problems, much easier. This is manifested when investigating common *design patterns*. Properties of encapsulation are informally described with pattern descriptions; attached *formal* specification (as it is done for functional properties, for instance in Bubel and Hähnle [2005]) would increase the precision of pattern descriptions.

The *way*, encapsulation properties are made specifiable to developers, is important to the acceptance of this technique. We thus analyse in detail what the requirements are for a specification language capable of expressing encapsulation properties. We will finally decide to extend existing specification languages like JML or UML/OCL to meet these requirements. To show how this extension works, we will perform it at the example of JavaFOL specifications.

**Outline.** We sketch requirements and design considerations for the way we specify encapsulation properties in Sect. 4.1. The state-of-the-art solutions to deal with encapsulation in real-world object-oriented languages are only partially satisfactory. We review these approaches in Sect. 4.1.2. As a consequence of our analysis, we present the basic extensions to JavaFOL and to functional specification languages in Sect. 4.2, before we provide means to conveniently specify important patterns of encapsulation on top of them as described in Sect. 4.3.

## 4.1 Requirements for Specifying Encapsulation

Encapsulation is important in object-oriented designs. Evidence that this so, can be found for instance in 'good' software designs, usually documented in design pattern catalogues. Further evidence is the fact that other recent research approaches are concerned with related issues; these concepts shall be called *alias control* approaches in the following. Of course the already mentioned, and in later chapters in more detail explained, need for encapsulation to allow for durable correctness of open programs, is a reason that encapsulation is important. In this section, we analyse the two former fields: how does encapsulation occur in design patterns and alias control approaches, and what conclusions can be drawn for a new powerful way to specify encapsulation.

### 4.1.1 Design Patterns

We investigate the pattern catalogues Gamma et al. [1995], Buschmann et al. [1996], Grand [1998, 1999] for encapsulation properties. A selection of patterns that affect encapsulation is listed below; the list is not complete, but these patterns are clear manifestations of real encapsulation properties:

**Whole-Part.** This is a structural pattern [Buschmann et al., 1996] which provides a very strict encapsulation policy. There is an *aggregate object* (`Whole`) at work which hides access to other objects which are called `Parts`: 'Clients should see the aggregate object as an atomic object that does not allow any direct access to its constituent parts.' [Buschmann et al., 1996]

**Memento.** This pattern [Gamma et al., 1995] captures the internal state of an object in an extra *Memento* object in order to set the object back to that state later. The access to internals of the *Memento* is forbidden to clients.

**Proxy.** This pattern [Gamma et al., 1995] restricts the access to an object: Accesses are only allowed through a *Proxy* object. Sample purposes are to protect the access according to an access policy, or to avoid unnecessary remote calls if the object to be accessed is located remotely. Since the proxy might store or cache data, the direct access ignoring the proxy might result in inconsistencies.

**Copy Mutable Parameters** and
**Return New Objects from Accessor Method.**
These patterns [Grand, 1999] ensure that, at a method call, the passed mutable objects are copied before being stored at field locations and the returned objects are copied before being returned. The purpose of both patterns is to achieve encapsulation: No client of an object is allowed to directly access its internals.

**Iterator.** This behavioural pattern [Gamma et al., 1995] ensures that an aggregate object, like a linked list, does not expose its internal structure, though it provides an `Iterator` object that traverses the aggregate. Other clients of the list than iterators are not allowed to access its internals. They must however be enabled to put elements into the list, which makes the objects referenced by the internals also referenced by the clients.

These patterns have in common that they require some objects to be hidden from others in the one or the other way. If the graphs made up by the references between objects in all states of a system have such a property we speak of *encapsulation*. Often in literature, the term *data hiding* or *information hiding* is used for similar meanings. Our notion of an encapsulation property is by purpose rather vague: *An* encapsulation property *describes under which circumstances it is forbidden to have a reference from one object to another.*

We believe that there is no sharp distinction between encapsulation properties and functional properties. To require, for instance, an object stored in the field slot of an object $o$ to be different in all observed states from an object $p$ can be considered both an encapsulation property (since we restrict the accessibility between objects) *and* a traditional functional invariant property.

**Example 4.1.** To be more concrete, we take up the example of an application of the Whole-Part pattern given in Buschmann et al. [1996]. We have an object `Triangle` whose instances contain each three references (`p0`, `p1`, `p2`) to objects of class `Point`. `Points` themselves consist of a pair of primitive integer fields `x` and `y`. Though immutable `Point` objects would be preferable, we explicitly allow in our design that `Points` are mutable. This is to efficiently provide means to drag graphical objects like triangles with points around in the space. Applying the Whole-Part pattern, `Triangle` should play the role of a `Whole` object and `Point` should play the role of a `Part`.

Following the pattern, the `Point` objects must not be shared among other graphical objects, since otherwise, for instance, performing a `rotate` operation on another graphical object could unintendedly change the shape of the `Triangle`. Fig. 4.1 (without the grey parts) shows a UML class diagram of the design and an object diagram for a snapshot of the system; we disallow the reference labelled with ①.

For a comprehensive specification of the design, we want to specify, in addition to the mere functional behaviour (such as an invariant that the nodes of a triangle are not collinear), that instances of `Point` cannot be accessed by any other object than the specific triangle which it is a node of. Since the desired property describes a behaviour that must be observed in any visible state of an instance of `Triangle`, we would like to describe it as a class invariant of `Triangle`. *

**Example 4.2.** To increase the level of complexity a bit, we assume now that, in addition to Example 4.1, `Point` contains additional references to other objects, such as to instances of `Colour`; the colour of the triangle is determined to be the 'gradient' of the colours of its nodes. The representation of a `Colour` object is left open, it may consist of an 'RGB' triple of primitive integer fields, or may have references to further objects.

A possible design decision would be to make `Colours` in general sharable among other graphical objects such as `Points`, but not if they belong to `Points` that are constituent parts of *different* `Triangles`. This restriction still allows `Points` of the same triangle to reference the same `Colour`. So modifying a colour not belonging to a triangle $t$ does not affect the state of $t$: Each node together with its associated colour is in fact a true part of the

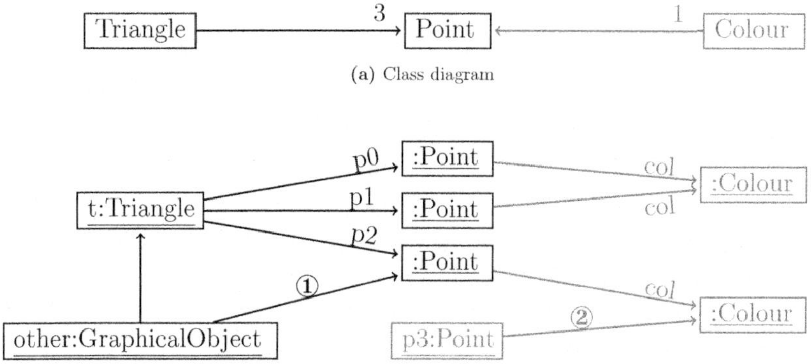


(a) Class diagram

(b) Object diagram

**Figure 4.1:** UML class diagrams (top) and object diagrams (bottom) for Example 4.1, extensions for Example 4.2 in grey

triangle, as the Whole-Part pattern requires. Like in the previous settings, `Point` objects being part of a `Triangle` must not be shared among other graphical objects.

Fig. 4.1 (including the grey extension) illustrates the design. The references ① and ② are not allowed in our design.

We would like to specify this more challenging encapsulation policy by means of an invariant of `Triangle`. $*$

The brief investigation of patterns should have shown the following three results:

(E1) Encapsulation is the result of purposely made design decisions.

(E2) There is not *the* encapsulation property, but there are many varying—and arbitrarily complex—encapsulation properties.

(E3) There is no sharp line between functional and encapsulation properties.

### 4.1.2 Alias Control: Related Work on Encapsulation

Quite a number of techniques have been published in recent years that aim at reducing the complexity introduced by aliasing in programs with pointers, as for example *islands* [Hogg, 1991], *balloons* [Almeida, 1997], *uniqueness* [Boyland, 2001], and different types of *ownership* [Clarke et al., 1998, Müller, 2002, Boyapati et al., 2003]. We refer to them as *alias control policies*. Overviews are, for instance, in Noble et al. [2003]. According to our criteria, these policies ensure properties that can be classified as encapsulation properties.

Most, if not all, of these policies are however technology driven, that is the properties are mostly statically checkable (for instance by means of a type checker), which is the major justification that the approach exists. We claim that we can formulate each of the properties summarised in Noble et al. [2003] with our approach, and we will demonstrate this at some examples below. Moreover we can observe that the investigated design patterns require more generality concerning their encapsulation properties than the existing encapsulation policies provide. Finally, users are facing two ways of writing specifications: the one they are usually used to, *design by contract*, writing invariants and pre-/postcondition contracts, and on the other hand, a completely different way of denoting encapsulation properties, for instance, by labelling fields with a special modifier. We believe that this distinction is unnecessary and unnatural, thus confusing for developers, especially for those who are sceptical towards formal specification anyway.

To sum up, we can state the following weaknesses of the existing *alias control* approaches to master encapsulation:

(R1) In recent approaches, there is an irritating difference between how functional properties and how encapsulation properties are specified.

(R2) The way encapsulation properties are specified is closely coupled to technologies that check them, which makes it likely that not all desired properties can be formulated.

## 4.1.3 Guidelines for Specifying Encapsulation

Taking the results of our reviews of design patterns and alias control policies into account, the central idea of our work is thus: Programmers know how they encapsulate data (E1), they should be enabled to easily specify their encapsulation concept formally and to check these properties with machine assistance. Especially, (R1) and (E3) encourage us to make encapsulation specifiable in a way traditional functional properties are, i.e. by applying *design by contract* and using an extended specification language. Moreover, the latter has the flexibility required by (E2) and the independence from concrete techniques required by (R2).

The obvious way to get new features, like encapsulation properties, into specification languages is to make them accessible as special predicates of the specification language. As any other predicate they can then be connected with other expressions of the language. Language expressions containing the predicates may then serve as preconditions, postconditions, or class invariants.

## 4.2 Basic Encapsulation Predicates

In this section, the two basic encapsulation predicates, the Acc and the Reach predicate, are defined for JavaFOL. Although we introduce them as extensions to JavaFOL, they can likewise be defined for any specification language that is capable of making statements about program states, like JML or UML/OCL. In the next section these basic predicates are complemented with a mere convenience layer, that is, we provide handy abbreviations. This however means that this section presents all the *needed* extensions to express encapsulation properties. All applications to design patterns and alias control properties (Sect. 4.3), as well as those in Chapter 9 could be done with the basic predicates of this section only. The formulae would just be more intricate.

### 4.2.1 The Acc Predicates

In object-oriented specification languages as well as in JavaDL there are only means to reason about concrete field accesses but there is no way to talk about an *arbitrary* field access, such as 'there is a field such that...'. Without getting too much into the spheres of higher order logic, this restriction needs to be relaxed by defining an Acc predicate [Roth, 2005]. It represents the relation of objects which can be accessed with exactly one field or array access from a list of allowed fields. We may omit the list of allowed symbols, with the meaning that *every* field or array access counts. In extension to Roth [2005] a variant is needed: An $\overline{\text{Acc}}$ predicate which expresses that one object can be accessed by another one *but not* through fields of an attached list. This predicate will be needed for a modular deductive treatment of Acc in Sect. 8.3.

We extend a JavaFOL signature as follows:

**Definition 4.1** (Syntax). Let $\Sigma = (\mathcal{T}, \mathcal{F}^{nr}, \mathcal{F}^{r}, \mathcal{P}^{nr}, \mathcal{P}^{r}, \preceq, \sigma, \tau)$ be a JavaFOL signature. Let $A$ be the set of symbols in $\Sigma$ which are either instance field symbols or array access symbols. Then $\mathrm{Acc}(\Sigma)$ is defined as

$$\begin{aligned} P^{nr*} \;:=\; P^{nr} & \cup \{\mathrm{Acc}[A'](\cdot,\cdot) \mid A' \subseteq A, A' \text{ not empty}\} \\ & \cup \{\mathrm{Acc}(\cdot,\cdot)\} \\ & \cup \{\overline{\mathrm{Acc}}[A'](\cdot,\cdot) \mid A' \subseteq A, A' \text{ not empty}\} \end{aligned}$$

$$\sigma^*(f) \;:=\; \begin{cases} (\texttt{Object}, \textsc{Any}) & \text{if } f \in \{\mathrm{Acc}[A'](\cdot,\cdot), \mathrm{Acc}(\cdot,\cdot), \overline{\mathrm{Acc}}[A'](\cdot,\cdot)\} \\ \sigma(f) & \text{otherwise} \end{cases}$$

$$\mathrm{Acc}(\Sigma) \;:=\; (\mathcal{T}, \mathcal{F}^{nr*}, \mathcal{F}^{r}, \mathcal{P}^{nr}, \mathcal{P}^{r}, \preceq, \sigma^*, \tau)$$

That is, the binary non-rigid predicate symbols $\mathrm{Acc}[\cdot](\cdot,\cdot)$, $\mathrm{Acc}(\cdot,\cdot)$, and $\overline{\mathrm{Acc}}[\cdot](\cdot,\cdot)$, extend an existing signature.

Our definition of *accessibility* from an object $e_0$ to an object $e_1$ in a state $s$ will require that $e_0$ holds a direct reference to $e_1$ in one of its field (or array) slots. Of course, this statement needs a justification as it must be possible to adequately model the notion of accessibility in the description of design patterns. In the Whole-Part pattern, the restricted accessibility is supposed to ensure that the state of Parts cannot be modified by clients others than from the corresponding Whole. State changes on a Part object $p$ are performed by invoking methods of $p$ or directly assigning to field or array slots of $p$. Both possibilities require that the object that performs the modification holds a reference to $p$. References may be held either in a local variable, a field, or an array slot. Like when invariants are considered, we are however at most interested in observed states directly before and after method invocations. Since such a method invocation cannot change the assignments to local variables, all local variables can be ignored. There is however one exception: the return value must be taken into account because it can afterwards be assigned by the caller to a field for instance. The return value is captured if we assume in the post-state that an (arbitrary) object references the returned object or value (see Sect. 8.1). This justifies the following two possibilities of how to access an object $e_1$ directly from a given one $e_0$ (for now, without further restrictions by the set $A$):

**Definition 4.2** (Access). An object $e_0$ *accesses* an object $e_1$

- by an arbitrary field $a$: if there is an instance field $a$ in the class of $e_0$ with $e_0.a = e_1$

- by an arbitrary array access: if $e_0$ is an array and there is an $i \in \{0, \ldots, e_0\texttt{.length} - 1\}$ with $e_0\texttt{[}i\texttt{]} = e_1$.

This is reflected in the semantics of the Acc symbols:

**Definition 4.3** (Semantics). Let $A$ be a non-empty set of instance field symbols and array access symbols, and $e_0 \in \mathrm{Dom}(\texttt{Object}) \setminus \{\texttt{null}\}, e_1 \in \mathrm{Dom}(\textsc{Any})$. The interpretations of the Acc symbols of a signature $\mathrm{Acc}(\Sigma)$ in a state $s$, $\mathrm{Acc}[A]^{s,P}$, $\mathrm{Acc}^{s,P}$, and $\overline{\mathrm{Acc}}[A]^{s,P}$ are relations $\mathrm{Dom}(\texttt{Object}) \times \mathrm{Dom}(\textsc{Any})$. Moreover we require:

1. $(e_0, e_1) \in \mathrm{Acc}[A]^{s,P}$ iff $e_0$ accesses $e_1$ by either a field $a$ or an array access $\texttt{[]}_T$ and the symbol representing $a$ is in $A$ or $\texttt{[]}_T \in A$ (resp.).

2. $(e_0, e_1) \in Acc^{s,P}$ iff $e_0$ accesses $e_1$ by a field $a$ or an array access.

3. $(e_0, e_1) \in Acc[A]^{s,P}$ iff $e_0$ accesses $e_1$ by a field or array access symbol $a$ *not* represented by a symbol in $A$.

Note that we do not care, at this stage, which visibilities the access providing fields have. For now, every reference counts, no matter if it is declared as `private` or as `protected` (these were the visibilities we have allowed earlier).

For a finite $A$, adding $\mathrm{Acc}[A]$ is no real extension to JavaFOL, since an equivalent formula could be written in the unextended JavaFOL. Also if we were considering only closed programs, no extension would be needed, we would just have to enumerate all fields in the program.

**Example 4.3.** Consider the following program:

```
public class C {
  public Object a;
}

public class D {
  public Object a;
  public Object b;
}
```

```
public class M {
  public static void main() {
    D d = new D();
    C c = new C();
    d.a = c;
    d.b = null;
    c.a = null;
  }
}
```

In the state after the execution of `main()` the following formulae are

| valid: | not valid: |
|---|---|
| $\mathrm{Acc}[a@(D)](d,c)$ | $\mathrm{Acc}[a@(C)](c,d)$ |
| $\mathrm{Acc}(d,c)$ | $\mathrm{Acc}(c,d)$ |
| $\overline{\mathrm{Acc}}[b@(D)](d,c)$ | $\overline{\mathrm{Acc}}[a@(D)](d,c)$ |

*

### 4.2.2 The Reach and Conn Predicates

Reasoning about encapsulation often means reasoning about the accessibility of all objects *reachable* from a root object. In this section a parameterised Reach predicate is defined which can be used to reason about reachability. For use only in Sect. 8.4, when we exploit the Universe type system to prove encapsulation properties, we define a similar predicate called Conn which does not care about the direction of references.

Essentially, reachability is the reflexive and transitive closure of the Acc relation defined in the last section. So we define Reach, a binary predicate for each set of fields, as follows:

**Definition 4.4** (Syntax of Reach). With $\Sigma = (\mathcal{T}, \mathcal{F}^{nr}, \mathcal{F}^{r}, \mathcal{P}^{nr}, \mathcal{P}^{r}, \preceq, \sigma, \tau)$, let again $A$ be the set of symbols in $\Sigma$ which are either instance field symbols or array access symbols. Then $\mathrm{Reach}(\Sigma)$ is defined as

$$P^{nr*} := P^{nr} \cup \{\mathrm{Reach}[A'](\cdot,\cdot,\cdot) \mid A' \subseteq A, A' \text{ not empty}\} \cup \{\mathrm{Reach}(\cdot,\cdot,\cdot)\}$$

$$\sigma^*(f) := \begin{cases} (\texttt{Object}, \textsc{Any}, \textsc{Integer}) & \text{if } f \in \{\mathrm{Reach}(\cdot,\cdot,\cdot), \mathrm{Reach}[A'](\cdot,\cdot,\cdot)\} \\ \sigma(f) & \text{otherwise} \end{cases}$$

$$\mathrm{Reach}(\Sigma) := (\mathcal{T}, \mathcal{F}^{nr*}, \mathcal{F}^{r}, \mathcal{P}^{nr}, \mathcal{P}^{r}, \preceq, \sigma^*, \tau)$$

For the formulae $\mathrm{Fma}^{\mathrm{Reach}(\Sigma)}$, we define the following abbreviation:

$$\mathrm{Reach}[A](t_0,t_1) \quad :\Leftrightarrow \quad \exists n\!:\!\textsc{Integer}.\ \mathrm{Reach}[A](t_0,t_1,n)$$

**Definition 4.5** (Semantics of Reach). Let $A$ be a non-empty set of instance field symbols and array access symbols, $e_0 \in \mathrm{Dom}(\texttt{Object})$, $e_1 \in \mathrm{Dom}(\textsc{Any})$, $e_2 \in \mathrm{Dom}(\textsc{Integer})$. We define the interpretations of the Reach symbols of a signature $\mathrm{Reach}(\Sigma)$ in a state $s$ as follows:

1. $\text{Reach}[A]^{s,P}$ is a relation Dom(`Object`) × Dom(ANY) × Dom(INTEGER) with the following property: $(e_0, e_1, e_2) \in \text{Reach}[A]^{s,P}$ iff $n \geq 0$ and there is a finite sequence $(e'_0, \ldots, e'_n)$ with $e'_0, \ldots, e'_n \in \mathcal{U}$, $e'_0 = e_0$, , $e'_n = e_1$, $n = e_2 \geq 0$, and for all $i = 1, \ldots, n$: $(e'_{i-1}, e'_i) \in \text{Acc}[A]^{s,P}$.

2. $\text{Reach}^{s,P}$ is a relation Dom(`Object`) × Dom(ANY) × Dom(INTEGER) with the following property: $(e_0, e_1, e_2) \in \text{Reach}^{s,P}$ iff $n \geq 0$ and there is a finite sequence $(e'_0, \ldots, e'_n)$ with $e'_0, \ldots, e'_n \in \mathcal{U}$, $e'_0 = e_0$, , $e'_n = e_1$, $n = e_2 \geq 0$, and for all $i = 1, \ldots, n$: $(e'_{i-1}, e'_i) \in \text{Acc}^{s,P}$.

As already said we also need a special predicate for the purpose of a better integration of the Universe type system (see Sect. 8.4).

**Definition 4.6** (Syntax of Conn)**.** Let $\Sigma$ and $A$ be as before. Then $\text{Conn}(\Sigma)$ is defined as

$$P^{nr*} := P^{nr} \cup \{\text{Conn}[A'](\cdot,\cdot,\cdot) \mid A' \subseteq A, A' \text{ not empty}\}$$

$$\sigma^*(f) := \begin{cases} (\text{ANY}, \text{ANY}, \text{INTEGER}) & \text{if } f = \text{Conn}[A](\cdot,\cdot,\cdot) \\ \sigma(f) & \text{otherwise} \end{cases}$$

$$\text{Conn}(\Sigma) := (\mathcal{T}, \mathcal{F}^{nr*}, \mathcal{F}^{r}, \mathcal{P}^{nr}, \mathcal{P}^{r}, \preceq, \sigma^*, \tau)$$

Again we use the following abbreviation:

$$\text{Conn}[A](t_0, t_1) \quad :\Leftrightarrow \quad \exists n{:}\text{INTEGER}.\ \text{Conn}[A](t_0, t_1, n)$$

**Definition 4.7** (Semantics of Conn)**.** $\text{Conn}[A]^{s,P}$ is a relation

$$\text{Dom}(\text{ANY}) \times \text{Dom}(\text{ANY}) \times \text{Dom}(\text{INTEGER})$$

with the following property: $(e_0, e_1, e_2) \in \text{Conn}[A]^{s,P}$ iff there is a finite sequence $(e'_0, \ldots, e'_n)$ with $e'_0, \ldots, e'_n \in \mathcal{U}$, $e'_0 = e_0$, $e'_n = e_1$, $n = e_2 \geq 0$, and for all $i = 1, \ldots, n$: $(e'_{i-1}, e'_i) \in \text{Acc}[A]^{s,P}$ or $(e'_i, e'_{i-1}) \in \text{Acc}[A]^{s,P}$ and for all $i = 1, \ldots, n$: $e'_i \neq \texttt{null}$

The last alternative is the only change to the Reach predicate: we allow accesses in both direction between objects.

In the sequel of this chapter we assume to have only signatures which contain all of the extensions defined above, that is we only have signatures $\Sigma$ with $\Sigma = \text{Conn}(\text{Reach}(\text{Acc}(\Sigma)))$.

## 4.3 Macro Encapsulation Predicates

Though the predicates Acc and Reach provide a basic vocabulary for specifying encapsulation behaviour, their use is still tedious. We thus provide handy abbreviations, or *macro encapsulation predicates*, for useful application patterns. Below, their practicability is measured by formulating properties of the design patterns and the alias control approaches. In the end, all predicates introduced throughout this section are summarised in Table 4.1.

For notational convenience, we use in this section the convention that quantification over logical variables without type information, means quantification over the type `java.lang.Object`. For instance, $\forall x.\ \varphi$ is a shorthand for $\forall x$:`Object`. $\varphi$.

### 4.3.1 The Enc predicate

The main task of encapsulation is to allow access (in the sense of the last section) to a set $E_1$ of objects or values only from another set of designated objects $E_0$. So we want to express that for all $e_z \in E_1$, if there is an access from an object $e_y$ to an object $e_z$ then $e_y \in E_0$. Usually it should be allowed that the objects of $E_1$ access each other. So we will additionally allow $e_y \in E_1$. So in short: if $e_y$ accesses $e_z \in E_1$ then $e_y \in E_0 \cup E_1$.

The characterisation of which objects belong to $E_0$ and $E_1$, can be done using formulae with free variables which characterise those objects being part of the respective set. The most general macro encapsulation predicate, called Enc and defined in the following, imposes no *a priori* restrictions on these sets or formulae. The objects to be *protected* from arbitrary access (i.e. belonging to $E_1$) are formalised as those $z$ satisfying the formula $p(z)$. And the objects which are the only ones allowed to access the protected objects from outside (i.e. belonging to $E_0$) are formalised as those *guarding* objects $y$ which satisfy the formula $g(y)$. The formula defining Enc says: *if* there is an access from an object $y$ to an object $z$, and $p(z)$ holds, that is $z$ should be protected, *then* (a) $y$ is either satisfying $g(y)$, or (b) $y$ is itself a protected object (that is, $p(y)$ holds).

Figure 4.2 illustrates these settings. The boxes depict objects in a certain state. There are four areas marked by the two ellipses. Those objects $y$ which satisfy $g(y)$, those $z$ which satisfy $p(z)$, those objects which satisfy both, and those which satisfy none of both. There are some references depicted by arrows between the objects. The references represented by bold and crossed-out arrows are disallowed by the Enc predicate.

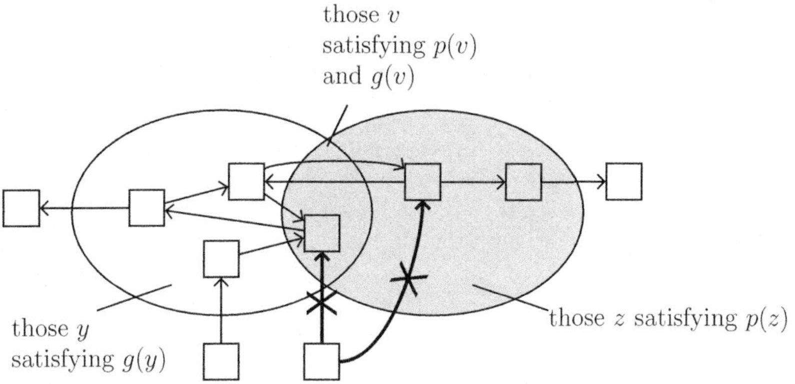


**Figure 4.2:** The Enc predicate illustrated. The bold and crossed-out references are disallowed

For a proper definition of the new predicate (as well as of all defined in this section) we would need to extend the signature $\Sigma$ and define an interpretation for the added symbols. Since the semantics of all predicates introduced in this section can be expressed by means of an extended signature $\Sigma$ = Reach(Acc($\Sigma$)) as defined in the last section, we simply say that formulae with one of the new predicate symbols are just abbreviations for a regular formula over $\Sigma$, which is expanded to these as needed. Again, the Enc predicate comes in two versions, one of which is parameterised with a list of fields (and additionally array access operators) which restrict the considered accesses. So here follows the syntax of the predicates and their defining formula:

$$\begin{aligned} \mathrm{Enc}_{y,z}\,[A; g(y), p(z)] \;&:\Leftrightarrow\; \dot\forall y.\ \dot\forall z.\ \big(\mathrm{Acc}[A](y,z) \wedge p(z) \rightarrow p(y) \vee g(y)\big) \\ \mathrm{Enc}_{y,z}\,[g(y), p(z)] \;&:\Leftrightarrow\; \dot\forall y.\ \dot\forall z.\ \big(\mathrm{Acc}(y,z) \wedge p(z) \rightarrow p(y) \vee g(y)\big) \end{aligned}$$

All encapsulation tasks needed to be accomplished for modular verification (see Sect. 9.3.3) are captured by this general predicate. However, often even more specialised patterns of encapsulation turn up. For a developer who needs to specify encapsulation, it is extremely helpful if these patterns are reflected in the vocabulary with which he can formalise encapsulation. The following paragraphs thus define useful instances of Enc.

### 4.3.2 The GuardObj and UniqueAcc Predicates

We define a predicate for the following property: If there is an access from a *guard* object $y$ to an object $u$ then $y$ must satisfy $\varphi(y)$. Or in other words: With the formula $\varphi(y)$, the set of guard objects $y$ are defined which are allowed to hold a reference to $u$. In JavaFOL over a signature extended as described above, we formalise this property as:

$$\begin{aligned}
\mathrm{GuardObj}_y[A;\varphi(y)](u) \;&:\Leftrightarrow\; \mathrm{Enc}_{y,z}\,[A;\varphi(y), z \doteq u] \\
&\Leftrightarrow\; \dot{\forall} y.\ \big(\mathrm{Acc}[A](y,u) \rightarrow \varphi(y) \vee y \doteq u\big)
\end{aligned}$$

$$\begin{aligned}
\mathrm{GuardObj}_y[\varphi(y)](u) \;&:\Leftrightarrow\; \mathrm{Enc}_{y,z}\,[\varphi(y), z \doteq u] \\
&\Leftrightarrow\; \dot{\forall} y.\ \big(\mathrm{Acc}(y,u) \rightarrow \varphi(y) \vee y \doteq u\big)
\end{aligned}$$

This predicate is illustrated in Fig. 4.3 in the same manner as before.

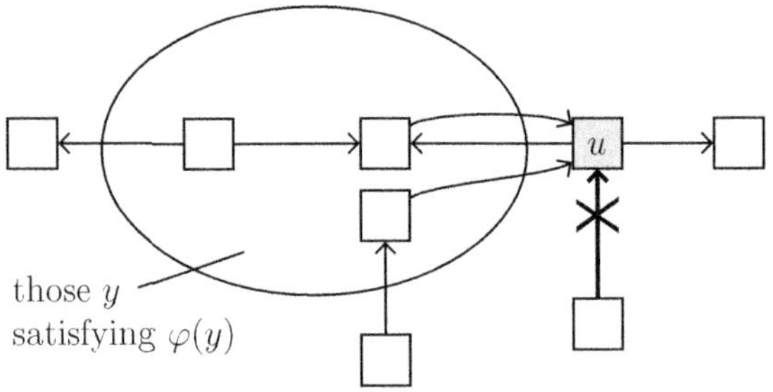


**Figure 4.3:** The GuardObj predicate illustrated. The bold and crossed-out reference is disallowed

In the easiest and most common case, $\varphi(y)$ will consist just of an equality $y \doteq g$, thus having just one guard object $g$. This specification pattern is in fact so common that we introduce another macro predicate called UniqueAcc which is defined as follows:

$$\text{UniqueAcc}(g, u) :\Leftrightarrow \text{GuardObj}_x[g \doteq x](u)$$

We continue with some examples of formalisations of approaches in literature using these two encapsulation predicates.

**Example 4.4** (Unique Pointer). A *unique object* is an object that is referenced by at most one object [Boyland, 2001]. The GuardObj predicate can easily be used to model this property, for instance to say that $u$ is a unique object, we require that for every object $y$ that has a direct reference to $u$, all other objects referencing $u$ must be equal to $y$. Or simpler, $y$ is the only guard object:

$$\dot{\forall} y.\ (\text{Acc}(y, u) \rightarrow \text{GuardObj}_x[x \doteq y](u))$$

Moreover there is an equivalent formulation with UniqueAcc:

$$\dot{\forall} y.\ (\text{Acc}(y, u) \rightarrow \text{UniqueAcc}(y, u))$$

By inserting the definition of GuardObj and simplifying we get the following formula, which obviously fits our expectations of a unique object:

$$\dot{\forall} y_0.\ \dot{\forall} y_1.\ \big(\text{Acc}(y_0, u) \land \text{Acc}(y_1, u) \rightarrow y_0 \doteq y_1 \lor y_0 = u\big)$$

This formalisation allows that $u$ may reference itself, as $\ldots \lor y_0 = u$ indicates. If this is not desired it is of course possible to define a macro predicate which requires stricter uniqueness. *

**Example 4.5** (Balloons). For balloons, it is required [Almeida, 1997] that for an object $b$ of a balloon type and the objects $B$ indirectly referenced by $b$ the property holds: $b$ is accessed at most once, the referencing object is not in $B$, and all objects in $B$ are only accessed by objects in $B \cup \{b\}$. Formalised in JavaFOL, this property is:

$$\dot{\forall} v.\ \big(\text{Acc}(v, b) \rightarrow \text{UniqueAcc}(v, b) \land \neg\, \text{Reach}(b, v)\big) \\ \land \text{Enc}_{y,z}\,[y \doteq b, \text{Reach}(b, z) \land z \not\doteq b] \quad *$$

**Example 4.6** (Whole-Part Pattern). The GuardObj or the UniqueAcc predicate can be employed for simple versions of the Whole-Part pattern, namely if the part's state does not depend on additional objects. In this case, the

Whole-Part pattern requires that there is no direct access to the parts (instances of `Part`), only indirect accesses through the `Whole` object are allowed. We can now formally denote this property as

$$\dot{\forall} p{:}\mathtt{Part}.\ \dot{\exists} w{:}\mathtt{Whole}.\ \mathrm{GuardObj}_x[x \doteq w](p)$$

or if we already know that the value in field `p` is a part of a `Whole` and using UniqueAcc, we write simpler: $\dot{\forall} w{:}\mathtt{Whole}.\ \mathrm{UniqueAcc}(w, w.\mathtt{p})$

For the settings in Example 4.1, we would require the following invariant:

$$\dot{\forall} t{:}\mathtt{Triangle}.\ \big(\mathrm{UniqueAcc}(t, t.\mathtt{p0}) \wedge \mathrm{UniqueAcc}(t, t.\mathtt{p1}) \\ \wedge \mathrm{UniqueAcc}(t, t.\mathtt{p2})\big)$$

This describes exactly the desired property that nodes may only be accessed by means of `Triangle`. It is however *not* sufficient for the settings of Example 4.2 since references to `Colour` objects would be allowed, even if they 'bypass' the corresponding `Triangle` object. *

**Example 4.7** (Copy Mutable Parameters, Return New Objects from Accessors). These two patterns help to ensure that an object stored in a field $a$ of object $o$ is only accessed through $o$ itself, denoted in JavaFOL as

$$\mathrm{GuardObj}_x[x \doteq o](o.a)$$

In contrast to many other patterns, these two patterns exactly define *how* encapsulation must be achieved, namely by copying parameters and return values. Obviously only the effect of the pattern can be specified with encapsulation predicates. *

**Example 4.8** (Confinement). Confinement defined by Vitek and Bokowski [2001] allows developers to mark certain types as *confined*. Instances of these types are required not to be accessed from outside the package in which the type is defined. The formula that specifies the confinement demonstrates that it is useful to have the possibility to use a formula $\varphi(x)$ to qualify guard objects.

We assume that we have a unary predicate $\mathit{confined}_p$ which holds for every object whose type is marked as being confined to package $p$. Let $T_1, \ldots, T_n$ be the types in package $p$. Only these classes may access types confined to $p$. The following formula describes this property:

$$\dot{\forall} y.\ \big(\mathit{confined}_p(y) \\ \rightarrow \mathrm{GuardObj}_x[\mathrm{ExactInstanceOf}_{T_1}(x) \vee \ldots \vee \mathrm{ExactInstanceOf}_{T_n}(x)](y)\big)$$

ExactInstanceOf$_T(t)$ is a variation of InstanceOf$_T(y)$ which requires that $t$ is not a strict subtype of $T$. A more formal definition of ExactInstanceOf() can be found in Sect. 6.2.4. $*$

### 4.3.3 The GuardReg and UniqueReg Predicates

The GuardObj predicate restricts the accessibility of one single object. Often however, it is necessary to restrict the access to *all* objects indirectly referenced by a particular one. To ensure, for instance, that in the object graph of Fig. 4.1 references ① and ② are not allowed, it must be required that all objects reachable from `t.p0` are only reachable through `t`. No restriction should however be imposed on references within the group of objects reachable from `t.p0`.

Using the GuardObj predicate we can formalise such properties as follows and define the GuardReg predicate:

$$\begin{aligned}&\mathrm{GuardReg}_x[A; \varphi(x)](u)\\&:\Leftrightarrow \dot{\forall} z.\ \big(\mathrm{Reach}[A](u,z) \rightarrow z \doteq u \vee \mathrm{GuardObj}_x[\varphi(x) \vee \mathrm{Reach}[A](u,x)](z)\big)\end{aligned}$$

or equivalently:

$$\begin{aligned}&\mathrm{GuardReg}_x[A; \varphi(x)](u)\\&\Leftrightarrow \dot{\forall} y.\ \dot{\forall} z.\ \big(\mathrm{Reach}[A](u,z) \wedge \mathrm{Acc}(y,z) \rightarrow z \doteq u \vee \mathrm{Reach}[A](u,y) \vee \varphi(y)\big)\end{aligned}$$

In this formalisation one can associate the objects of the protected 'region' as those objects $z$ which are reachable with fields $A$ starting from an object $u$. Any reference from an object $y$ to such a $z$ must either satisfy $\varphi(y)$ or is itself part of this region (i.e. reachable from $u$ via fields $A$). Fig. 4.4 describes GuardReg visually.

Like there was a UniqueAcc predicate introduced for the GuardObj predicate we define a UniqueReg predicate as follows to capture the most common application of GuardReg:

$$\mathrm{UniqueReg}(g,u) :\Leftrightarrow \mathrm{GuardReg}_x[x \doteq g](u)$$

Again, a survey of design patterns and alias control policies follows intended to demonstrate the usefulness of the two additional macro predicates. In addition, we mention how the predicate enables us to formally specify the *compositions*-type associations of the modelling language UML.

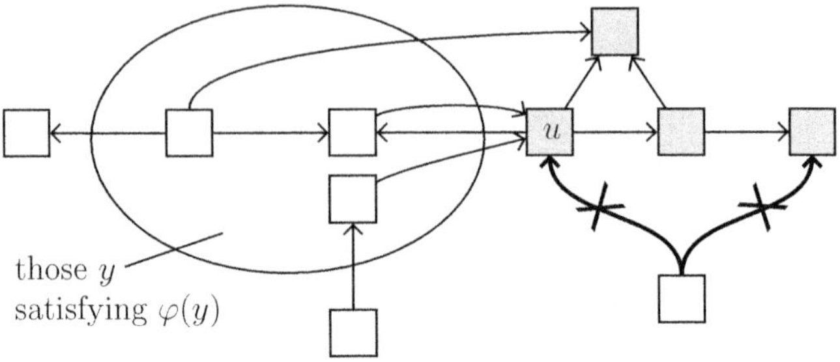


**Figure 4.4:** The GuardReg predicate illustrated. The bold and crossed-out references are disallowed. The grey boxes are all objects reachable from $u$

**Example 4.9** (Islands). An object $b$ plays the role of a bridge [Hogg, 1991] if in all states the formula

$$\dot{\forall} x.\ (\mathrm{Acc}(b, x) \to \mathrm{UniqueReg}(b, x))$$

holds. By applying the definition and simplifying we get:

$$\dot{\forall} x.\ \dot{\forall} y.\ \dot{\forall} z.\ \big(\mathrm{Acc}(b, x) \wedge \mathrm{Acc}(y, z) \wedge \mathrm{Reach}(x, z) \to \mathrm{Reach}(x, y) \vee b \doteq y\big) \quad *$$

**Example 4.10** (Whole-Part Pattern, continued). The Whole-Part pattern requires that there is no direct access to the parts (instances of `Part`), only indirect accesses through the `Whole` object are allowed. For simple structures, we have already observed above that it is sufficient to use a formulation using the GuardObj predicate.

If, however, the `Part` objects' representations consist of a more complex object structure, this formulation is insufficient as Example 4.6 has illustrated. Instead, we can express the desired property with the help of GuardReg. The basic formalisation is:

$$\dot{\forall} p{:}\texttt{Part}.\ \dot{\exists} w{:}\texttt{Whole}.\ \mathrm{UniqueReg}(w, p) \tag{4.1}$$

The validity of this formula implies that all objects that are (indirectly) referenced by a `Part` are only accessed among each other or by a particular `Whole` object.

We take up the settings of Example 4.2. The special variant of the Whole-Part pattern imposed there is that parts of the same aggregate may access internals of each other. The guard object is thus not only the `Whole` instance but also all objects reachable from the parts are guard objects, i.e. those $x$ satisfying

$$\varphi_g := x \doteq t \lor \mathrm{Reach}(t.\mathtt{p0}, x) \lor \mathrm{Reach}(t.\mathtt{p1}, x) \lor \mathrm{Reach}(t.\mathtt{p2}, x)$$

The desired property is now formalised in JavaFOL as follows:

$$\dot\forall t{:}\mathtt{Triangle}.\ \big(\mathrm{GuardReg}_x[\varphi_g](t.\mathtt{p0}) \land \mathrm{GuardReg}_x[\varphi_g](t.\mathtt{p1}) \land \mathrm{GuardReg}_x[\varphi_g](t.\mathtt{p2})\big) \qquad *$$

**Example 4.11** (Proxy Pattern). The proxy pattern requires exactly the same property:

$$\dot\forall s{:}\mathtt{Subject}.\ \dot\exists p{:}\mathtt{Proxy}.\ \mathrm{UniqueReg}(p, s)$$

Note, that we can easily enable variations of the pattern, for instance we might allow some objects (specified by the terms $t_0, \ldots t_n$) to bypass the proxy and have direct access to the subject:

$$\dot\forall s{:}\mathtt{Subject}.\ \dot\exists p{:}\mathtt{Proxy}.\ \mathrm{GuardReg}_x[x \doteq p \lor x \doteq t_0 \lor \ldots \lor x \doteq t_n](s) \qquad *$$

**Example 4.12** (Iterator Pattern). With this pattern, it is demonstrated that the parameterisation of the predicate with a set of fields $A$ is in fact useful. The objects that should only be accessible through the guard objects are the internals of the aggregate object. For simplicity, we assume that the aggregate object is a linked list `LinkedList` (like the Java implementation `java.util.LinkedList`). We assume that the internals of the list are made up by objects of a class `Entry` connected by a `next` field. The first object of this region is stored in the `header` field of a `LinkedList`. The guard objects are both the `LinkedList` instance and the `ListItr` iterator object (this could be made more precise by describing only `ListItr` instances of the particular list). The encapsulation property required for the Iterator pattern is thus:

$$\dot\forall l{:}\mathtt{LinkedList}.\ \mathrm{GuardReg}_x[\{\mathtt{next}\}; x \doteq l \lor \mathrm{InstanceOf}_{\mathtt{ListItr}}(x)](l.\mathtt{header}) \qquad *$$

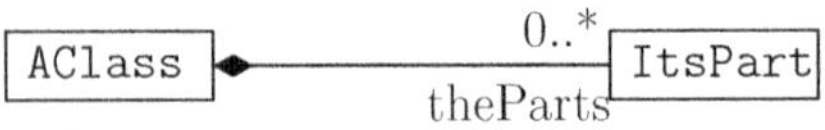


**Figure 4.5:** UML composition

**Example 4.13** (UML Compositions)**.** In the UML, classes and their interrelation can be modelled in class diagrams. The relation between instances of classes are denoted as *associations* between classes. There are special kinds of associations, for instance *compositions*. These are depicted with a filled diamond adornment (see Fig. 4.5) and emphasise that one partner in the relation has sole responsibility for managing the parts of the other partner. As a consequence, accessing these objects directly is forbidden. We can capture this property formally as in (4.1):

$$\dot{\forall} p{:}\texttt{ItsPart}.\ \dot{\exists} w{:}\texttt{AClass}.\ \mathrm{UniqueReg}(w, p) \qquad *$$

## 4.3.4 Expressing Advanced Ownership Systems

Ownership type systems are the most advanced technique to enforce encapsulation. In their first definition [Clarke et al., 1998], the expressible encapsulation properties were rather strict: All objects are owned by another object and only the owner and objects with the same owner are allowed to reference owned objects. The ownership relation is acyclic and is enforced by annotating variables with the modifier `rep`. Annotating a variable reference $v$ as `rep` makes objects stored in this location being owned by the object which declares the variable reference $v$. Objects indirectly referenced by such a `rep` reference belong to the object's representation. In more recent incarnations, restrictions have been lifted [Clarke et al., 1999, Müller, 2002, Boyapati et al., 2003, Banerjee and Naumann, 2005].

As an example we consider Müller's variant called *Universe type system* as described in Müller [2002], Müller and Poetzsch-Heffter [2001]. The major progress of the Universe type system is to allow for *readonly* references, which forbid to write to objects obtained by such references.

Central paradigm of ownership systems is that every object has an owner which is not transferable to other objects.[1] Assume we have an acyclic partial

[1] In fact, there are ownership type systems which aim at owner transfer [Boyapati et al., 2003]. Universes do not allow it however.

| Predicate | Definition |
|---|---|
| $\mathrm{Acc}(t_1, t_2)$ | (Axiom, 'there are direct references from $t_1$ to $t_2$') |
| $\mathrm{Reach}(t_1, t_2)$ | (Axiom, 'there are access paths from $t_1$ to $t_2$') |
| $\mathrm{Enc}_{y,z}\,[A; g(y), p(z)]$ | $\dot\forall y.\ \dot\forall z.\ \mathrm{Acc}[A](y, z) \land p(z) \rightarrow p(y) \lor g(y)$ |
| $\mathrm{GuardObj}_x[\varphi(x)](u)$ | $\dot\forall y.\ \mathrm{Acc}(y, u) \rightarrow \varphi(y)$ |
| $\mathrm{UniqueAcc}(g, u)$ | $\mathrm{GuardObj}_x[g \doteq x](u)$ |
| $\mathrm{GuardReg}_x[A; \varphi(x)](u)$ | $\dot\forall y.\ \dot\forall z.\ ((\ \mathrm{Reach}[A](u, z) \land \mathrm{Acc}(y, z)) \rightarrow (z \doteq u \lor \mathrm{Reach}[A](u, y) \lor \varphi(y)))$ |
| $\mathrm{UniqueReg}(g, u)$ | $\mathrm{GuardReg}_x[g \doteq x](u)$ |

**Table 4.1:** Overview of encapsulation predicates

function $\mathrm{Own}[R; F]^s$ being the interpretation of a binary predicate symbol $\mathrm{Own}[R; F]$ which we include into our signatures. This relation defines which object is owned by which other one. It is parameterised with the fields $R$ declared as `rep` and the fields $F$ declared as `readonly`. Every object referenced through a `rep` field is owned by the object which declares this field. Additionally, every object referenced by an owned object is owned by the same owner unless this reference is in $R \cup F$.

The ownership invariant then requires that only the owner of an object $e$ or objects owned by the same owner access $e$ and that this access happens using a field in $R$ or that the reference is readonly. We can formalise this in JavaFOL over the extended signature as follows:

$$\dot\forall x.\ \dot\forall y.\ \dot\forall z.\ \Big(\mathrm{Own}[R](x, z) \rightarrow \big(\mathrm{Acc}[R](y, z) \rightarrow y \doteq x\big) \land \big(\overline{\mathrm{Acc}}[R \cup F](y, z) \rightarrow \mathrm{Own}[R](x, y)\big)\Big)$$

In Sect. 8.4 we will present a technique which infers encapsulation properties automatically using a very similar formalisation.

## 4.4 Summary

In this chapter we have investigated how encapsulation properties can be formalised. For a seamless integration with functional specification, we decided to extend traditional specification languages, and as prototype JavaFOL, with encapsulation predicates. Basic encapsulation predicates are the Acc family of predicates and the Reach predicate. On top of these a number of macro predicates (see Table 4.1) have been defined, the most powerful being the Enc predicate restricting access from one set of objects to another, each defined by a characteristic formula. Examples from alias control approaches and common design patterns have shown the feasibility of the approach.

In Sect. 8 we will investigate how encapsulation properties can be checked, possibly exploiting procedures developed in the area of type systems. In Sect. 9.3.3 encapsulation predicates will turn out to be the important ingredient from the specification side to enable modular verification of invariants.

# 5 Component Specifications

Facilius per partes in
cognitionem totius adducimur.

*(Seneca)*

The basic principle of contracts is to divide obligations between two parties, so that one party can rely on the services of the other. In Chapter 3 these two parties were caller and callee of an operation. Callers were responsible to ensure the precondition of an operation contract which in turn made the callee promise to assert the corresponding post-condition, the correctness of the assignable clause, a certain termination behaviour, and all invariants.

In this chapter the notion of contracts is extended to *component contracts*. Though traditional contracts will not disappear they get wrapped in a second layer of mutual responsibilities, which is quite similar to the first notion of contract.

Operation contracts, more precisely their preconditions, restrict the set of allowed calls to an operation; the caller, possibly not located within the considered open program, is responsible to ensure the precondition, according to the statement: *If* a caller ensures the precondition *then* the callee promises to establish the postcondition. While there, we were concerned with the dynamic caller/callee interface, we are now interested in the static program/extension interface. The contract metaphor is used here as follows: *If* an extension, that is, classes that use the open program, satisfies certain conditions, *then* the considered open program fulfils its specification.

The new 'preconditions' are obligations the user of a component has to establish. They are written up as *extension contracts* as presented in Sect. 5.1, while the new 'post-conditions', the properties the component ensures, are the classical contracts from Chapter 3.

To impose restrictions on the context as 'preconditions' is ambivalent: On the one hand, this is not desired at all in an open world, since it is the contrary of our original goal to have trusted components no matter in which environment they are employed. On the other hand it is obviously necessary and comes with no surprise that one needs to rely on contexts which adhere to certain criteria: In a re-use context one deliberately *wants to adapt* behaviour to the new context; it can then quite easily happen that, with this change, behaviour is affected which is sensitive to the correctness of the re-used program.

So the new preconditions are *not* a desired feature, they are a pure necessity with languages which aim at making programs easily extensible (or re-usable). Especially *object-oriented* programming has ever been promoted with this goal. From the perspective of formal methods, one ideally would want component contracts with an empty set of extension contracts, but this could only be achieved at the cost of an inextensible system.

There are two places where we need restrictions on the context:

- Modular proofs: subclasses *must* be behavioural subtypes.
- Ensuring invariants in an open poorly encapsulated context: For instance, encapsulation behaviour is propagated to subclasses in the context, or the context itself is made responsible to maintain invariants.

**Outline.** We describe the 'preconditions' of component contracts, that is, generic extension contracts in the next section. In Sect. 5.2 contracts for components are defined.

## 5.1 Generic Extension Contracts

This section defines how requirements on the *context* a program is used in are specified. When we reason about correctness issues, this context can be identified with the notion of an observer as defined in Chapter 3.

The obvious problem with specifying a context is, that a lot of information is unavailable at the time such a specification is written: For instance, no type or operation names of the context are known at the time of specification. Thus specifications cannot simply be attached to a type or an operation. Instead it is needed to

1. *generically* describe the context elements a specification is attached to, and
2. provide *conditions*, which must be satisfied, if a context type should comply to a specification.

In the following we describe how we achieve this for JavaFOL specifications. Since specifications are usually written in 'real' specification languages, these features must be added to such languages. We exemplify these additions for UML/OCL and JML in this section. Note that generic extension contracts are not part of these languages but are proposals for extending them.

### 5.1.1 Syntax

Like for generic types in some programming languages (like Java 5 [Gosling et al., 2005]), we introduce *type parameters* to make contracts generic. Type parameters must be declared in a *header* in front of the specification which uses them. They are accompanied with conditions (*instantiation constraints*) on allowed instantiations of the parameters.

Every specification in JavaFOL or in a specification language has to name the type(s) it imposes constraints on. We extend JavaFOL and specification languages by allowing for type variables replacing these type names. More generally, wherever a type name is expected according to the specification language's syntax, a type parameter may be used.

Instantiation constraints allow for specifying *which* classes may be instantiated for the type parameter. For a type parameter `T`, the following instantiation constraints are provided:

1. `extends* <TypeName>`
2. `unconstrained`

Note that these instantiation constraints are just those needed in this work, for other applications one may think of other patterns, like for instance, `T` are all classes in package $p$.

A header entry with the declaration of generic parameters and the instantiation constraints looks as follows:

```
<TypeParameterName> <InstantiationConstraint> ;
```

A headers contains at least one of such entries.

**Example 5.1.** The following is a header which specifies that the type parameter `T` stands—in the following specification—for an arbitrary subtype of `Period`.

```
T extends* Period;
```

*

Altogether, a generic contract consists of a header and a specification written as usual in the considered specification language except that type names may be replaced by type parameters. A generic contract is additionally bordered by the key words `generic contract` and a pair of curly braces. A generic contract thus has the following shape:

```
generic contract {
  (<TypeParameterName> <InstantiationConstraint> ;)+
  <SpecificationWithTypeParameters>
}
```

In the sequel, the concept is clarified by concrete applications using JavaFOL, JML, and UML/OCL.

### JavaFOL Specifications

In JavaFOL specifications, types appear

- in quantifications, e.g. as $T$ in $\forall x{:}T.$ ,
- as sorts of terms, and
- as part of the operation designation in an operation contract.

We allow that type parameters replace these concrete types. Therefore an extension Generic($\Sigma$) of a JavaFOL signature $\Sigma$ is defined which comprises the declared type parameters as part of their type symbols:

**Definition 5.1.** For a signature $\Sigma$ with types $\mathcal{T}$, the signature Generic($\Sigma$) augmented with type parameters $R_1, \ldots, R_n$ is identical to $\Sigma$ except that its types are $\mathcal{T} \cup \{R_1, \ldots, R_n\}$.

We call specifications (according to Def. 3.1) over a signature augmented by type parameters declared in a header *generic specifications*. Furthermore we explicitely allow that a type parameter may occur in the description of an operation (in extension to Def. 3.2).

### JML

JML specifications are (in principal) annotations to Java source files. It is however possible to separate specifications from implementations by using extra files which contain copies of the signatures of the Java type to be specified. So even then, JML specifications keep the appearance of Java source files. Consequently in JML, the type a specification is belonging to is indicated by the Java class or interface declaration it is located in. For instance, to specify class `Period` the specification of invariants and operations follows the declaration of the class

```
public class Period { //...
```

In our modifications for extension contracts, type parameter may now simply replace the type name. We give three examples on the realisation of extension contracts in JML.

**Example 5.2.** In order to specify that all (indirect) subclasses of `Period` must satisfy an instance invariant $\varphi$(`self`) we write:

```
generic contract {
  T extends* Period;
  class T {
    /*@ instance invariant φ(this) */
  }
}
```

*

**Example 5.3.** We formalise that all methods declared as `void m(int p)` in all (indirect) subclasses of `Period` behave according to an operation contract with precondition $\varphi_{\mathrm{pre}}$, post-condition $\varphi_{\mathrm{post}}$ and assignable clause *Mod* as follows:

```
generic contract {
  T extends* Period;
  class T {
    /*@ public behavior
      @ requires φ_pre;
      @ ensures φ_post;
      @ assignable Mod;
      @*/
    public void m(int p);
  }
}
```

*

**Example 5.4.** Even *all* classes can be required to satisfy a (static) invariant $\varphi$. This is done as follows:

```
generic contract {
  T unconstrained;
  class T {
    /*@ static invariant φ*/
  }
}
```

Note that it is usually not possible to write instance invariants in generic contracts where the type parameter is unconstrained. Instance invariants typically refer to instance members, but since we are in a generic context it is impossible to refer to instance members (except from those present in all objects, like `equals(Object)`. *

### OCL

In OCL the constrained type is usually given following the keyword `context`. To have generic contracts, this type name is replaced by a generic parameter. Ex. 5.2 would thus be expressed in OCL as follows:

```
generic contract {
  T extends* Period;
  context T
  inv:     φ
}
```

## 5.1.2 Semantics

For defining a semantics of generic contracts we transform generic contracts into regular specifications of the base specification languages. Therefore, we replace or *instantiate* the type parameters with concrete types of a program $P$ and check whether the instantiation constraints are satisfied. If this is not the case these contracts are sorted out. Otherwise the result (without header) forms the new specification of $P$.

The first step is to assign classes and interfaces of a program to the type parameters. In the sequel, let $par(gct)$ be the set of type parameters occurring in a generic contract $gct$.

**Definition 5.2.** An instantiation $\iota$ of $gct$ to a program $P$ is a total function

$$\iota : par(gct) \rightarrow \text{Typenames}(P)$$

where Typenames($P$) is the set of names of the types of $P$. An instantiation is canonically continued on instantiation constraints and whole generic contracts over $G$ (i.e. generic JavaFOL, JML, or UML/OCL specifications).

**Example 5.5.** Let `MyPeriod` be a subclass of `Period` and `SomeClass` be no (even indirect) subclass of `Period`. Instantiations of the generic contract *gct* from Example 5.2 to a program {`MyPeriod`, `SomeClass`} are the functions $\iota_i : \{\mathtt{T}\} \rightarrow \{\mathtt{MyPeriod}, \mathtt{SomeClass}\}$ for $i = 1, 2$ with $\iota_1(\mathtt{T}) = \mathtt{MyPeriod}$ and $\iota_2(\mathtt{T}) = \mathtt{SomeClass}$.

Further we have the instantiated generic contracts:

$\iota_1(gct)$ =

```
generic contract {
  MyPeriod extends* Period;
  class MyPeriod {
    /*@ instance invariant φ(this) */
  }
}
```

$\iota_2(gct)$ =

```
generic contract {
  SomeClass extends* Period;
  class SomeClass {
    /*@ instance invariant φ(this) */
  }
}
```

*

Then we can check the instantiation constraints (containing only concrete types) whether they are satisfied.

**Definition 5.3.** Let $C$ and $D$ be names of Java classes or interfaces. Instantiation constraints are *satisfied* as described below:

- An instantiation constraint $D$ `extends*` $C$ is satisfied if $D \preceq C$.
- The instantiation constraint $C$ `unconstrained` is always satisfied.

Suppose *gct* is a generic contract and $P$ a program. An instantiation $\iota$ of *gct* to $P$ is *legal* if all instantiation constraints of $\iota(gct)$ are satisfied.

**Example 5.6.** Continuing Ex. 5.5, the instantiation constraint in $\iota_1(gct)$ :

```
MyPeriod extends* Period;
```

is satisfied, while the instantiation constraint in $\iota_2(gct)$:

```
SomeClass extends* Period;
```

is not. $\iota_1(gct)$ is thus legal, while $\iota_2(gct)$ is not. *

From now on we restrict the number of *type parameters per contract to* 1, which covers all cases we need in this work. The final step is to say that legally instantiated generic contracts are the resulting *generated* specification.

**Definition 5.4.** A generic contract *gct generates* the specification $S$ for program $P$ if $S$ is the union of all legal instantiations from *gct* to $P$; hereby the headers and the key word `generic contract` and the enclosing braces are omitted such that syntactically valid specifications emerge.

Given now a set of generic contracts $GCt$. $GCt$ generates the specification $S$ for a program $P$ if $S$ is the union of those specifications generated by the generic contracts $gct \in GCt$.

**Example 5.7.** We continue Ex. 5.6. The generic contract *gct* generates the following regular JML specification for the set {`MyPeriod`} of classes:

```
class MyPeriod {
  /*@ instance invariant φ(this) @*/
}
```

*

### 5.1.3 Relative-Durable Correctness

Generic extension contracts enable us to weaken durable correctness, which was defined in Def. 3.11. In that definition, we were utilising an *arbitrary* closure of the considered program and had thus an *arbitrary* observer[1]. This arbitrariness is now lost: We require from an observer that contracts generated from an extension contract are fulfilled.

**Definition 5.5** (Relative-Durable Correctness). Let $S$ be a specification of an open program $P$. Let further $GCt$ be a set of generic contracts. Suppose $P^{cl}$ is a closure of $P$ and $GCt$ generates the specification $S'$ for $Obs := P^{cl} \backslash P$. Furthermore we assume that every method or constructor *op* of $P$ with an operation contract in $S$ is called by $Obs$ only in a state where the precondition of at least one fitting operation contract from $S$ is satisfied. $P$ is durable correct *relative to* $GCt$ w.r.t. $S$ if

[1]Note, that arbitrariness is weakened in the sense that the observer must respect preconditions of operations.

- *Obs* is naively correct w.r.t. $S'$,
- all invariants hold after an arbitrary method of *Obs* has terminated,
- all invariants are valid in the initial state of $P$,
- all operations *op* of $P$ fulfil the operation contracts for *op* in $S$.

For restrictions on extensions of the context we use here the naive correctness as defined in Def. 3.9. Since we want to make it as easy as possible for developers extending or reusing a program to satisfy conditions which make the used component correct and naive correctness is quite easy to establish, this is a natural choice.

**Example 5.8.** We come back to the introductory example from Sect. 1.2. We have seen that by overriding `earlierOrEqual(Date)` in `Date2` in a context, is was possible to violate an invariant, though the open program {`Period`} seemed to be durable correct otherwise (with the original use of defensive copies). We can now constrain a context in a way that arbitrarily overriding `earlierOrEqual(Date)` is disallowed. We require `earlierOrEqual(Date)` to conform to the specification in `Date`. This can be achieved with the generic contract $gct_{\texttt{earlierOrEqual(Date)}}$

```
generic contract {
  T extends* Date;
  class T {
    /*@ normal_behavior
      @ requires cmp !=null;
      @ ensures \result == (year<cmp.year || (year==cmp.year
      @                      && month.val<=cmp.month.val));
      @*/
    /*@pure@*/ boolean earlierOrEqual(Date cmp);
  }
}
```

Then all subclasses which override `earlierOrEqual(Date)` must fulfil the operation contract as defined in `Date`. The code in `Period` can rely on a proper implementation of this method and can thus establish (in the sense of durable correctness) its invariant.

It can easily be seen that a similar effect is possible for the method `copy()` which is called from the constructor of `Period`. Here we impose the generic extension contract $gct_{\texttt{copy()}}$:

```
generic contract {
  T extends* Date;
  class T {
    /*@ normal_behavior
      @ ensures ( \result.month.val==month.val
      @         & \result.year==year
      @         & \fresh(\result) & \fresh(\result.month);
      @*/
    /*@pure@*/ Date copy();
  }
}
```

We will later (in Sect. 10.2) aim to show that {Period} is durable correct relative to $\{gct_{\texttt{earlierOrEqual(Date)}}, gct_{\texttt{copy()}}\}$. *

Note that it might be sometimes useful to strengthen generic contracts in order to hide implementation details from the context. It is always possible to

- make invariants stronger than originally required,
- likewise make postconditions stronger,
- weaken preconditions,
- allow for a subset of the original assignable clause,
- and require the same termination behaviour as before or *total*.

Concerning assignable clauses, we could even be more liberal by allowing locations which are only present in the extensions to be part of the new strengthened clause. This however requires more thorough investigations, which is object of future work.

## 5.2 Component Contracts

As already motivated in the introductory notes to this chapter, a component contract for a component consists of

- a set $GCt$ of generic extension contracts (as defined in the last section) and
- a specification $S$ imposed for classes and operations of the component in question.

More precisely we define:

**Definition 5.6.** Let $P$ be a component (or equivalently an open program). Let further be $S$ a specification (Def. 3.1) of $P$. Let $GCt$ be a set of generic contracts. Then the pair $(GCt, S)$ is a component contract for $P$.

$GCt$ plays the role of a 'precondition', in the sense that it is an obligation for the 'outside' of the component to fulfil the specification generated by $GCt$ for this context. If it is fulfilled however, the component must in turn fulfil its specification $S$.

With this, obligations for the clients of a component are introduced. Remember that, according to Def. 3.11, a client (or observer) was only required to establish local operation preconditions before an operation was called. Still though, no invariants of the considered component need to be established, instead all invariants of the component are guaranteed.

**Definition 5.7.** A component $P$ is correct w.r.t. the component contract $(GCt, S)$ for $P$ if $P$ is durable correct relative to $GCt$ and with respect to $S$ (see Def. 5.5).

**Example 5.9.** Let $P$ be the component consisting only of the class `Period`. Let *cct* be the component contract consisting of the specification given by the annotated JML specification and $gct_{\texttt{earlierOrEqual(Date)}}$, $gct_{\texttt{copy()}}$. Provided all other requirements were met as assumed in Ex. 5.8, $P$ is correct w.r.t. *cct*. $*$

## 5.3 Summary

This chapter introduced the notion of a component contract. Analogously to operation contracts, clients making use of a component can benefit from the promises of a component contract only if they fulfil certain preconditions. These preconditions are expressed by means of generic extension contracts, a formalism introduced here, which transfers the concept of type parameters to specifications.

We show how to verify component contracts in Chapter 10. Generic extension contracts are needed there and in Chapter 6 to allow for a liberal notion of modular proofs.

# Part II

# Modular Verification

# 6 Modular Program Proofs

> Omnia iam fient fieri quae posse negabam.
>
> *(Ovid)*

In Sect. 2.3, we have defined the validity of formulae, the soundness of rules, and closed proofs relative to a closed program context. When dealing with extensible or even open programs there is however no such unique closed program. In a modular environment we give up a fixed context, but have an unchanged core context with unknown extensions.

And in fact it is difficult to extend the notion of validity of JavaDL formulae to programs which can arbitrarily be extended. Consider again the extension made to Ex. 1.1 by subclassing `Date` with the class `Date2` (see Sect. 1.2). A formula which states that, after a `Period` object is constructed, the start date lies before the end date in the usual sense:

$$\begin{aligned} &\forall d_1{:}\texttt{Date}.\ \forall d_2{:}\texttt{Date}.\ \{\texttt{d1} := d_1, \texttt{d2} := d_2\} \\ &\qquad [\texttt{p = new Period(d1,d2);}] \\ &\qquad\qquad (\texttt{p.start.year} < \texttt{p.end.year} \\ &\qquad\qquad \vee(\ \texttt{p.start.year} = \texttt{p.end.year} \\ &\qquad\qquad\quad \wedge \texttt{p.start.month.val} \leq \texttt{p.end.month.val})) \end{aligned} \tag{6.1}$$

is valid in a program context {`Period`, `Date`}, but it is *not* valid in the context {`Period`, `Date`, `Date2`}. The reason for this is obviously that the call to the method `earlierOrEqual(Date)` is bound *dynamically* w.r.t. to the (statically unknown) runtime type of the object argument of the constructor call. Without fixing or at least constraining a particular program context (6.1) cannot be valid, in the presence of dynamic binding.

Dynamic binding is the primary vehicle to foster re-use of object-oriented programs by making it possible to adapt programs. It would thus be no help to forbid the use of dynamically bound methods in programs we verify. Instead it must be supported adequately. On the other hand it is the most problematic one to deal with when we adapt JavaDL in this chapter for more modularity. We investigate in this section how a definition of validity can be achieved which is independent from additions to the underlying program. Such a validity is called *modular validity.* By declaring `earlierOrEqual(Date)` final, we would forbid that this method is overridden. It would be thus possible to achieve this strict notion of modular validity in our example. If more reusability is desired however, we need a less restrictive version. Modular validity is thus weakened by imposing restrictions on the reuse context. In this case we speak of *relative* modular validity.

Since we are approaching validity with a calculus, all notions of modular validity are transferred to notions of soundness of rules in the JavaDL calculus.

**Overview.** First, we modify the notion of validity and soundness in a modular sense. In Sect. 6.2 we investigate the JavaDL rules according to these new notions. Since it turns out that adaptations are needed, Sect. 6.3 defines the weaker notion of relative modularity and soundness. In the subsequent section the JavaDL calculus is made compliant to these relativised criteria.

## 6.1 Modular Validity and Modular Soundness

In Sect. 2.3 we have evaluated a JavaDL formula in one fixed context. Now we know just a part of the context, the *core context*, in which the evaluation happens while all the rest of the context is unknown.

Let $\Sigma$ be a JavaDL signature and $P$ a closed $\Sigma$-program. Let $P'$ be a closed program with $P \subseteq P'$. A JavaDL-formula $\varphi \in \mathrm{DLFma}^{\Sigma}$ which is valid in $P$ is *not* necessarily valid in context $P'$.

**Example 6.1.** We consider the following three Java classes:

```
class A {
  public int p() {
    return 0;
  }
}
class B extends A {
  public int p() {
    return 1;
  }
}
```

```
class Main {
  public static int main(A a) {
    return a.p();
  }
}
```

With $P = \{\texttt{A}, \texttt{Main}\} \cup \text{JCl}$, and $P' = \{\texttt{A}, \texttt{Main}, \texttt{B}\} \cup \text{JCl}$, the JavaDL formula

$$\forall a{:}A.\ \{\texttt{a} := a\}(a \neq 0 \rightarrow \langle\ \texttt{x=Main.main(a);}\rangle\, \texttt{x} \doteq 0) \tag{6.2}$$

is valid in $P$ but not valid in $P'$ because the method call `a.p()` in `main` is bound dynamically. *

In this example the core context has been a closed program. We liberalise this from now on, by allowing the core context to be an open program. This gives rise to the following definition:

**Definition 6.1.** Let $\Sigma$ be a JavaFOL signature and $P$ a (possibly open) $\Sigma$-program. A JavaDL formula $\varphi \in \text{DLFma}^{\Sigma}$ is *modularly valid in a core context* $P$ if it is valid in all closures $P'$ of $P$. We write: $\models^{\emptyset}_{P} \varphi$.

The reason for the notation $\models^{\emptyset}_{P} \varphi$ will become clear in Sect. 6.3 when we allow for other sets than $\emptyset$ as parameter.

**Example 6.2.** In the settings of Ex. 6.1, (6.2) is not modularly valid in the core context $P$.

We may declare method `p()` in class `A` as `final`, which means, according to the Java semantics that `p()` must not be overridden. Then (6.2) is modularly valid in the core context $\{\texttt{Main}, \texttt{A}\}$. The subclass `B`, which overrides `p()` is illegal, which will already be detected by the Java compiler. *

So far we have noticed that adding a class to a context could invalidate JavaDL formulae. This is the interesting (and dangerous) case for modular correctness. As a side-remark however, there is also the analogous phenomenon that *removing* a class from the context can make a valid formula invalid, though syntactic validity of the formula and compilability of the context is maintained. Interestingly however, an example is much harder to find than before, and seems impossible to find by exploiting the effects of dynamic dispatching only. By referring to dynamic types of objects it is however possible: The formula

$$\exists x{:}A.\ (\text{Reach}[\texttt{<nextToCreate>}](\texttt{A.<first>}, x) \wedge \neg\, \text{InstanceOf}_{A}(x))$$

states that there is an instance of `A` which is no *direct* instance of `A`, that is it must be an instance of a subclass of `A`. For the used specification-only fields please refer to Sect. 2.3.6. This formula is valid in the context

$P' = \{\texttt{A}, \texttt{Main}, \texttt{B}\}$ but not in the subset $P = \{\texttt{A}, \texttt{Main}\}$. Thus in general, a valid formula $\varphi \in \text{DLFma}^{\Sigma}$ in context $P'$ is not necessarily valid in context $P \subseteq P'$.

The definition of modular soundness is a variation of the regular soundness for a fixed context in Def. 2.21. After having clarified what *modularly valid* means, the definition of rule soundness is however straightforward:

**Definition 6.2.** A rule

$$\frac{seq_1 \quad \cdots \quad seq_k}{seq_0}$$

(with $seq_0, \ldots, seq_k \in \text{Seq}^{\Sigma}$) is *modularly sound* in the core context of a $\Sigma$-program $P$ which is a $\Sigma$-program if the following implication holds: If $seq_1, \ldots, seq_k$ are defined for $P$ and are modularly valid in the core context $P$ then $seq_0$ is modularly valid in the core context $P$ (Def. 6.1).

A rule $r$ is modularly sound if for all signatures $\Sigma$ with $seq_0, \ldots, seq_k \in \text{Seq}^{\Sigma}$: $r$ is modularly sound in all core contexts $P$ which are $\Sigma$-programs.

The following section analyses whether the rules of the JavaDL calculus are modularly sound.

## 6.2 Modularity of the JavaDL Rules

Fortunately the JavaDL calculus is already well suited for modularity. Only a few rules depend on the whole context. Thus only these few rules must be specially adapted. We cope with this issue in the next section.

First we present and discuss the rules of the JavaDL calculus which turn out to be problematic for extensible programs. In Sect. 6.2.4 the other rules, which all pose no problem, are discussed.

### 6.2.1 Method calls

Method calls to methods which are not static and not private must be dispatched dynamically [Gosling et al., 2000], that is, the (dynamic type of the) receiver object determines which concrete method body is invoked. In the preceding example we have seen that the resolution of method calls which are to be dynamically dispatched is problematic to treat in a modular way.

## Inlining methods

One possibility to deal with methods in the JavaDL calculus is to symbolically execute (*inline*) their method body, like the virtual machine would do. If dynamic binding is required, that is we have a non-private non-static method call, a preprocessing step simulates dynamic binding by constructing a cascade of `if (...){...} else {...}` statements. The cascade discriminates according to the dynamic type of the receiver expression. If static binding is required only the method body is determined according to the static type of the receiver object. Beckert [2000] describes this rule in more detail.

Let $\texttt{e.m(p}_1\texttt{, ..., p}_n\texttt{)}$ be a (correctly typed) method reference, $\texttt{e}, \texttt{p}_1, \ldots, \texttt{p}_n$ being expressions which are (already by their syntactical shape) side-effect free, and let `r` be a program variable of the return type of the referenced method. In JavaDL, we have the following rule scheme to resolve method references which assign their return value to `r`[1]:

$$\frac{\Gamma \vdash \left\langle \texttt{..} \begin{array}{l} \texttt{if (e instanceof } C_1\texttt{) r=e.m(p}_1\texttt{,..., p}_n\texttt{)@}C_1\texttt{;} \\ \texttt{else if (e instanceof } C_2\texttt{) r=e.m(p}_1\texttt{,...,p}_n\texttt{)@}C_2\texttt{;} \\ \quad\vdots \\ \texttt{else if (e instanceof } C_\ell\texttt{) r=e.m(p}_1\texttt{,...,p}_n\texttt{)@}C_k\texttt{;} \end{array} \texttt{...} \right\rangle \varphi, \Delta}{\Gamma \vdash \langle \texttt{.. r = e.m(p}_1\texttt{,..., p}_n\texttt{) ...} \rangle \varphi, \Delta} \tag{6.3}$$

The used symbols are explained in the following:

- $C_1, \ldots, C_k$ is a topological order (i.e. $C_i \preceq C_j$ implies $i < j$) of those $k$ classes in the context which have a non-abstract method declaration which is applicable [Gosling et al., 2000] to the method reference $\texttt{m(p}_1\texttt{,...,p}_n\texttt{)}$.
- if a static or a private method is referenced, then $k = 1$ and $C_1 = T$ if $T$ is the (static) type of `e`.
- the notation $\texttt{r=e.m(p}_1\texttt{,...,p}_n\texttt{)@}C_i$ is called *method body statement* and is a placeholder for the method body of the method declaration which is applicable to $\texttt{m(p}_1\texttt{,...,p}_n\texttt{)}$ in class $C_i$ and assigns return values to `r`, as defined in 2.3.4.

[1] When we consider method references, here and throughout this chapter, we only give rules for assignments from method references (to a variable). The rules for method references which do not assign the returned type or which reference `void`-methods are analogously defined.

- As a general remark for JavaDL rule schemas, note, that the symbol .. stands for a sequence of opening braces or `trys`, etc., and the symbol ... represents a continuation of the program which is not interesting for the rule, since a JavaDL rule processes only the first active statement. See Beckert [2000] for details.

For a more concise presentation, we ignore the fact that static analyses might provide optimisations to this rule, for instance by reducing alternatives. In particular, the sequence of classes $C_1, \ldots, C_k$ can always stop at the smallest supertype of the static type of `e` which provides a method declaration (if there is one). Furthermore the sequence does not need to incorporate classes which are no subtypes or supertypes of the static type of `e`. These optimisations are in place in the original JavaDL calculus and implemented in KeY. Though Rule (6.3) produces trivially closeable branches, it correctly simulates dynamic dispatching according to the Java language specification. Proving the soundness of this rule is however out of scope of this work; see Sect. 2.3.5 for approaches to verify JavaDL rules. We thus postulate with the help of Lemma 2.2: For every given context $P$, Rule (6.3) is sound in $P$.

If we identified the word *context* in Rule (6.3) with *core context*, Rule (6.3) would *not* be modularly sound. Consider the following JavaDL derivation with the (core) program context $P = \{\texttt{A}, \texttt{Main}\} \cup \text{JCl}$ as introduced in Ex. 6.1:

$$\frac{\langle \texttt{if (a instanceof A) r=a.p()@A;} \rangle\, \texttt{r} \doteq 0}{\langle \texttt{r = a.p();} \rangle\, \texttt{r} \doteq 0}$$

The premise is modularly valid in $P$, since—independent from the context—the method body in `A` is executed, which returns 0. The conclusion is *not* modularly valid in $P$: Though it is valid in context $P$, it is not valid in $P \cup \{\texttt{B}\}$. Altogether this rule (application) shows the non-modularity of (6.3).

Moreover we run into problems since open programs are in general allowed as core context: Some types are only provided as skeletons but their methods are possibly referenced. Method bodies as requested by the method body statements used in this rule may thus not exist.

#### Using Operation Contracts

There is an equivalent rule to (6.3) in JavaDL. It requires the existence of a specification $S$ which is over the same signature $\Sigma$ as the sequents involved in the rule. Let the program context be a $\Sigma$-program $P$. The rule is more suited to cope with open core program contexts. It requires, to be sound, that additional conditions, namely the correctness of the needed operation contracts in $S$, are proven in separate proofs but with the same program context. The rule is defined as follows (with the same legend as in Rule (6.3)); the differences to that rule are described directly below:

$$\frac{\Gamma \vdash \left\langle ..\begin{array}{l}\texttt{if (e instanceof } D_1\texttt{) m}'_{D_1}\texttt{(e;p}_1\texttt{,...,p}_n\texttt{;r);}\\ \texttt{else if (e instanceof } D_2\texttt{) m}'_{D_2}\texttt{(e;p}_1\texttt{,...,p}_n\texttt{;r);}\\ \quad\vdots\\ \texttt{else if (e instanceof } D_\ell\texttt{) m}'_{D_\ell}\texttt{(e;p}_1\texttt{,...,p}_n\texttt{;r);}\end{array} ...\right\rangle \varphi, \Delta}{\Gamma \vdash \langle ..\ \texttt{r = e.m(p}_1\texttt{,..., p}_n\texttt{);}...\rangle \varphi, \Delta} \tag{6.4}$$

We use in this rule a sequence $D_1, \ldots, D_\ell$ instead of the sequence $C_1, \ldots, C_k$ from above. If a static or a private method is referenced, then $\ell = 1$ and $D_1 = T$ if $T$ is the (static) type of `e`. Otherwise: In $D_1, \ldots, D_\ell$ we have, compared to $C_1, \ldots, C_k$, skipped complete subtrees in the subtype hierarchy, and included *all* method declarations, even those that are abstract and thus do not provide a method body. Formally we can state these properties as the existence of a set $CS \subseteq P$ (called *cut-set*) with the following properties:

- $D'_1, \ldots, D'_{\ell'}$ is a topological order[2] (i.e. if $D'_i \preceq D'_j$ then $i < j$) of those $\ell$ interfaces or classes in the context which declare a method that is applicable [Gosling et al., 2000] to the method reference $\texttt{m(p}_1\texttt{,...,p}_n\texttt{)}$.
- $D_1, \ldots, D_\ell$ is a subsequence of $D'_1, \ldots, D'_{\ell'}$,
- $CS \subseteq \{D_1, \ldots, D_\ell\}$,
- for all $i = 1, \ldots, \ell$ and all supertypes $T$ of $D_i$: $T \in \{D_1, \ldots, D_\ell\}$, and
- $D_1, \ldots, D_\ell$ does not contain strict subtypes of $CS$.

We can now define what $\texttt{m}'_C(\texttt{e};\texttt{p}_1, \ldots, \texttt{p}_n;\texttt{r})$ means. This expression stands for $r = \texttt{e.m}(\texttt{p}_1, \ldots, \texttt{p}_n)@C$ *or* for a virtual method body that fulfils all operation contracts in $S$ which are for the method declaration in $C$ under the assumption of invariants $I$. We write $\texttt{m}_C^{S,I}(\texttt{e};\texttt{p}_1, \ldots, \texttt{p}_n;\texttt{r});$ for such a method

[2] Since interfaces are involved we are now considering a DAG instead of a tree

body; we will see later how we proceed with it in the calculus. Precisely, we have:

$$\texttt{m}'_C\texttt{(e;}\,\texttt{p}_1,\ldots,\texttt{p}_n\texttt{;}\,\texttt{r);} = \begin{cases} \texttt{e.m(}\texttt{p}_1,\ldots,\texttt{p}_n\texttt{)@}C\texttt{;} & \text{if } C \notin CS \text{ and if there is an applicable non-abstract method for } \texttt{m(p}_1,\ldots,\texttt{p}_n\texttt{)} \text{ declared in } C. \\ \texttt{m}_C^{S,I}\texttt{(e;}\,\texttt{p}_1,\ldots,\texttt{p}_n\texttt{;}\,\texttt{r);} & \text{otherwise} \end{cases}$$

Two issues with this rule need to be clarified in the following:

1. Under which circumstances is this rule sound?
2. How is $\texttt{m}_C^{S,I}\texttt{(e;}\,\texttt{p}_1,\ldots,\texttt{p}_n\texttt{;}\,\texttt{r);}$ precisely defined and how can it be resolved in the JavaDL calculus?

For Rule (6.4) to be sound for a method $m$ requires that for all $C \in CS^{\preceq}$ and all operation contracts $ct$ of $S$ applicable to the method declaration of $m$ in $C$: $m$ fulfils $ct$ under the assumption of a subset $I$ of Inv.

Let us assume that this condition holds. Let $C'$ be an arbitrary subclass of $C$ and $\varphi$ a formula. Moreover we assume that e is an instance of $C'$. Then:

$$\models_P \langle \texttt{e.m(}\texttt{p}_1,\ldots,\texttt{p}_n\texttt{)@}C'\texttt{;}\rangle\, \varphi \tag{6.5}$$

implies

$$\models_P \left\langle \texttt{m}_C^{S,I}\texttt{(e;}\,\texttt{p}_1,\ldots,\texttt{p}_n\texttt{;}\,\texttt{r);} \right\rangle \varphi$$

Thus (6.5) also implies

$$\models_P \left\langle \cdots \begin{array}{l} \texttt{if (e instanceof } C'_1\texttt{) r=e.m(p}_1\texttt{,}\ldots\texttt{,p}_n\texttt{)@}C'_1\texttt{;} \\ \texttt{else if (e instanceof } C'_2\texttt{) r=e.m(p}_1\texttt{,}\ldots\texttt{,p}_n\texttt{)@}C'_2\texttt{;} \\ \quad\vdots \\ \texttt{else if (e instanceof } C'_k\texttt{) r=e.m(p}_1\texttt{,}\ldots\texttt{,p}_n\texttt{)@}C'_k\texttt{;} \end{array} \cdots \right\rangle \varphi$$

if $C'_1, \ldots, C'_k$ are all subclasses of $C$. With this implication we can further conclude that the soundness of Rule (6.3) implies the soundness of Rule (6.4).

Like Rule (6.3), this rule is neither modularly sound as can be demonstrated with the same settings as in Ex. 6.1. Since concrete method bodies of all classes are not needed, but specifications suffice, open programs can however be dealt with.

To resolve the construct $\mathtt{m}_C^{S,I}(e;\mathtt{p}_1,\ldots,\mathtt{p}_n;\mathtt{r});$, 'the method body that fulfils the operation contracts for $m@C$ in $S$ under the assumption of invariants $I$' the calculus provides the following rule:

$$\frac{\begin{array}{l}\Gamma \vdash \varphi_{\text{pre}}(\mathtt{e};\mathtt{p}_1,\ldots,\mathtt{p}_n),\Delta \\ \Gamma \vdash I,\Delta \\ \Gamma \vdash (\quad \varphi_{\text{pre}}(\mathtt{e};\mathtt{p}_1,\ldots,\mathtt{p}_n) \land I \\ \qquad\quad \land \{u\}\varphi_{\text{post}}(\mathtt{e};\mathtt{p}_1,\ldots,\mathtt{p}_n;\mathtt{r};\mathtt{exc})) \rightarrow \{u\}\varphi,\Delta\end{array}}{\Gamma \vdash \left\langle \mathtt{m}_C^{S,I}(\mathtt{e};\mathtt{p}_1,\ldots,\mathtt{p}_n;\mathtt{r}); \right\rangle \varphi,\Delta} \tag{6.6}$$

where $ct$ is an operation contract of $S$ with the precondition $\varphi_{\text{pre}}(\mathtt{e};\mathtt{p}_1,\ldots,\mathtt{p}_n)$ and the post-condition $\varphi_{\text{post}}(\mathtt{e};\mathtt{p}_1,\ldots,\mathtt{p}_n;\mathtt{r};\mathtt{exc})$. The update $u$ is generated from the assignable clause $Mod = Mod(\mathtt{e};\mathtt{p}_1,\ldots,\mathtt{p}_n)$ of $ct$ according to Def. 2.13: $u = u(Mod)$. Furthermore $I$ is the subset of all invariants Inv in $S$ under the assumption of which $ct$ is fulfilled.

This soundness of Rule (6.6) (under the assumption that $C$ fulfils the operation contract given for method declaration $m$ in $C$) is proven in Katz [2003] and Beckert and Schmitt [2003].

We would like to note that the interplay of Rules (6.4) and (6.6) requires a sophisticated proof management system which we have integrated into the KeY system. It keeps track of rule applications of (6.6) and of proofs of the underlying contract. It forbids 'cyclic applications' of that rule. Imagine, for instance, we would use (6.6) for $\mathtt{m}_C^{S,I}(\mathtt{e};\mathtt{p}_1,\ldots,\mathtt{p}_n;\mathtt{r});$ in the proof of the correctness of a method `p` and would then try to use $\mathtt{p}_C^{S,I'}(\mathtt{e};\mathtt{p}_1,\ldots,\mathtt{p}_n;\mathtt{r});$ in the proof of `m`, we would not be able to argue as before that proofs using Rules (6.4) and (6.6) can be transformed in proofs using only Rule (6.3).

**Example 6.3.** As illustrative example consider the following class:

```
public class A {
  /*@ ensures \result==3 @*/
  int m0() {
    return m1()-1;
  }
```

```
  /*@ ensures \result==4 @*/
  int m1() {
    return m0()+1;
  }
}
```

The following formula, which tries to show the correctness of the method contract of `m0()` (as annotated in JML), is not valid:

$$\langle \texttt{r=m0();} \rangle\, \texttt{r} \doteq 3$$

Using the annotated specifications during proof construction and applying Rules (6.4) and (6.6) with the annotated contracts *without* proof management interdicting cyclic applications of lemmas, it is possible to prove this formula. When we prove `m0()` we use the contract that `m1()` returns 4. And when we prove `m1()` the contract that `m0()` returns 3 is employed. Proof management intervenes when the second action is attempted. $*$

### 6.2.2 Static Analysis for Valid Array Store

According to Gosling et al. [2000] an `ArrayStoreException` is thrown if an object $e$ is assigned to an array slot of an array $arr$ and $e$ is not assignment compatible [Gosling et al., 2000] to the element type of $arr$.

When KeY symbolically executes an assignment to an array slot, formulae are created which contain a binary predicate ArrayStoreValid (relating the array $arr$ and the right hand side $e$). It is used to distinguish between the case that an array store exception is thrown and the case that this does not happen. The interpretation of this predicate is defined as follows: $(e_1, e_2) \in \text{ArrayStoreValid}^{s,P}$ iff $e_1 \neq \texttt{null}$ is an array and for all integers $i$ in the range of $e_1$ the assignment $e_1\texttt{[}i\texttt{]=}e_2\texttt{;}$ does not raise an array store exception.

The JavaDL calculus contains a rule to resolve ArrayStoreValid formulae by statically analysing $e_1$ and $e_2$. It determines, depending on all possible dynamic types of the involved array and the right hand side of the assignment, whether

1. an array store exception cannot arise from an assignment $e_1\texttt{[}i\texttt{]=}e_2\texttt{;}$,
2. an array store exception must necessarily arise from $e_1\texttt{[}i\texttt{]=}e_2\texttt{;}$,
3. no decision if an array store exception is thrown can be met with the given information.

In the first two cases the rule invoking the static procedure will replace the predicate ArrayStoreValid by true or false (resp.). In the other case the formula remains unchanged.

As one suspects, analysing all dynamic types of an expression, that is, all subtypes of its static type, is non-modular. As an example we look at the following application of this rule.

**Example 6.4.** Given a class `A` and a subclass `B` of `A` and the following Java program:

```
public class Main {
  public static boolean foo(A[] arr) {
    try {
      arr[0] = new A();
    } catch (ArrayStoreException e) {
      return false;
    }
    return true;
  }
}
```

Let us assume that we work in the (core) context $P = \{\texttt{Main}, \texttt{A}\}$. During symbolic execution we perform the step

$$\frac{\Gamma \vdash \mathrm{true}}{\Gamma \vdash \mathrm{ArrayStoreValid}(\texttt{arr}, \texttt{A.<nextToCreate>})}$$

This rule instance is however not modularly correct. While the premise is trivially valid in all contexts, the conclusion is valid in context $P$ but not necessarily in context $P \cup \{\texttt{B}\}$, since the argument `arr` could be an array of type `B[]`. $*$

### 6.2.3 Enumerating Dynamic Types

Consider the following rule which explicitely enumerates the dynamic types the evaluation of an expression may have. The rule schema is denoted as follows:

$$\frac{\Gamma, \quad \bigvee_{T' \preceq T} \mathrm{ExactInstanceOf}_{T'}(e) \lor e \doteq \texttt{null} \;\vdash\; \varphi(e), \Delta}{\Gamma \vdash \varphi(e), \Delta} \tag{6.7}$$

where $T$ is the static type of $e$.

The predicate $\mathrm{ExactInstanceOf}_T(t)$ is syntactic sugar for

$$\mathrm{Reach}[\texttt{<nextToCreate>}](\texttt{T.<first>}, t)$$

describing that a term $t$ of type $T$ is not of a strict subtype of $T$. So this predicate is part of the calculus as a matter of fact. We can note, that for arbitrary terms $t$, $\mathrm{ExactInstanceOf}_T(t)$ is *not* modularly valid:

$$\forall x\!:\!\texttt{A}.\ (\mathrm{ExactInstanceOf}_{\texttt{A}}(x) \lor x \doteq \texttt{null})$$

says that all objects of type A are exact instances of A. In context {A} this sequent is valid. When a subclass of A is added to the context, the formula loses validity.

The following derivation step using Rule (6.7) is modularly unsound:

$$\frac{\mathrm{ExactInstanceOf}_C(e) \lor e \doteq \texttt{null} \ \vdash\ \mathrm{ExactInstanceOf}_C(e) \lor e \doteq \texttt{null}}{\vdash\ \mathrm{ExactInstanceOf}_C(e) \lor e \doteq \texttt{null}}$$

The conclusion is true in all contexts while the conclusion is only valid in contexts where only class $C$ has instances. If a subclass of $C$ is added, the premise is not modularly valid; thus this rule is not modularly sound.

### 6.2.4 The Other Rules

We claim that all other rules of JavaDL are modularly sound. In particular we can make the following observations:

1. Rules expressible as taclets [Beckert et al., 2004] without meta construct are modularly sound if they are sound for some program context.

   The justification for this claim lies in the design of taclets: the premises 'produced' by a taclet without meta construct only depend on the (syntactical shape of the) conclusion. There is no dependency to the set of types as a whole. Consider for instance the rule *all-right*:

   $$\frac{[x/c]\varphi}{\forall x\!:\!T.\ \varphi}$$

   where $c$ is a new constant of type $T$. This rule is modularly sound: Let $P$ be an arbitrary context. We assume that $[x/c]\varphi$ is modularly valid and the rule is sound in $P$. Then $\forall x\!:\!T.\ \varphi$ is valid in $P$.

2. The update simplification and update rules [Beckert et al., 2006a] of JavaDL are modularly sound if they are sound for some program context.

   No program context is involved when an update rule is applied. Their definition is completely possible without referring to a program context or the set of types of the underlying signature.

3. Rules expressible with taclets containing meta constructs which do not get type information on the whole program context are modularly sound if they are sound for some program context.

   If there is no access to information on all types of the signature, non-modular effects cannot be achieved.

According to our investigations, all rules, except the treatment of dynamic method binding and array store exceptions, are covered by these criteria. Thus, all rules of the JavaDL calculus can be considered modularly sound. A more formal investigation of all rules is however considered future work.

## 6.3 Relative Modular Validity and Soundness

So far we have considered a very strict notion of soundness. The fact that, in reality of open programs, the program context must satisfy certain requirements, has not yet been taken into account. The instrument to constrain the context has however already been introduced in Sect. 5.1: generic extension contracts. It is a small step to use them for a relativised notion of modular validity and soundness.

**Definition 6.3.** Let $\Sigma$ be a signature, $P$ be a possibly open $\Sigma$-program. $\varphi \in \mathrm{DLFma}^{\Sigma}$ is modularly valid in the core context $P$ *relative* to a set of generic contracts $GCt$ if for all closures $P'$ of $P$ and for the specification $S'$ which $GCt$ generates for $P' \backslash P$: The *naive* correctness of $P' \backslash P$ w.r.t. $S'$ implies $\models_{P'} \varphi$. We write: $\models_P^{GCt} \varphi$.

Note that we used $\models_P^{\emptyset}$ to denote (not relativised) modular validity. The following lemma justifies these notations:

**Lemma 6.1.** A JavaDL formula $\varphi$ is valid in a core context $P$ relative to the empty set iff $\varphi$ is modularly valid in the core context $P$.

*Proof.* '⇐': Let $\varphi \in \mathrm{DLFma}^{\Sigma}$ and $\varphi$ be modularly valid in the core context $P$. Then $\varphi$ is valid in all closures of $P$, even in those which have a completion which is naively correct w.r.t. the empty specification. The empty set generates the empty specification. Thus $\varphi$ is valid in a core context $P$ relative to $\emptyset$.
'⇒': Let $\varphi \in \mathrm{DLFma}^{\Sigma}$ and $\varphi$ be valid in a core context $P$ relative to the empty set. Let $P'$ be a closure of $P$. $GCt = \emptyset$ generates the empty specification for $P' \setminus P$. Since $P' \setminus P$ is trivially naively correct w.r.t. the empty specification, it follows that $\models_{P'} \varphi$. Thus $\varphi$ is modularly valid in the core context $P$. □

**Example 6.5.** Let *gct* be the following generic contract:

```
generic contract {
  T extends* A;
  class T {
    /*@ ensures \result == 0; @*/
    public int p();
  }
}
```

With $P = \{\texttt{A}, \texttt{Main}\} \cup \mathrm{JCl}$ and $P' = \{\texttt{A}, \texttt{Main}, \texttt{B}\} \cup \mathrm{JCl}$, this generates the following concrete contract for $P' \setminus P = \{\texttt{B}\}$:

```
class B extends A {
  /*@ ensures \result == 0; @*/
  public int p();
}
```

If B is naively correct with respect to this specification, that is it fulfils the operation contract defined by this JML specification (what it does not in the implementation on p. 116),

$$\forall a{:}A.\ \{\texttt{a} := a\}(a \not\doteq 0 \rightarrow \langle\ \texttt{x=Main.main(a);}\rangle\, \texttt{x} \doteq 0)$$

would be valid in the core context $P$ relative to $\{gct\}$. *

Finally the soundness definition for the relative modular case goes straightforward:

**Definition 6.4.** Let $\Sigma$ be a signature, $P$ be a possibly open $\Sigma$-program, and $GCt$ a set of generic contracts. A rule $r \in \mathrm{Rule}^{\Sigma}$ defined as

$$\frac{seq_1 \quad \cdots \quad seq_k}{seq_0}$$

is *modularly sound relative* to *GCt in the core context P* if the following implication holds: If $seq_1, \ldots, seq_k$ are modularly valid in the core context $P$ relative to $GCt$ then $seq_0$ is modularly valid in the core context $P$ relative to $GCt$.

The rule $r \in \text{Rule}^{\Sigma}$ is *modularly sound relative* to $GCt$ if, for all signatures $\Sigma'$ with $r \in \text{Rule}^{\Sigma'}$, $r$ is modularly sound in all core contexts $P$ which are $\Sigma'$-programs relative to $GCt$.

## 6.4 Relative Modular Dynamic Logic for Java

This section proposes a variation of the JavaDL calculus which is relative modularly sound and establishes modular validity of JavaDL formulae.

### 6.4.1 Relative Modular Method Call Rule

Overriding methods and relying on the dynamic dispatching procedure is the main feature of object-oriented programs to achieve re-use and extensibility. It is thus no surprise that it is impossible to find an entirely modular rule which would replace the modularly unsound method call rule (6.3). We can at most achieve an acceptable compromise by aiming at *relative* modular soundness.

Rule (6.4) already has a flavour of modularity since it allowed to disregard *some* classes (namely those below a class in a cut-set). It is natural to vary the rule by setting the cut-set to $\{D_1, \ldots, D_k\}$, where again $D_1, \ldots, D_k$ are the classes or interfaces with an applicable method declaration for the considered method reference.

$$\frac{\Gamma \vdash \left\langle .. \begin{array}{l} \texttt{if (e instanceof } D_1\texttt{) } \texttt{m}'_{D_1}\texttt{(e;p}_1\texttt{,...,p}_n\texttt{;r);} \\ \texttt{else if (e instanceof } D_2\texttt{) } \texttt{m}'_{D_2}\texttt{(e;p}_1\texttt{,...,p}_n\texttt{;r);} \\ \quad\vdots \\ \texttt{else if (e instanceof } D_\ell\texttt{) } \texttt{m}'_{D_k}\texttt{(e;p}_1\texttt{,...,p}_n\texttt{;r);} \end{array} \ldots \right\rangle \varphi, \Delta}{\Gamma \vdash \langle ..\ \texttt{r = e.m(p}_1\texttt{,...,p}_n\texttt{);}\ldots\rangle\, \varphi, \Delta} \tag{6.8}$$

with $D_1, \ldots, D_k$ is a topological order of those $k$ interfaces or classes in the context which declare a method that is applicable [Gosling et al., 2000] to the method reference $\texttt{m(p}_1\texttt{,...,p}_n\texttt{)}$.

For this rule, we re-define $\mathtt{m}'_C\mathtt{(e,\ p_1,\ldots,p_n,\ r);}$ as follows; the rest of the used designations is the same as in Rule (6.4).

$$\mathtt{m}'_C\mathtt{(e;\ p_1,\ldots,\ p_n,\ r);} = \begin{cases} \mathtt{r=e.m(p_1,\ldots,p_n)@}C\mathtt{;} & \text{if } C \text{ or } m \text{ is final} \\ & \text{or } m \text{ is private} \\ & \text{or static} \\ \mathtt{m}_C^{S,I}\mathtt{(e;\ p_1,\ldots,p_n;\ r);} & \text{otherwise} \end{cases}$$

This re-definition reflects the fact that all but final, static, and private methods and methods in final classes can be overridden by the unknown part of the context. For all other methods the method specification must be used, since we may not use more knowledge about the method than encoded in the method contract. Otherwise overriding classes in a program extension would not have the chance to behave like the overridden method.

For each $\mathtt{m}_C^{S,I}\mathtt{(e,\ p_1,\ldots,\ p_\ell,\ r);}$ an extension contract $gct^I_m(C)$ is derived. The purpose of $gct^I_m(C)$ is to constrain extensions of the context: If $gct^I_m(C)$ generates a specification which the extension of the context fulfils then Rule (6.8) is relative modular correct. Let the set $Ct$ consist of all the operation contracts from $S$ applicable to the method declaration of `m` in class $C$.

Then $gct^I_m(C)$ is defined as follows:

```
generic contract {
  T extends* C;
  (Ct', ∅)
}
```

where $Ct'$ is a set of operation contracts over $\Sigma$. $Ct'$ emerges from $Ct$ by

- adding $I$ conjunctively to the preconditions of $Ct$ and
- replacing all occurrences of $C$ in descriptions of operation declarations by the type parameter `T`.

**Example 6.6.** Let the specification for a method `p` in class `A` emerge from this JML specification:

```
class A {
  /*@ normal_behavior
    @ ensures \result == 0;
    @*/
  public int p();
}
```

Then, from $\mathtt{p}_{\mathtt{A}}^{S,\emptyset}(r)$ the generic contract of Ex. 6.5 is derived. *

The following lemma shows that Rule (6.8) improves the modularity of Rules (6.3) and (6.4) at least a bit.

**Lemma 6.2.** Rule (6.8) is modularly sound relative to $\{gct_{\mathtt{m}_{D_1}}^{I_1}, \ldots, gct_{\mathtt{m}_{D_\ell}}^{I_m}\}$ for some sets of formulae $I_i$ $(i = 1, \ldots, m)$ in a core context $P$.

*Proof.* Let the premise of (6.8) be modularly valid in core context $P$ relative to $GCt$. Let $P'$ be a closure of $P$ and let $\bar{P} := P' \setminus P$. Let $S'$ be the specification which $\{gct_{\mathtt{m}_{D_1}}^{I_1}, \ldots, gct_{\mathtt{m}_{D_\ell}}^{I_m}\}$ generates for $\bar{P}$. Let $\bar{P}$ be naively correct w.r.t. $S'$. Then the premise (6.8) is valid in $P'$. Thus all subclasses of $D_i$ $(i = 1, \ldots, \ell)$ in $\bar{P}$ fulfil all operation contracts of $S'$ applicable to the method declaration of `m` in $D_i$. This is the case under the assumption of the empty set since no invariants are in $S'$. Because of the soundness of (6.4) in $\text{JavaDLRule}_{P'}^{\Sigma}$, the conclusion of $\text{JavaDLRule}_{P'}^{\Sigma}$ is valid in $P'$. □

**Example 6.7.** The following rule or derivation step is modularly sound relative to the generic contract given in Ex. 6.5:

$$\frac{\left\langle \mathtt{if\ (a\ instanceof\ A)\{p_A^{\mathit{S},\emptyset}(a,\ r);\}} \right\rangle \mathtt{r} \doteq 0}{\langle \mathtt{r\ =\ a.p();} \rangle\, \mathtt{r} \doteq 0}$$

With it, we can derive the original conjecture

$$\forall a\!:\!A.\ \{\mathtt{a} := a\}(a \not\doteq 0 \rightarrow \langle\ \mathtt{x=Main.main(a);} \rangle\, \mathtt{x} \doteq 0)$$

in our calculus. Note again, that this is only a valid statement under the precondition that classes inheriting from `A`, like `B`, satisfy the specification generated from the generic contract from above. *

### 6.4.2 Other Non-modular Rules

**Static Analysis of Valid Array Store.** We propose quite a weak analysis as substitute for the analysis sketched in Sect. 6.2.2. It resolves formulae with top-level operator ArrayStoreValid to true if the first argument's static element type is final, otherwise the formula remains unmodified. Then no subtypes are allowed which can give rise to an array store exception. Obviously this rule is modularly sound.

**Dynamic Type Enumeration.** Apparently it is not possible to enumerate the possible dynamic types of an expression unless the static type is declared as final. Then there is only one possibility what the dynamic type of an expression is: it is just the static type.

### 6.4.3 Modular Proofs with Generated Extension Contracts

We consider now the calculus consisting of the JavaDL rules except from the method call rules (6.3) and (6.4) but including the 'more modular' method call rule (6.8) and the weak analysis of array store exceptions as defined before. This calculus shall further be called JavaDL$^m$.

In the following definition, the notion is introduced that a proof *generates* generic extension contracts whenever a method call is symbolically executed.

**Definition 6.5.** A *(closed) modular proof with generated contracts* of a formula $\varphi \in \mathrm{DLFma}^{\Sigma}$ with a $\Sigma$-program $P$ as core context (in JavaDL$^m$) is a closed proof of $\varphi$ with program $P$, but each node which is a result of an application of rule (6.8) is marked with a set of extension contracts $gct_m(C)$ corresponding to the occurrences of $\mathtt{e.m}_C^S\mathtt{(p}_1,\ldots,\mathtt{p}_n\mathtt{;r);}$ in the node's sequent.
We call the set of all of these extension contracts the *generated extension contracts* of the proof.

**Lemma 6.3** ((Relative) Modular Soundness of Proofs)**.** Let $\Sigma$ be a signature and $P$ a $\Sigma$-program.

1. If there is a closed modular proof with generated contracts $GCt$ in JavaDLRule$^{\Sigma}$ of a formula $\varphi \in \mathrm{DLFma}^{\Sigma}$ with core context $P$, then $\varphi$ is modularly valid in the core context $P$ relative to $GCt$.

2. If there is a closed modular proof with generated contracts of a formula $\varphi \in \mathrm{DLFma}^{\Sigma}$ with core context $P$ and the set of generated extension contracts is empty, then $\varphi$ is modularly valid in the core context $P$.

*Proof.* 1. Follows from Lemma 6.2 and the modular soundness of all other rules in JavaDL$^m$.

2. Follows from (1) and Lemma 6.1.

□

If a proof generates the empty set of extension contracts we have a completely modular proof. This is however only possible if

- only private or static method calls have been performed,
- all involved non-private and non-static method calls were `final`, or
- with the help of more detailed type information it can be ensured that a public method call does not target subclasses.

The last case shows that the definitions and lemmas from above are in fact not precise enough, since they do not cover this case.

**Example 6.8.** In Sect. 1.2 the class `Date` has been subclassed by `Date2`, which overrides the method `earlierOrEqual(Date)` in a way that violates the invariant imposed on the overridden method.

We consider now the formula (6.1)

$$\begin{array}{l} \forall d_1\texttt{:Date}.\ \forall d_2\texttt{:Date}.\ \{\texttt{d1} := d_1 \mid \texttt{d2} := d_2\} \\ \qquad [\texttt{p = new Period(d1,d2);}] \\ \qquad\qquad (\texttt{p.start.year} < \texttt{p.end.year} \\ \qquad\qquad \lor(\ \texttt{p.start.year} = \texttt{p.end.year} \\ \qquad\qquad\quad \land\texttt{p.start.month.val} \leq \texttt{p.end.month.val})) \end{array}$$

In the core context {`Period`, `Date`, `Month`}, $\varphi$ is *not* modularly valid as `Date2` demonstrates: If the core context is extended by this class, dynamic dispatching might choose the overridden version of `earlierOrEqual(Date)` in `Date2` and would not establish the given post-condition.

We are however able to change the constructor of `Date` in a way that $\varphi$ is modularly valid:

```
public Period(Date d1, Date d2) {
  Date d1new=new Date(new Month(d1.getMonth().getVal()),
                      d1.getYear());
  Date d2new=new Date(new Month(d2.getMonth().getVal()),
                      d2.getYear());
  if (d1new.earlierOrEqual(d2new)) {
    this.start=d1new; this.end=d2new;
  } else {
    this.start=d2new; this.end=d1new;
  }
}
```

The reason that this helps is that the invocation of `earlierOrEqual(Date)` is now guaranteed to happen on an exact instance of `Date` with a correct implementation of `earlierOrEqual(Date)`. *

The problem occurring in this example can however not be dealt with Rule (6.8). That rule would still generate extension contracts for all subclasses of `Date` which is unnecessary since we have precise knowledge on the runtime type of the receiver object. We can thus introduce the following additional modularly sound method call rule for every class $C$ in the core context:

$$\frac{\Gamma \vdash \langle ..\texttt{r=e.m(p}_1\texttt{, ..., p}_n\texttt{)@}C\texttt{;}...\rangle\, \varphi, \Delta \qquad \Gamma \vdash \text{ExactInstanceOf}_C(\texttt{e}), \Delta}{\Gamma \vdash \langle ..\texttt{r = e.m(p}_1\texttt{, ..., p}_n\texttt{);}...\rangle\, \varphi, \Delta}$$

This rule allows to discharge the proof in Ex. 6.8.

## 6.5 Summary

In this chapter we have seen how to cope with an open world on the logic and the calculus level. A calculus designed for a fixed closed program context has been adapted to an open program context. This was only possible with the cost of a constrained program context, and the weaker notion of relative validity and soundness w.r.t. these constraints. Here, generic extension contracts have been employed to constrain the program context. Apparently in the presence of dynamic binding, an object-oriented feature that is desired for the benefit of extensibility, this is an inconvenience which cannot be avoided.

When dealing with proof obligations for durable correctness of open programs in Chapter 10, we will make use of (relative) modular validity and modular proofs.

# 7 Non-modular Verification of Call Correctness

Non est ad astra mollis
e terris via.

*(Seneca)*

In Part I of this work we have defined under which circumstances a program is considered correct. How the required conditions can be verified in practice has not been an issue yet.

This chapter takes the first step from the mere theoretical notion of correctness to *proof obligations* with the help of which correctness can be proven deductively. Here, we are only concerned with the not so intricate observed-state *call* correctness. Our goal for this chapter is to have a set of proof obligations, abstractly defined in terms of *proof obligation templates*, which ensures—if all elements can be proven—that a program is entirely call correct.

Moreover, since this chapter is the first concerned with proof obligations, there are also some general and re-usable proof obligation templates which will turn up over and over again in the rest of this work. These single proof obligation templates serve also another purpose, which is to enable developers to check for single properties of interest instead of a *post mortem* analysis of the whole program. Such proof obligations are thus also called *lightweight* proof obligations. So they are not only part of a complex proof obligation template which checks entire correctness but are as well available directly to users of a program analysis tool like KeY.

In the following chapters we will refer to these single proof obligations and arrange them in an advanced manner to optimise and modularise verification and take the step towards durable correctness and open programs.

Technically, we describe in this chapter, how to build JavaDL formulae, the proof obligations, from JavaFOL formulae and terms which come from JavaFOL specifications.

**Outline.** First we briefly review the definitions of correctness and introduce auxiliary notations. In Sect. 7.2, we define lightweight proof obligations which are the starting points to prove correctness properties of programs. Most extensively, we look at proofs for assignable clauses in Sect. 7.2.7. In Sect. 7.3 we compose them to a simple system of proof obligations which ensure call correctness of a program. Sect. 7.4 covers an optimisation which allows to skip some proofs. Finally an improvement concerning the presentation of proof obligations to the user of a prover is proposed.

## 7.1 Towards Proof Obligations for Call Correctness

Except from the proof obligation on the correctness of an assignable clause, proof obligation for a correctness property follow a specific shape, also known as a *Hoare triple* $\{\psi\}\alpha\{\varphi\}$, for first order formulae $\psi$ (the precondition) and $\varphi$ (the postcondition) and a sequence of statements $\alpha$. In JavaDL such a Hoare triple is encoded as the following implication:

$$\psi \rightarrow [\alpha]\varphi \tag{7.1}$$

In Chapter 3 it was already discussed which contents $\psi$, $\varphi$, and $\alpha$ should have. There, we referred to $\psi$ as the *assumption*, to $\varphi$ as the *assertion*, and to $\alpha$ as the *operation call*. We keep these designations in order not to get confused with pre and post conditions in operation contracts.

As a summary of the discussion, the assumption $\psi$ contains at least the general assumption $\mathcal{A}_{op}(o; p_1, \ldots, p_n)$ and possibly a more specific precondition from an operation contract on *op*. It is not possible to include—formalised in JavaFOL—the condition that the state described by $\psi$ is reachable. Instead we have to rely on the adequateness of the invariants describing admissible states. Of course however, we lose precision by not taking into account the reachability assumption, while correctness is maintained.

The assertion $\varphi$ covers all invariants of the considered program and the postcondition of an operation contract. Moreover, the assignable clause must be proven correct. Remember that we added a standard operation contract to `<clinit>()` and an implicit invariant to appropriately reflect static initialisation.

We have as well discussed how the generic shape of sequences of statements $\alpha$ looks like, which the observer of a program invokes.

According to a termination marker from $\{total, partial\}$, JavaFOL specifications distinguish whether an operation must terminate or if termination can be assumed and must not be proven. This is not reflected in (7.1) yet, where the 'box' modality of JavaDL is used and thus termination is assumed. To be more flexible when formulating concrete proof obligation templates we define the following function $\mathcal{M}(\cdot,\cdot)$, which maps marker $\tau \in \{partial, total\}$ and a program $\alpha$ to a modal operator:

$$\mathcal{M}(\tau,\alpha) := \begin{cases} [\alpha] & \text{if } \tau = partial \\ \langle\alpha\rangle & \text{if } \tau = total \end{cases}$$

The general shape of a proof obligations is thus rather:

$$\psi \rightarrow \mathcal{M}(\tau,\alpha)\varphi$$

## 7.2 Lightweight Program Correctness Proof Obligations

Often while writing code one is not interested in the correctness of the whole program but only in certain *lightweight* properties, for instance that a method preserves its invariant. This section presents *lightweight proof obligations* suited to such kind of verification. The section serves also to define single proof obligations needed for a full verification of a program. Appropriate systematic combinations of the lightweight proof obligations can be found in Sect. 7.3 and Chapters 9 and 10.

### 7.2.1 The Basic Proof Obligation Template

Most proof obligation presented in the sequel are structured according to the following proof obligation template:

**Proof Obligation Template:** $\mathit{Ensures}(op; \Psi; \Phi; \tau; \mathtt{self}; \mathtt{p}_1, \ldots, \mathtt{p}_n, \mathtt{r}; \mathtt{exc})$.

for an operation $op$, sets of formulae $\Phi$ and $\Psi$, $\tau \in \{partial, total\}$ and program variables $\mathtt{self}, \mathtt{p}_1, \ldots, \mathtt{p}_n, \mathtt{r}, \mathtt{exc}$:

$$\bigwedge_{\psi\in\Psi} \psi \wedge \mathcal{A}_{op}(\mathtt{self}; \mathtt{p}_1, \ldots, \mathtt{p}_n) \rightarrow \mathcal{M}(\tau, \widetilde{\alpha}_{op}(\mathtt{self}; \mathtt{p}_1, \ldots, \mathtt{p}_n; \mathtt{r}; \mathtt{exc})) \bigwedge_{\varphi\in\Phi} \varphi$$

Informally, *Ensures* describes the following property: if the operation *op* is called on an object `self` with the parameters $\mathtt{p}_1, \ldots, \mathtt{p}_n$ assigning the returned value in `r` and the thrown exception to `exc` in a state which satisfies $\psi$ and the general assumption then all formulae in $\Phi$ hold in the post-state if it exists. Furthermore, the call must terminate if $\tau$ is *total*.

Sometimes we skip the pre-condition in *Ensures*, which is then interpreted as being true:

**Proof Obligation Template:** $\mathit{Ensures}(op; \Phi; \tau; \mathtt{self}; \mathtt{p}_1, \ldots, \mathtt{p}_n; \mathtt{r}; \mathtt{exc})$. with the designations from above:

$$\begin{aligned}&\mathit{Ensures}(op; \{\text{true}\}; \Phi; \tau; \mathtt{self}; \mathtt{p}_1, \ldots, \mathtt{p}_n; \mathtt{r}; \mathtt{exc})\\ =&\mathcal{A}_{op}(\mathtt{self}; \mathtt{p}_1, \ldots, \mathtt{p}_n) \rightarrow \mathcal{M}(\tau, \widetilde{\alpha}_{op}(\mathtt{self}; \mathtt{p}_1, \ldots, \mathtt{p}_n; \mathtt{r}, \mathtt{exc})) \bigwedge_{\varphi \in \Phi} \varphi\end{aligned}$$

Remark: Often we instantiate the parameters `self`, $\mathtt{p}_1, \ldots, \mathtt{p}_n$, `r`, and `exc` with fresh program variables of the appropriate types. If this is the case, we may omit occurrences of these parameters. For instance, we would just write

$$\mathit{Ensures}(op; \Psi; \Phi; \tau)$$

for

$$\mathit{Ensures}(op; \Psi; \Phi; \tau; \mathtt{self}; \mathtt{p}_1, \ldots, \mathtt{p}_n; \mathtt{r}; \mathtt{exc})$$

if `self`, $\mathtt{p}_1, \ldots, \mathtt{p}_n$, `r`, `exc` are instantiated with fresh program variables of the suitable types.

As another convention we can omit the `self` parameter if we are dealing with static methods and we omit the `r` parameter if the operation is a void method or a constructor.

These conventions apply to all the proof obligations in the sequel.

### 7.2.2 Invariant Preservation

Let $I$ be a set of closed formulae. We think of them as static or (quantified) instance invariants. Let now *op* be a method or constructor declaration in type $D$. According to our discussion in Chapter 3, the invocation of *op* in a state satisfying the general assumption must establish only post-states in which all formulae of $I$ hold.

**Proof Obligation Template:** *PreservesInv*$(op; I; \texttt{self}; \texttt{p}_1, \ldots, \texttt{p}_n)$.
where `self` is a suitable receiver object for *op* and $\texttt{p}_1, \ldots, \texttt{p}_n$ are suitable parameters for *op*:

$$Ensures(op; I; partial; \texttt{self}; \texttt{p}_1, \ldots, \texttt{p}_n; \texttt{r}; \texttt{exc})$$

with a fresh program variable `exc`. This can be simplified to

$$\mathcal{A}_{op}(\texttt{self}; \texttt{p}_1, \ldots, \texttt{p}_n) \rightarrow [\widetilde{\alpha}_{op_D}(\texttt{self}; \texttt{p}_1, \ldots, \texttt{p}_n; \texttt{r})] \bigwedge_{\varphi \in I} \varphi$$

We abbreviate *PreservesInv*$(op; \mathrm{Inv}; \texttt{self}; \texttt{p}_1, \ldots, \texttt{p}_n)$ with

$$PreservesInv(op; \texttt{self}; \texttt{p}_1, \ldots, \texttt{p}_n)$$

### 7.2.3 Invariant Preservation Under Weaker Assumptions

Sometimes, even a stronger proof obligation than *PreservesInv* is useful. Essentially, we skip the assumption that *all* invariants of the whole program hold and assume just a subset of all invariants, for instance just those that are to be established. The *PreservesInvAssumpt* proof obligation is thus defined as follows for an operation *op*, two sets of invariants $I$ and $I'$, and program variables $\texttt{self}, \texttt{p}_1, \ldots, \texttt{p}_n$ that suit to the signature of *op*:

**Proof Obligation Template:**
*PreservesInvAssumpt*$(op; I'; I; \texttt{self}; \texttt{p}_1, \ldots, \texttt{p}_n)$.

$$Ensures(op; I'; I; partial; \texttt{self}; \texttt{p}_1, \ldots, \texttt{p}_n; \texttt{r}; \texttt{exc})$$

which is equivalent to

$$\bigwedge_{\varphi' \in I'} \varphi' \rightarrow [\widetilde{\alpha}_{op}(\texttt{self}; \texttt{p}_1, \ldots, \texttt{p}_n; \texttt{r})] \bigwedge_{\varphi \in I} \varphi$$

**Lemma 7.1.**

$$\begin{aligned} &\models_P PreservesInvAssumpt(op; I'; I; \texttt{self}; \texttt{p}_1, \ldots, \texttt{p}_n) \\ \text{implies } &\models_P PreservesInv(op; I; \texttt{self}; \texttt{p}_1, \ldots, \texttt{p}_n) \end{aligned}$$

if $I' \subseteq I$.

An interesting special case is that an operation *op* preserves the static and quantified instance invariants $I$ of the class it is declared in only. This lightweight proof obligation is thus defined as follows for suitable program variables $\mathtt{self}, \mathtt{p}_1, \ldots, \mathtt{p}_n$:

**Proof Obligation Template:**
$PreservesOwnInvAssumpt(op; \mathtt{self}; \mathtt{p}_1, \ldots, \mathtt{p}_n)$.

$$\begin{aligned} &PreservesInvAssumpt(op; I) \\ &= \bigwedge_{\varphi \in I} \varphi \rightarrow [\widetilde{\alpha}_{op}(\mathtt{self}; \mathtt{p}_1, \ldots, \mathtt{p}_n; \mathtt{r})] \bigwedge_{\varphi \in I} \varphi \end{aligned}$$

where *op* is declared in a class $D$ and $I$ are the quantified instance invariants and static invariants of $D$.

### 7.2.4 Invariant Initialisation

As pointed out in Sect. 3.2.5, invariants have to hold in the initial state. This must be checked by a proof obligation. It is simple to construct one according to what has been said in Sect. 3.2.5. Remember from Sect. 2.3.6 that $\varphi_{\text{init}}$ is defined as

$$\bigwedge_{C \in P} C.\mathtt{<classPrepared>} \doteq \text{FALSE}$$

**Proof Obligation Template:** $InitInv(I)$**.**
for a set of invariants $I$

$$\varphi_{\text{init}} \rightarrow \bigwedge_{\varphi \in I} \varphi$$

As mentioned earlier, instance invariants, that is, invariants of the shape $\dot{\forall} x : C.\ \varphi'$, trivially pass this proof obligation. It is thus unnecessary to invoke this proof obligation if the formula already has this shape.

### 7.2.5 Postcondition Assurance

For an operation *op* and an operation contract *opct* on *op*, we might want to prove that *op* establishes the post-condition of *opct*. As discussed in Sect. 3.2.1, the general assumption can be assumed, as the pre-condition of *opct* can be. We thus formalise the proof obligation as follows for suitable program variables $\mathtt{self}, \mathtt{p}_1, \ldots, \mathtt{p}_n$ for the invocation of *op* and a program variable `r` to store the returned value and `exc` to capture the possibly thrown exception:

**Proof Obligation Template:** $\mathit{EnsuresPost}(\mathit{opct}; \mathtt{self}; \mathtt{p}_1, \ldots, \mathtt{p}_n; \mathtt{r}; \mathtt{exc})$.

$$\begin{aligned}
&\mathit{Ensures}(op; \{\psi_{opct}\}; \{\varphi_{opct}\}; \tau_{opct}; \mathtt{self}; \mathtt{p}_1, \ldots, \mathtt{p}_n; \mathtt{exc}) \\
&= \mathcal{A}_{op}(\mathtt{self}; \mathtt{p}_1, \ldots, \mathtt{p}_n) \wedge \psi_{opct} \\
&\qquad \rightarrow \mathcal{M}(\tau_{opct}, \widetilde{\alpha}_{op}(\mathtt{self}; \mathtt{p}_1, \ldots, \mathtt{p}_n; \mathtt{r}; \mathtt{exc}))\varphi_{opct}
\end{aligned}$$

which can further be simplified to

$$\begin{aligned}
&\bigwedge_{\varphi \in \mathrm{Inv}} \varphi \wedge \psi_{opct} \wedge \mathtt{self.<created>} \doteq \mathrm{TRUE} \\
&\qquad \wedge \bigwedge_{i=1,\ldots,n} (\mathtt{p}_i\mathtt{.<created>} \doteq \mathrm{TRUE} \vee \mathtt{p}_i \doteq \mathtt{null}) \\
&\qquad\qquad \rightarrow \mathcal{M}(\tau_{opct}, \widetilde{\alpha}_{op}(\mathtt{self}; \mathtt{p}_1, \ldots, \mathtt{p}_n; \mathtt{r}; \mathtt{exc}))\varphi_{opct}
\end{aligned}$$

where we abbreviated

- $\psi_{opct}(\mathtt{self}; \mathtt{p}_1, \ldots, \mathtt{p}_n)$ as $\psi_{opct}$ and
- $\varphi_{opct}(\mathtt{self}; \mathtt{p}_1, \ldots, \mathtt{p}_n; \mathtt{r}; \mathtt{exc})$ as $\varphi_{opct}$.

### 7.2.6 Postcondition Assurance Under Weaker Assumptions

As for invariants, it is possible to show a stronger proof obligation than *EnsuresPost*, namely one with weaker assumptions by skipping some invariants:

**Proof Obligation Template:**
$\mathit{EnsuresPostAssumpt}(\mathit{opct}; I; \mathtt{self}; \mathtt{p}_1, \ldots, \mathtt{p}_n; \mathtt{r}; \mathtt{exc})$.

$$\mathit{Ensures}(op; I \cup \{\psi_{opct}\}; \{\varphi_{opct}\}; \tau_{opct}; \mathtt{self}; \mathtt{p}_1, \ldots, \mathtt{p}_n; \mathtt{r}; \mathtt{exc})$$

or equivalently:

$$\bigwedge_{\varphi \in I} \varphi \wedge \psi_{opct} \wedge \texttt{self.<created>} \doteq \text{TRUE}$$
$$\wedge \bigwedge_{i=1,\ldots,n} (\texttt{p}_i\texttt{.<created>} \doteq \text{TRUE} \vee \texttt{p}_i \doteq \texttt{null})$$
$$\rightarrow \mathcal{M}(\tau_{opct}, \widetilde{\alpha}_{op}(\texttt{self}; \texttt{p}_1, \ldots, \texttt{p}_n; \texttt{r}; \texttt{exc}))\varphi_{opct}$$

## 7.2.7 Assignable Clauses

An assignable clause for an operation specifies the locations that it can *at most* modify. Its semantics has been defined in Sect. 3.2.3. Checking assignable clauses belongs amongst the most difficult tasks in program verification. The reason is that the focus is on those locations which are *not* explicitely mentioned in the specification. All of them must be proven to be unmodified.

Sasse [2004] aims at a 'straightforward' approach for checking assignable clauses with the help of JavaDL by enumerating all locations which are *not* described by an assignable clause and checking for their unchangedness. Unfortunately this approach produces huge proof obligations; their sizes grow linear in the number of fields in the considered program. Moreover the approach is not modular in the sense that if the program context is extended, the whole proof obligation changes.

In the following a new kind of proof obligation template to check assignable clauses is presented which produces compact and readable formulae and which remains unchanged if the program context changes. However, the idea behind the proof obligation is, due to the nature of the problem, not as intuitive as the other proof obligations in this chapter are. We thus proceed in small steps to motivate the structure.

An assignable clause of an operation contract *opct* of an operation *op* consists of a set of location terms $Mod \subseteq \text{LocTerm}^{\Sigma}$. Intuitively, *Mod* is correct if a call $\alpha$ to *op* (which satisfies the general assumption and the pre-condition of *opct*) assigns at most to the locations described in *Mod*. Temporary violations of this rule, not visible to the observer, are however allowed.

Let $S_{\text{pre}}$ be the set of states in which the pre-condition of *opct* and the general assumption hold. Imagine that in these states the locations $\text{Loc}_{S_{\text{pre}}}(Mod)$

described by *Mod* are assigned fixed but unknown values. Let us call the resulting set of states $S_1$.

We consider now an arbitrary *anonymous* method `anon()` of which we only specify the following behaviour: `anon()` terminates if invoked in a state of $S_1$. All the rest of the behaviour of `anon()` is unknown. Thus, for all the other states we must assume that termination is not specified. In particular it could be possible that `anon()` does not terminate when invoking it from other states than $S_1$.

Let us look at a different set $S_2$ of states which originate again from $S_{\text{pre}}$ but by invoking *op* and, after that, assigning the locations $\text{Loc}_{S_{\text{pre}}}(\mathit{Mod})$ the same values as above.

Assume now that `anon()`, characterised as above, terminates if started in $S_2$. Because `anon()` is arbitrary and only our assumptions from above about the termination behaviour are known, we can conclude that $S_2 \subseteq S_1$. Thus no other locations than $\text{Loc}_{S_{\text{pre}}}(\mathit{Mod})$ (and locations irrelevant to the termination behaviour of `anon()`, i.e., local variables) have been modified by *op*. Hence *Mod* is a correct assignable clause for *op*.

As follows, we formalise these considerations as a JavaDL proof obligation. First of all, the states $S_{\text{pre}}$ have to be characterised by

$$\psi_{opct}(\mathtt{self};\mathtt{p}_1,\ldots,\mathtt{p}_n) \land \mathcal{A}_{op}(\mathtt{self};\mathtt{p}_1,\ldots,\mathtt{p}_n)$$

for the pre-condition of *opct* and the general assumption. Further, we formalise the assignment of $\text{Loc}_{S_{\text{pre}}}(\mathit{Mod})$ to certain values as an update. In order to reflect that the values assigned to these locations are arbitrary, we use the anonymising update $u(\mathit{Mod})$ introduced in Sect. 2.3.1. The update has as top level operators of its right hand side expressions *rigid* symbols matching the signature of the top-level non-rigid symbols of the updated terms. Termination of `anon()` is expressed, as usual, as $\langle\mathtt{anon();}\rangle\,\text{true}$.

When formalising the update, we must take some care since the update occurs one time inside the scope of a modality; the locations that are to be updated refer to the pre-state of this modality however. In Sect. 2.3.4 the instruments needed to refer to pre-states have been defined: rigid functions and predicates $f^{@pre}$ for every non-rigid function and predicate (resp.) $f$, which are appropriately axiomatised by $\text{Def}(F^{@pre})$ if $F^{@pre}$ is the mapping between normal function / predicate symbols and the *@pre* versions. So we must modify the update $u(\mathit{Mod})$ according to the following definition.

**Definition 7.1** (Updates of Pre-State Objects). We extend the function pre (see Def. 2.19) to updates. pre applied on an update delivers a tuple $(t^{@pre}, F^{@pre})$ where $t^{@pre} \in \text{Upd}^{\Sigma}$ and $F^{@pre}$ is a mapping from non-rigid function or predicate symbols $f$ to rigid function or predicate (resp.) symbols $f^{@pre}$. pre on updates is inductively defined as follows:

- $\text{pre}(f(t_1, \ldots, t_n) := t_0) = (f(t'_1, \ldots, t'_n) := t'_0, \bigcup_{i=0,\ldots,n} F_i^{@pre})$
  with $\text{pre}(t_i) = (t'_i, F_i^{@pre})$ (for $i = 0, \ldots, n$)
- $\text{pre}(u_1|u_2) = (u'_1|u'_2, F_1^{@pre} \cup F_2^{@pre})$ with $\text{pre}(u_i) = (u'_i, F_i^{@pre})$ (for $i = 1, 2$)
- $\text{pre}(\text{for } x ; \varphi ; u) = ((\text{for } x ; \varphi' ; u'), F_1^{@pre} \cup F_2^{@pre})$
  with $\text{pre}(\varphi) = (\varphi', F_1^{@pre})$, $\text{pre}(u) = (u', F_2^{@pre})$

**Lemma 7.2.** If $\text{pre}(u) = (u', F^{@pre})$ and $s_{\text{pre}} \models_P \text{Def}(F^{@pre})$ then for all $l \in L_{\Sigma}$ and all states $s$: $\text{updval}_{s,\beta}(u')(l) = \text{updval}_{s_{\text{pre}},\beta}(u)(l)$

Altogether the proof obligation to prove that an assignable clause is correct is as follows:

**Proof Obligation Template:** *RespectsModifies*$(opct; \texttt{self}; \texttt{p}_1, \ldots, \texttt{p}_n)$.

$$\begin{aligned} &\psi_{opct}(\texttt{self}; \texttt{p}_1, \ldots, \texttt{p}_n) \wedge \mathcal{A}_{op}(\texttt{self}; \texttt{p}_1, \ldots, \texttt{p}_n) \\ &\wedge \text{Def}(F^{@pre}) \wedge \{u\} \langle \texttt{anon();} \rangle \, \text{true} \\ &\qquad \rightarrow [\widetilde{\alpha}_{op}(\texttt{self}; \texttt{p}_1, \ldots, \texttt{p}_n)]\{u'\} \langle \texttt{anon();} \rangle \, \text{true} \end{aligned}$$

with $u = u(Mod(opct))$ as defined in Sect. 2.3.1 and $\text{pre}(u) = (u', F^{@pre})$

**Lemma 7.3.** If $\models_P$ *RespectsModifies*$(opct; \texttt{self}; \texttt{p}_1, \ldots, \texttt{p}_n)$ then in all states $s_{\text{pre}}$ and $s_{\text{post}}$ with

$$\begin{aligned} s_{\text{pre}} \models_P \psi_{opct}(\texttt{self}; \texttt{p}_1, \ldots, \texttt{p}_n) \wedge \mathcal{A}_{op}(\texttt{self}; \texttt{p}_1, \ldots, \texttt{p}_n) \\ \text{and} \quad s_{\text{post}} = \rho_{\widetilde{\alpha}_{op}(\texttt{self}; \texttt{p}_1, \ldots, \texttt{p}_n)}(s_{\text{pre}}) \end{aligned}$$

the assignable clause $Mod(opct) \subseteq \text{LocTerm}^{\Sigma}$ is satisfied (in the pre-state $s_{\text{pre}}$ and the post-state $s_{\text{post}}$).

Before we start to prove this lemma, a helper lemma is needed:

**Lemma 7.4.** For all $t \in \mathrm{LocTerm}^\Sigma$:
$l \in \mathrm{Loc}_{s,P,\beta}(t)$ iff $\mathrm{updval}_{s,P,\beta}(u(t))(l) \neq \bot$

*Proof.* By structural induction on $\mathrm{LocTerm}^\Sigma$:
(a) $t = f(t_1, \ldots, t_n)$. Then:

$$\begin{aligned} l \in Loc(t,s) &\Leftrightarrow l = (f, (\mathrm{val}_{s,P,\beta}(t_1), \ldots, \mathrm{val}_{s,P,\beta}(t_n))) \\ &\Leftrightarrow \{(f, (\mathrm{val}_{s,P,\beta}(t_1), \ldots, \mathrm{val}_{s,P,\beta}(t_n))) \mapsto \mathrm{val}_{s,P,\beta}(t)\}(l) \neq \bot \\ &\Leftrightarrow \mathrm{updval}_{s,P,\beta}(u(f(t_1, \ldots, t_n)))(l) \neq \bot \\ &\Leftrightarrow \mathrm{updval}_{s,P,\beta}(u(t))(l) \neq \bot \end{aligned}$$

(b) $t = (\text{for } x \ ; \varphi \ ; t')$. Then:

$$\begin{aligned} l \in \mathrm{Loc}_{s,P,\beta}(t) &\Leftrightarrow l \in \bigcup_{\substack{\text{exists } e \in \mathcal{U}: \\ \beta_x^e \models_P \varphi}} \mathrm{Loc}_{s,\beta_x^e}(t') \\ &\Leftrightarrow l \in \mathrm{Loc}_{s,\beta_x^e}(t') \text{ for some } e \text{ with } \beta_x^e \models_P \varphi \\ &\Leftrightarrow \mathrm{updval}_{s,\beta_x^e}(u(t'))(l) \neq \bot \text{ for some } e \text{ with } \beta_x^e \models_P \varphi \\ &\Leftrightarrow \text{there exists an } e \in \mathcal{U} \\ &\qquad \text{with } \mathrm{updval}_{s,\beta_x^e}(u(t')(l) \neq \bot \text{ and } s, \beta_x^e \models_P \varphi \\ &\Leftrightarrow \mathrm{updval}_{s,P,\beta}((\text{for } x \ ; \varphi \ ; u(t')))(l) \neq \bot \\ &\Leftrightarrow \mathrm{updval}_{s,P,\beta}(u((\text{for } x \ ; \varphi \ ; t')))(l) \neq \bot \\ &\Leftrightarrow \mathrm{updval}_{s,P,\beta}(u(t))(l) \neq \bot \end{aligned}$$ □

*Proof of Lemma 7.3.* Choose an arbitrary $f \in F^{nr}$ and $e_1, \ldots, e_n \in \mathcal{U}$. Further abbreviate $l := (f, (e_1, \ldots, e_n))$. We can assume:

$$\models_P \mathit{RespectsModifies}(opct, \mathtt{self}, (\mathtt{p}_1, \ldots, \mathtt{p}_n)) \tag{7.2}$$

$$f^{s_{\mathrm{pre}}, P}(e_1, \ldots, e_n) \neq f^{s_{\mathrm{post}}, P}(e_1, \ldots, e_n) \tag{7.3}$$

For a proof by contradiction we assume:

$$l = (f, (e_1, \ldots, e_n)) \notin \bigcup_{t \in Mod(opct)} \mathrm{Loc}_{s_{\mathrm{pre}},\beta}(t) \tag{7.4}$$

From (7.4) we can conclude that for all $t \in Mod(opct) : l \notin \mathrm{Loc}_{s_{\mathrm{pre}},\beta}(t)$. With Lemma 7.4: $\mathrm{updval}_{s_{\mathrm{pre}},\beta}(u(t))(l) = \bot$. Thus:

$$f^{\rho_{u(t)}(s_{\mathrm{pre}}), P}(e_1, \ldots, e_n) = f^{s_{\mathrm{pre}}, P}(e_1, \ldots, e_n)$$

Because of (7.2) we know: $\mathrm{pre}(u(t)) = (u', F^{@pre})$ and $s_{\mathrm{pre}}, \beta \models_P \mathrm{Def}(F^{@pre})$. Then, with Lemma 7.2, $\mathrm{updval}_{s_{\mathrm{pre}},\beta}(u(t))(l) = \mathrm{updval}_{s_{\mathrm{post}},\beta}(u')(l)$. And because of $\mathrm{updval}_{s_{\mathrm{post}},\beta}(u')(l) = \mathrm{updval}_{s_{\mathrm{pre}},\beta}(u(t))(l) = \bot$ we can conclude:

$$f^{s_{\mathrm{post}},P}(e_1, \ldots, e_n) = f^{\rho u'(s_{\mathrm{post}}),P}(e_1, \ldots, e_n)$$

We use the following designations for different intermediate states:

$$s'_{\mathrm{pre}} = \rho u(t)(s_{\mathrm{pre}}), \qquad s'_{\mathrm{post}} = \rho u'(s_{\mathrm{post}})$$

From (7.2) we get $\models_P \rho_{\mathtt{anon()}}(s'_{\mathrm{pre}}) \neq \bot$ implies $\rho_{\mathtt{anon()}}(s'_{\mathrm{post}}) \neq \bot$ and can conclude that $s'_{\mathrm{pre}} = s'_{\mathrm{post}}$. Altogether we have

$$f^{s_{\mathrm{pre}},P}(e_1, \ldots, e_n) = f^{s_{\mathrm{post}},P}(e_1, \ldots, e_n)$$

in contradiction to (7.3). □

**Example 7.1.** In Ex. 1.1 we had the empty assignable clause attached to the operation `earlierOrEqual(Date)`. Its correctness can be proven with *RespectsModifies* instantiated as follows:

$$\begin{array}{l} \mathcal{A}_{\mathtt{earlierOrEqual(Date)}}(\mathtt{self}; d) \wedge \{\mathrm{skip}\}\,\langle\mathtt{anon();}\rangle\,\mathrm{true} \\ \quad \to [\; \mathtt{try\{\ r=self.earlierOrEqual(d)@Date;\}} \\ \qquad\;\; \mathtt{catch\ (Throwable\ e)\ \{\}}] \quad \{\mathrm{skip}\}\,\langle\mathtt{anon();}\rangle\,\mathrm{true} \end{array}$$

By the symbolic execution of the method body no updates are accumulated so that the proof can easily be closed. *

## 7.3 A System of Proof Obligations for Entire Call Correctness

The properties presented so far may help developers when questions concerning single correctness issues occur during development. At some point, the question might arise whether the complete program, finally finished being programmed, is entirely correct. Of course, the proofs originating from lightweight correctness proof obligations (with the unmodified underlying program context) remain useful in order to prove the entire correctness and might thus be re-used here.

The following proof obligation consists of several elementary proof obligations and ensures observed-state call correctness as defined in Def. 3.10. That definition is directly formalised:

**Lemma 7.5.** Let $\Sigma$ be a signature, $P$ a $\Sigma$-program, and $S$ a JavaFOL specification of $P$. If for all non-private operations *op* of $P$ the following proof obligations are valid in $P$ then $P$ is observed-state call correct w.r.t. $S$:

$$\text{for all operation contracts } opct \in \mathrm{OpCt}_{op} : \mathit{EnsuresPost}(opct) \tag{7.5}$$

$$\text{for all operation contracts } opct \in \mathrm{OpCt}_{op} : \mathit{RespectsModifies}(opct) \tag{7.6}$$

$$\text{for all invariants } \varphi \in \mathrm{Inv} : \mathit{PreservesInv}(op, \{\varphi\}) \tag{7.7}$$

$$\text{for all invariants } \varphi \in \mathrm{Inv} : \mathit{InitInv}(\{\varphi\}) \tag{7.8}$$

*Proof.* We simply write $\alpha$ instead of $\widetilde{\alpha}_{op}(\mathtt{self}; \mathtt{p}_1, \ldots, \mathtt{p}_n; \mathtt{r}; \mathtt{exc})$. According to Def. 3.10, the fulfilment of all operation contracts and the preservation of invariants must be shown:

- (Fulfilled Operation Contracts) Let *opct* be an operation contract of $s$ applicable to *op*. Further assume that for all states $s_{\mathrm{pre}}$:

$$s_{\mathrm{pre}} \models_P \mathit{EnsuresPost}(opct) \tag{7.9}$$
$$s_{\mathrm{pre}} \models_P \mathit{RespectsModifies}(opct) \tag{7.10}$$
$$s_{\mathrm{pre}} \models_P \mathcal{A}_{op}(\mathtt{self}; \mathtt{p}_1, \ldots, \mathtt{p}_n) \tag{7.11}$$
$$s_{\mathrm{pre}} \models_P \psi_{opct}(\mathtt{self}; \mathtt{p}_1, \ldots, \mathtt{p}_n) \tag{7.12}$$

  - If the *total* marker is set in *opct*, then $\mathcal{M}(\tau_{opct}, \alpha) = \langle \tau_{opct} \rangle\, \alpha$. Because of $s_{\mathrm{pre}}, \beta \models_P (\langle \tau_{opct} \rangle\, \alpha)$, there exists a state $s_{\mathrm{post}}$ with $s_{\mathrm{post}} = \rho_\alpha(s_{\mathrm{pre}})$ and $s_{\mathrm{post}}, \beta \models_P \langle \alpha \rangle\, \varphi$.
  - Assume now there is a state $s_{\mathrm{post}} = \rho_\alpha(s_{\mathrm{pre}})$. Because of the validity (7.11) and (7.12) the validity of *EnsuresPost*(*opct*) yields:

$$s_{\mathrm{post}} \models_P \varphi_{\mathrm{post}}$$

  - Assume again the existence of $s_{\mathrm{post}} = \rho_\alpha(s_{\mathrm{pre}})$. Then the satisfaction of the assignable clause follows directly from Lemma 7.3.

  Altogether the contract *opct* on *op* of $S$ is fulfilled (Def. 3.6).

- (Preserved Invariants) Let *op* be an arbitrary operation of $P$. With (7.11) and

$$s_{\mathrm{pre}} \models_P \mathit{PreservesInv}(op, \mathrm{Inv}) \tag{7.13}$$
$$s_{\mathrm{post}} = \rho_\alpha(s_{\mathrm{pre}}) \tag{7.14}$$

$s_{\text{post}} \models_P \text{Inv}$ follows directly from (7.13). □

The proof obligations (7.7) are equivalent to the following larger one:

$$PreservesInv(op, \text{Inv}) \tag{7.15}$$

## 7.4 Non-modular Optimisations

With the system of proof obligations of the last section, the number of generated proof obligations *explodes*: with $i$ the number of invariants in the program and $j$ the number of operations, we get $i \cdot j$ proof obligations, whereas there are only $2 \cdot j$ proof obligations for ensuring that the operation contracts are fulfilled.

The following chapters are devoted to alleviate this problem. The strategy is to modularly analyse invariants and finding out which invariants must be checked for which operations. *Modularly* in this sense means that we can derive from the invariants which operations are affected and that other operations than those do not need to be considered. Obviously, this approach is the only one viable for open programs.

Nevertheless, in the section, we describe an alternative way to deal with the problem. We analyse operations without having to symbolically execute the operation body and without a need to pre-analyse the invariant.

**Example 7.2.** In Ex. 1.1 we have the invariant:

$$\dot{\forall} m{:}\texttt{Month}.\ (0 \leq m.\texttt{val} \land m.\texttt{val} \leq 12)$$

It is intuitively clear that this invariant cannot be violated by `setYear(int)` in `Period`. There should thus be no need to check that `setYear(int)` preserves this particular invariant, though in this case symbolic execution would be trivial. Clearly however there could be methods where a huge effort would be needed to get deductively rid of the code, although the method has no means to affect the evaluation of the considered invariant. *

The intuition of a developer recognises quite immediately if a method cannot influcnce the evaluation of a certain invariant, since the locations that get changed by the method on the one side and those that an invariant depends on are distinct.

We have already familiarised ourselves with the fact that those locations an operation may assign values to are specified in assignable clauses. If assignable clauses are checked as described above, we can make safe use of this kind of specifications to decide that an operation cannot be affected by an invariant.

More precisely we make use of Lemma 3.1 which states that if $\{u(\mathit{Mod})\}\varphi$ is valid then $\varphi$ is valid after the execution of a program for which *Mod* is an assignable clause. So instead of symbolically executing the operation body we can apply the update $u(\mathit{Mod})$ derived from the assignable clause *Mod* of the operation. If this does not already affect a considered invariant, the actual body will neither.

We exploit all these considerations in the following proof obligation and lemma:

**Proof Obligation Template:** *InvNotModified*$(op;\varphi)$.
if $\varphi$ is an invariant, *op* an operation and $\mathit{Mod}(op)$ the union of the assignable clauses of all operation contracts in $S$ applicable to *op*

$$\mathcal{A}_{op}(\mathtt{self};\mathtt{p}_1,\ldots,\mathtt{p}_n)\wedge\varphi\rightarrow\{u(\mathit{Mod}(op))\}\varphi$$

**Lemma 7.6.** For an invariant $\varphi$ and an operation *op*, if

$$\begin{array}{l}\models_P \ \mathit{InvNotModified}(op,\varphi)\\ \models_P \ \mathit{RespectsModifies}(opct) \text{ for all } opct \text{ applicable to } op \text{ in } S\end{array}$$

then *op* preserves $\varphi$.

*Proof.* Let $s_{\mathrm{pre}}$ be a state. $\alpha := \widetilde{\alpha}_{op}(\mathtt{self};\mathtt{p}_1,\ldots,\mathtt{p}_n)$. We assume:

$$\begin{array}{rcl}s_{\mathrm{pre}} & \models_P & \mathit{InvNotModified}(op,\varphi)\\ s_{\mathrm{pre}} & \models_P & \mathit{RespectsModifies}(opct) \text{ for all } opct \text{ applicable to } op \text{ in } S\\ s_{\mathrm{pre}} & \models_P & \mathcal{A}_{op}(\mathtt{self};\mathtt{p}_1,\ldots,\mathtt{p}_n)\\ s_{\mathrm{post}} & = & \rho_\alpha(s_{\mathrm{pre}})\end{array}$$

Let *opct* be an arbitrary operation contract in $S$ which has a pre-condition which holds in $s_{\mathrm{pre}}$. There must be such an operation contract since the general assumption is valid in $s_{\mathrm{pre}}$. Since *RespectsModifies*$(opct)$ holds for this operation contract in $s_{\mathrm{pre}}$, we have $(s_{\mathrm{pre}},s_{\mathrm{post}})\models_P M$ for the assignable clause of *opct*. Since $M\subseteq \mathit{Mod}(op)$ also: $(s_{\mathrm{pre}},s_{\mathrm{post}})\models_P \mathit{Mod}(op)$. Because of the validity of the general assumption $s_{\mathrm{pre}}\models_P\varphi$. With $s_{\mathrm{pre}}\models_P$

*InvNotModified*$(op, \varphi)$ we have $s_{\mathrm{pre}} \models_P \{u(Mod(op))\}\varphi$. Lemma 3.1 yields: $s_{\mathrm{pre}} \models_P \langle\alpha\rangle\, \varphi$. And finally $s_{\mathrm{post}} \models_P \varphi$. □

**Example 7.3.** Coming back to Ex. 7.2, `setYear(int)` has {`self.year`} as union of assignable clauses of all applicable operation contracts. The *InvNotModified* proof obligation pattern is thus instantiated as follows:

$$\dot{\forall} m{:}\texttt{Month}.\ (0 \leq m\texttt{.val} \land m\texttt{.val} \leq 12) \\ \to \{\texttt{self.year} := f(\texttt{self})\}\dot{\forall} m{:}\texttt{Month}.\ (0 \leq m\texttt{.val} \land m\texttt{.val} \leq 12)$$

where $f$ is a rigid function. According to update application rules [Beckert et al., 2006b] this is equivalent to the tautology

$$\dot{\forall} m{:}\texttt{Month}.\ (0 \leq m\texttt{.val} \land m\texttt{.val} \leq 12) \\ \to \dot{\forall} m{:}\texttt{Month}.\ (0 \leq m\texttt{.val} \land m\texttt{.val} \leq 12)$$

The lemma above ensures that `setYear(int)` preserves the considered invariant. Note that we did not look at the implementation of `setYear(int)` to come to this statement. Of course an inspection of the code is needed when the correctness of the assignable clause is proven with *RespectsModifies*. *

As a consequence of the above lemma, if the assignable clause of an operation is (provably) empty, there is no need to check *PreservesInv* for that operation, since this property is trivially true. This is why methods of *immutable* objects always preserve all invariants.

**Lemma 7.7.** If all operation contracts *opct* applicable to an operation *op* have an empty assignable clause and $\models_P$ *RespectsModifies*(*opct*) then *op* preserves every invariant.

*Proof.* With $u(\emptyset) = \mathrm{skip}$ and $\mathrm{updval}_{s,P,\beta}(\mathrm{skip}) = \bot$ we get for every $\varphi$: $\models_P$ *InvNotModified*$(op, \varphi)$. With Lemma 7.6, the preservation of $\varphi$ can be concluded. □

**Example 7.4.** In Ex. 1.1, the assignable clause of `getMonth()` is empty in all applicable operation contracts. Tehere is thus no need to check for invariant preservation for any invariant at this method. *

## 7.5 Pragmatics

Usually, the formula described by a proof obligation is placed in the succedent of an (otherwise empty) sequent, and is then deduced with the sequent calculus rules of JavaDL. Unfortunately the general assumption involves *all* invariants of the whole context and is part of this formula. Thus the sequent presented to the user is huge and complex. Moreover, in practice it is unusual that all invariants are actually needed to conduct the proof, though this case can almost never be excluded *a priori*.

This gives rise to an advanced strategy how the general assumption is presented to the user. In this strategy, invariants contained in the general assumption are available to a user of the prover only *on demand*, that is, they are made visible in the antecedent of the sequent only if the user requests it.

Technically, we transform the formulae $\varphi$ arising from the proof obligations presented in this and the subsequent chapters into pairs $(\varphi', R)$ of formulae $\varphi'$ and sets $R$ of rules, realised by the function $\mathrm{simp} : \mathrm{Fma}^{\Sigma} \longrightarrow \mathrm{Fma}^{\Sigma} \times \mathrm{Rule}^{\Sigma}$. The rules are an extension to the regular calculus rules of JavaDL and introduce formulae in the antecedent. They are thus of the form:

$$\frac{\Gamma, \psi \vdash \Delta}{\Gamma \vdash \Delta}$$

simp is defined as follows:

$$\mathrm{simp}(\varphi) = \begin{cases} (\varphi', R) & \text{if } \varphi = \bigwedge\limits_{\psi \in \Psi} \psi \rightarrow \{\alpha\}\varphi'' \\ (\varphi, \emptyset) & \text{otherwise} \end{cases}$$

with sets of formulae $\Psi_0$, $\Psi_1$, $\Psi = \Psi_0 \uplus \Psi_1$ and:

$$\varphi' = \bigwedge_{\psi_0 \in \Psi_0} \psi_0 \rightarrow \{\alpha\}\varphi'' \qquad\qquad R = \bigcup_{\psi_1 \in \Psi_1} \frac{\Gamma, \psi_1 \vdash \Delta}{\Gamma \vdash \Delta}$$

**Lemma 7.8.** Assume: $\varphi = \left(\bigwedge\limits_{\psi \in \Psi} \psi \rightarrow \{\alpha\}\varphi''\right) \in \mathrm{Term}^{\Sigma}$, and $\mathrm{simp}(\varphi) = (\varphi', R)$. There is a closed proof in JavaDL of $\varphi$ with $\Sigma$-program $P$ if and only if for every choice of $\Psi_0$ there is a closed proof of $\varphi'$ with $P$ using the normal JavaDL rules extended by $R$.

*Proof.* There is a proof of $\vdash \varphi$ in JavaDL iff there is a proof for $\Psi \vdash \{\alpha\}\varphi''$ because of the soundness and completeness preserving of the imp-right and

and-left rules. There is however also a proof for $\vdash \varphi$ with the extended rule set iff there is a proof for $\Psi \vdash \langle\alpha\rangle\varphi''$ in that set because of the soundness and completeness preserving of imp-right, all-left, and $R$. □

A good heuristics is to put the conjuncts of the general assumption in $\Psi_1$ or to exclude from this set those invariants defined in the class of the receiver, since they are more likely to be needed in a proof for one of the receiver's operations.

**Example 7.5.** For the invariant in Ex. 1.1:

$$\dot{\forall} m{:}\texttt{Month}.\ (0 \leq m\texttt{.val} \land m\texttt{.val} \leq 12)$$

the following *PreservesInv* proof obligation for `setVal(int)` is generated:

$$\begin{array}{l} \dot{\forall} p{:}\texttt{Period}.\ (\ p\texttt{.start.year} < p\texttt{.end.year} \\ \qquad\qquad\qquad \lor(\ p\texttt{.start.year} \doteq p\texttt{.end.year} \\ \qquad\qquad\qquad\quad \land p\texttt{.start.month.val} \leq p\texttt{.end.month.val})) \\ \land \dot{\forall} m{:}\texttt{Month}.\ (0 \leq m\texttt{.val} \land m\texttt{.val} \leq 12) \\ \to [\widetilde{\alpha}_{\texttt{setVal(int)}}(\texttt{self};\texttt{p}_1,\ldots,\texttt{p}_n;\texttt{r})]\dot{\forall} m{:}\texttt{Month}.\ (0 \leq m\texttt{.val} \land m\texttt{.val} \leq 12) \end{array}$$

With the technique presented above we can instead have as proof obligation:

$$[\widetilde{\alpha}_{\texttt{setVal(int)}}(\texttt{self};\texttt{p}_1,\ldots,\texttt{p}_n;\texttt{r})]\dot{\forall} m{:}\texttt{Month}.\ (0 \leq m\texttt{.val} \land m\texttt{.val} \leq 12)$$

which is supposed to be discharged with the additional help of the following rules:

$$\frac{\begin{array}{l}\Gamma,\ \dot{\forall} p{:}\texttt{Period}.\ (\ p\texttt{.start.year} < p\texttt{.end.year} \\ \qquad\qquad\qquad \lor(\ p\texttt{.start.year} \doteq p\texttt{.end.year} \qquad\qquad \vdash \Delta \\ \qquad\qquad\qquad\quad \land p\texttt{.start.month.val} \leq p\texttt{.end.month.val}))\end{array}}{\Gamma \vdash \Delta}$$

$$\frac{\Gamma, \dot{\forall} m{:}\texttt{Month}.\ (0 \leq m\texttt{.val} \land m\texttt{.val} \leq 12) \vdash \Delta}{\Gamma \vdash \Delta}$$

Clearly this proof obligation formula is easier readable. Moreover, as already mentioned alternative, it is possible according to the lemma above to leave the invariant of `Month` in the formula and provide only the first (irrelevant) invariant as rule. The criterion to do so is that `Month` is the receiver class which makes it likely that its invariant is needed. *

For all operation contracts in $opct \in \mathrm{OpCt}$:

$EnsuresPost(opct)$ or $EnsuresPostAssumpt(I; opct)$ if $I \subseteq \mathrm{Inv}$,

$RespectsModifies(opct)$,

$$and \begin{cases} PreservesInv(op, \mathrm{Inv}) \text{ } or \\ \text{for all invariants } \varphi \in \mathrm{Inv}: \begin{cases} PreservesInv(op, \{\varphi\}), \\ InvNotModified(op, \{\varphi\}), \text{ } or \\ PreservesInvAssumpt(op; I; \{\varphi\}) \\ \quad \text{if } I \subseteq \mathrm{Inv} \end{cases} \end{cases}$$

**Figure 7.1:** Verification strategies for entire observed-state call correctness

By encoding assumed invariants as rules, it is also possible to have a finer grained proof management, since only the really applied rules of $R$ correspond to those invariants which the proof later depends on. Imagine the conducted proof $P_1$ is to prove the fulfilment of an operation contract. If one later wants to make use of this contract (according to Rule (6.6)) in a second proof $P_2$, one has to show the assumptions made by the contract. These are the preconditions and the assumed invariants. If however one particular invariant is not needed to conduct $P_1$ it is also not needed to prove the establishment of this invariant when the specification of the operation contract is used. Having an invariant encoded as a rule allows to easier determine whether the invariant has been used in $P_1$, whereas having it within the original proof obligation formula requires a much more intricate analysis of the proof.

## 7.6 Summary

We have discussed several single proof obligations, among others to verify the assurance of post-conditions, the correctness of assignable clauses, and the preservation of invariants. We have further seen that these single proof obligations can be utilised to prove entire observed-state call correctness in a non-modular way. There are several ways to establish this property, in particular we can make use of non-modular optimisations, and it is the choice of the individual developer to decide which of them to take. Fig. 7.1 illustrates the different options.

We have finally seen that there are different possibilities how these proof obligations are presented to the user. Ultimate goal is to reduce the complexity of proof obligations in the user presentation.

Chapters 9 and 10 will refine the system of proof obligations presented here with the focus on modular verification and on durable correctness of open programs. Before that, some further instruments have to be developed. In the next chapter the proof obligations presented here are especially adapted to cope with encapsulation predicates.

# 8 Verification of Encapsulation

Num negare audes? quid taces?
Convincam, si negas.

*(Cicero)*

This chapter deals with the question how specifications containing encapsulation predicates, as introduced in Chapter 4, can efficiently be checked against an implementation. The developed concept has been partly presented in Roth [2005].

Essentially there are two possibilities to check encapsulation properties:

- Using *deductive* methods for proving specifications of encapsulation is most natural, as this is the preferred way to verify programs w.r.t functional specifications. Since we make no distinction between encapsulation properties and functional properties—both are specified in the traditional design by contract way—they should be checkable the same way. The special challenge with deduction is that deductive reasoning should be modular as pointed out in Chapter 6.

- *Static analysis* methods are established means to check encapsulation properties. The approaches described in Sect. 4.1.2 all come with a fast static analysis. Static analyses have the appeal of a fully automated technique which should thus be made use of whenever possible. We must however find a save way back from the more general encapsulation predicates to the restrictive but checkable alias control approaches.

The approach described below aims at a framework which integrates both techniques, and which allows to check the easily statically checkable properties to be checked with static analysis and the others deductively.

**Outline.** Sect. 8.1 describes peculiarities with proof obligations for encapsulation properties. Compared to other proof obligations we must explicitely state a special worst case of the caller. In the subsequent section we look at a first non-modular approach to deal with encapsulation predicates with a deduction system. In Sect. 8.3, a modular approach, suited to the special encapsulation proof obligations, is proposed. Sect. 8.4 discusses the integration of established static analysis techniques into our approach.

## 8.1 Proof Obligations

In this section we customise the proof obligations from the last section so that they are applicable for formulae containing encapsulation predicates. More precisely we only adapt the *PreservesInv* proof obligation since encapsulation properties typically occur in invariants. All other proof obligations can be adapted analogously.

The following example motivates the necessity for customisations. Let $\varphi$ be the following formula:

$$\dot{\forall} x.\ \mathrm{Acc}(x, \texttt{self}.a) \rightarrow x \doteq \texttt{self}$$

Let `m` be a method assigning an argument `p` to the field `a`:

```
public void m(T p) {
  a = p;
}
```

If we put this formula in the normal *PreservesInv* proof obligation for `m` we obtain:

$$\mathcal{A}_{\texttt{m}}(\texttt{self};\texttt{p}) \rightarrow [\texttt{p=p0; try\{self.m(p0)\} catch(Throwable e)\{\}}]\varphi$$

This formula is valid in all states since Acc takes into account only fields and not local variables, so that it is not relevant that $\texttt{p} \doteq \texttt{self.a}$ holds in the post-state. However, an observer may keep this reference in a field and $\varphi$ would thus not be an invariant of the system. So we need to refine our proof obligations to match the observer model better. It is the worst case which we should assume here: our observer acquires as many references that can be obtained.

In general it must be modelled that the caller, that is, in our observer model, the observer, may hold references (a) to the parameter objects and (b) to the callee itself and (c) will, after the call has finished, hold a reference to the returned value. (a) and (b) can be modelled by providing additional pre-conditions for parameters $\mathtt{p}_1, \ldots, \mathtt{p}_n$ and callee `self`:

$$\psi_{acc}(\mathtt{self}; \mathtt{p}_1, \ldots, \mathtt{p}_n) := \bigwedge_{i=1,\ldots,n} \exists x.\ \mathrm{Acc}(x, \mathtt{p}_i) \wedge \exists x.\ \mathrm{Acc}(x, \mathtt{self})$$

That the return value `r` is afterwards possibly referenced, can be modelled by qualifying the invariant $\varphi$ appropriately, that is by referring to it as

$$\exists x.\ \mathrm{Acc}(x, \mathtt{r}) \rightarrow \varphi$$

An alternative is to use fields of an anonymous object as arguments of the call and assigning the return value to another field of that class as pointed out in Roth [2005]. Both alternatives are equally viable, though the first one is more explicit and does not need an extension of the model, that is, no special anonymous class must be added.

We thus obtain the following proof obligation template to prove that an invariant $\varphi \in \mathrm{Term}^{\mathrm{Acc}(\Sigma)}$ containing encapsulation predicates is preserved by an operation *op*:

**Proof Obligation Template:** $\mathit{PreservesInv}^*(op, \varphi, \mathtt{self}, (\mathtt{p}_1, \ldots, \mathtt{p}_n))$ .

$$\begin{aligned} &\mathit{Ensures}(op, \psi_{acc}(\mathtt{self}, (\mathtt{p}_1, \ldots, \mathtt{p}_n)) \wedge \varphi, \\ &\qquad \exists x.\ \mathrm{Acc}(x, \mathtt{r}) \rightarrow \varphi, \mathit{partial}, \mathtt{self}, (\mathtt{p}_1, \ldots, \mathtt{p}_n)) \end{aligned}$$

Note that this is the version of *PreservesInv* that *must* be used whenever encapsulation predicates are involved, that is when the formula is built over $\mathrm{Acc}(\Sigma)$. For all other proof obligations presented in this work, analogous starred versions can be derived. For convenience we maintain the un-starred versions to be used when no encapsulation predicate is in the considered formulae.

In order to prove the preservation of an (encapsulation) property $\varphi \in \mathrm{Term}^{\mathrm{Acc}(\Sigma)}$ for a method call `self.m(p);` (in an environment where no invariants and preconditions are specified) the following proof obligation is obtained:

$$\begin{aligned} &\exists x.\ \mathrm{Acc}(x, \mathtt{self}) \wedge \exists x.\ \mathrm{Acc}(x, \mathtt{p}) \wedge \varphi \\ &\qquad \rightarrow [\mathtt{r\ =\ self.m(p);}](\exists x.\ \mathrm{Acc}(x, \mathtt{r}) \rightarrow \varphi) \end{aligned}$$

**Example 8.1.** Let us take up the settings from Example 4.1. To class `Triangle`, we add a method `getPoint0()`. Our first attempt is to attach

to `getPoint0()` the implementation `return p0;`. This is however not acceptable since the caller references `p0` after `getPoint0()` returns, though the encapsulation specification requires unique access through the `Triangle` object.
Proof obligation template *PreservesInv**, instantiated as follows, is thus not valid:

$$\begin{aligned}\exists x.\ \mathrm{Acc}(x,\texttt{tria}) \wedge \forall t{:}\texttt{Triangle}.\ \mathrm{GuardObj}_x[x \doteq t](t.\texttt{p0})&\\ \rightarrow [\ \texttt{r = tria.getPoint0();}\ ]&\\ \exists x.\ \mathrm{Acc}(x,\texttt{r}) \rightarrow \forall t{:}\texttt{Triangle}.\ \mathrm{GuardObj}_x[x \doteq t](t.\texttt{p0})&\end{aligned}$$

If we change the implementation of `getPoint0()` to

```
return new Point(p0.getX(), p0.getY());
```

the above proof obligation is however, as desired, valid. *

## 8.2 Naive Deductive Approach

The two predicates defined in Sect. 4.2 must be axiomatised to deductively treat encapsulation predicates. Both, Acc and Reach predicates are challenging: Acc is beyond the original JavaDL expressibility if no set of fields is annotated and an open program is considered. For Reach a complete axiomatisation is impossible.

### The Acc Predicates

Let $\Sigma$ be a signature and $P$ a $\Sigma$-program, $t_0 \in \mathrm{Term}^{\Sigma}_{T_0}$, $t_1 \in \mathrm{Term}^{\Sigma}_{T_1}$. Moreover:

$$\mathrm{AccArr}\,[A]\,(t_0,t_1) := \begin{cases} \exists i{:}\textsc{Integer}.\ t_0\,[i] \doteq t_1 & \text{if } \texttt{[]} \in A \\ \text{false} & \text{otherwise} \end{cases}$$

The following axiomatisation of the Acc$[A]$ predicates is modularly sound:

$$\frac{\mathrm{AccArr}[A](t_0,t_1) \vee \bigvee_{\substack{a\in A\\ \tau(\mathrm{top}(t_0))\preceq\sigma(a)}} t_0.a \doteq t_1,\quad \Gamma \vdash \Delta}{\mathrm{Acc}[A](t_0,t_1),\quad \Gamma \vdash \Delta} \tag{8.1}$$

**Lemma 8.1.** Rules which are instances of Rule Scheme (8.1) are modularly sound.

*Proof.* Let $r \in \text{Rule}^{\Sigma}$ be an instance of (8.1) and $P$ a $\Sigma$-program. Let $s$ be a state and $\beta$ a variable assignment with

$$\text{val}_{s,P,\beta}(t_0) = e_0, \quad \text{val}_{s,P,\beta}(t_1) = e_1$$

The formula

$$\text{AccArr}[A](t_0, t_1) \lor \bigvee_{\substack{a \in A \\ \tau(\text{top}(t_0)) \preceq \sigma(a)}} t_0.a \doteq t_1$$

is modularly valid in core context $P$ if and only if one of these cases holds:

1. $s, \beta \models^{\emptyset}_{P} \bigvee_{\substack{a \in A \\ \tau(\text{top}(t_0)) \preceq \sigma(a)}} t_0.a \doteq t_1$. This holds iff for some field $a \in A$: $s, \beta \models^{\emptyset}_{P} t_0.a \doteq t_1$. This is true iff $e_0.a = \text{val}_{s,P,\beta}(t_0).a = \text{val}_{s,P,\beta}(t_1) = e_1$.
2. `[]` $\in A$ and $s, \beta \models \exists i.\ (t_0[i] \doteq y)$. This holds iff there is a $j$ with

   $$s, \beta^i_j \models x[i] \doteq y$$

   (We observe that $e_0 = val_s(t_0)$ must be an array since otherwise the value of this sub-formula would depend on expressions $ch(t_0[i])$ which cannot be evaluated further. Also, $0 \leq j < e_0$`.length` because otherwise $t_0[i]$ evaluated to $ch(t_0[i])$ and $s, \beta^i_j \models t_0[i] \doteq t_1$ did not hold.) So we have equivalently: $e_0[j] = \text{val}_{s,P,\beta}(t_0)[\text{val}_{s,P,\beta}(i)] = \text{val}_{s,P,\beta}(t_0[i]) = \text{val}_{s,P,\beta}(t_1) = e_1$.

By Def. 4.3 one of these cases holds iff $s, \beta \models^{\emptyset}_{P} \text{Acc}[A](t_0, t_1)$. □

## The other Acc Predicates

The predicate Acc (without a list of fields) can be soundly axiomatised for a fixed program context. We simply instantiate the above axiom with *all* fields of $P$. This axiomatisation is however *not* modularly sound. Consider the following classes:

```
class A { static A a;}
class B { static B b;}
```

```
class A2 extends A {
  private B b2;
  public static m() {
    a = new A2();
    a.b2 = B.b;
  }
}
```

Consider the core context $\{\texttt{A}, \texttt{B}\}$. Thus we get the following instantiation of the rule scheme; since there are no instance fields in `A` the disjunction in the premise is just false:

$$\frac{\text{false}, \Gamma \vdash \Delta}{\text{Acc}(a@(A), b@(B)), \Gamma \vdash \Delta}$$

The premise is thus valid in all contexts extending the core context. The conclusion is however not valid in the context $\{\texttt{A}, \texttt{B}, \texttt{A2}\}$. This shows the modular unsoundness of the rule scheme.

The same problem holds for the $\overline{\text{Acc}}[A]$ Predicates. We will deal with it in Sect. 8.3.

### The Reachable Predicate

The Reach predicate is axiomatised in a similar way as other attempts in the literature, for instance by Nelson [1983]. Basically it is the reflexive and transitive closure of Acc. The following axiomatisation is correct, that is, the following is a true statement for the Reach predicate:

$$\begin{aligned}\forall x{:}\texttt{Object}.\ \forall y{:}\text{ANY}.\ \forall n{:}\text{INTEGER}.\ \Big(&\text{Reach}[A](x,y)\\ \leftrightarrow \big(\ &(x \doteq y \wedge n \doteq 0)\\ &\vee \exists z{:}\texttt{Object}.\ (\text{Acc}[A](x,z) \wedge \text{Reach}[A](z,y,n-1))\big)\Big)\end{aligned} \tag{8.2}$$

$$\begin{aligned}\forall x{:}\texttt{Object}.\ \forall y{:}\text{ANY}.\ \forall n{:}\text{INTEGER}.\ \Big(&\text{Reach}[A](x,y,n)\\ \leftrightarrow \exists z{:}\texttt{Object}.\ \exists m{:}\text{INTEGER}.\ \big(\ &\text{Reach}[A](x,z,m)\\ &\wedge \text{Reach}[A](z,y,n-m)\big)\Big)\end{aligned} \tag{8.3}$$

It is well known that there is no complete axiomatisation of the transitive closure, and thus of Reach, in first order logic since the access graph may contain cycles and our domain is infinite [Baar, 2003]. That is there can be other predicates which satisfy the condition from above but which are not the Reach predicate. However, it seems that the above (incomplete) axiomatisation is sufficient for practical purposes.

The same axiomatisation can be done for the unparameterised version exactly the same way, except that Acc is used instead of Acc[$A$]. Note that this axiomatisation relies on the axiomatisation of the Acc predicates. Thus for the unparameterised version of Reach the same problems as for the unparameterised version of Acc arise.

## 8.3 Modular Treatment of Accessibility

The results on the axiomatisation of accessibility as described in the last section is not satisfactory. The reasons are that, with open programs, modular proofs are needed such that a given conjecture can be proven modularly valid as detailed in Sect. 6.4. The axiomatisation of Acc and $\overline{\text{Acc}}[A]$ as presented above does however refer to all types in the Java model and is thus not modularly sound.

A closer look at the proof obligations for encapsulation properties from Sect. 8.1 reveals that the involved sequents fortunately have a good-natured character: They deal with the *preservation* of properties (involving Acc) only. A typical sequent arising during a proof of an encapsulation property following the Enc pattern conducted *without* Axiom 8.1 looks roughly as follows:

$$\{u\}\,\text{Acc}(y_0, z_0), \Gamma \;\vdash\; \text{Acc}(y_0, z_0), \Delta$$

The succedent of the sequent originates from assuming the encapsulation property in the pre-state; since it was on the left side of an implication which was itself on the left side of the top level implication, it turns up in the succedent. The antecedent describes the post-state, syntactically expressed by an update $u$ applied to a formula with the non-rigid Acc predicate.

With this observation it can be concluded that it would already help a lot if Acc was modularly axiomatised for *state changes*, that is update applications.

In the following we will only discuss the $\overline{\text{Acc}}[A]$ predicate, though our primary focus is on Acc. It is however easy to see that Acc can be seen as abbreviation for $\overline{\text{Acc}}[\emptyset]$.

We only consider updates $u$ of the following *normalised* shape (for all $i = 1, \dots, n$):

$$\begin{aligned} u &:= u_1 | \dots | u_n \\ u_i &:= (\text{for } x^i_1, \dots, x^i_{m_i} \text{ ; } \varphi_i \text{ ; } u'_i) \\ u'_i &:= a_i(t^i_1, \dots, t^i_{k_i}) := t^i_0 \end{aligned}$$

Rümmer [2005] shows that this shape can always be achieved from an arbitrary update.

Our first type of update simplification rule 'moves' updates which cannot influence $\overline{\text{Acc}}[A](r_0, r_1)$ (since they modify locations $a \in A$) 'behind' the predicate (where $u$ is an update and $r_0$, $r_1$ are terms):

$$\frac{\{\bar{v}\}\overline{\text{Acc}}[A](\{v\}r_0, \{v\}r_1), \Gamma \vdash \Delta}{\{u\}\overline{\text{Acc}}[A](r_0, r_1), \Gamma \vdash \Delta} \qquad \frac{\Gamma \vdash \{\bar{v}\}\overline{\text{Acc}}[A](\{v\}r_0, \{v\}r_1), \Delta}{\Gamma \vdash \{u\}\overline{\text{Acc}}[A](r_0, r_1), \Delta} \tag{8.4}$$

where $v$ is the subsequence of $u$ with $v'_i = l := t^i_0$ and $\text{top}(l) \in A$ and $\bar{v}$ is the subsequence which complements $v$ to $u$.

Now we introduce a function $F$ which maps a term $\{u\}\overline{\text{Acc}}[A](r_0, r_1)$ to a term $F(\{u\}\overline{\text{Acc}}[A](y, z))$ (where again $u$ is an update and $r_0$, $r_1$ are terms). The intention is to obtain the following sound rules:

$$\frac{F(\{u\}\overline{\text{Acc}}[A](r_0, r_1)), \Gamma \vdash \Delta}{\{u\}\overline{\text{Acc}}[A](r_0, r_1), \Gamma \vdash \Delta} \qquad \frac{\Gamma \vdash F(\{u\}\overline{\text{Acc}}[A](r_0, r_1)), \Delta}{\Gamma \vdash \{u\}\overline{\text{Acc}}[A](r_0, r_1), \Delta}$$

Let $u$ be an update of the normalised shape with $u'_i = (l^i := t^i_0)$ , $A_0 = \{\text{top}(l^i) \mid i = 1, \dots, n\}$ (for $i = 1, \dots, n$), and $A \cap A_0 = \emptyset$. This form can be obtained by applying rule (8.4). Moreover we require that no clashes occur between the elements, this can be achieved (as a necessary condition) by requiring that all top level symbols $\text{top}(l^i)$ of left hand sides are distinct. We define:

$$F(t) := \left( \begin{array}{l} \quad (\exists x^n_1 : T^n_1 . \;\cdots \exists x^n_{m_n} : T^n_{m_n} . \; (\varphi_n \wedge t^n_1 \doteq \{u\}r_0 \wedge t^n_0 \doteq \{u\}r_1)) \\ \qquad\qquad\qquad\qquad \vdots \\ \vee \; (\exists x^1_1 : T^1_1 . \;\cdots \exists x^1_{m_1} : T^1_{m_1} . \; (\varphi_1 \wedge t^1_1 \doteq \{u\}r_0 \wedge t^1_0 \doteq \{u\}r_1)) \\ \vee \; \overline{\text{Acc}}[A \cup A_0](\{u\}r_0, \{u\}r_1) \end{array} \right)$$

**Lemma 8.2.** The following rules are modularly sound for normalised updates $u$ with $u'_i = (l^i := t^i_0)$ (for $i = 1, \dots, n$), $A_0 = \{\text{top}(l^i) \mid i = 1, \dots, n\}$, and $A \cap A_0 = \emptyset$:

$$\frac{F(\{u\}\overline{\mathrm{Acc}}[A](y,z)), \Gamma \vdash \Delta}{\{u\}\overline{\mathrm{Acc}}[A](y,z), \Gamma \vdash \Delta} \qquad \frac{\Gamma \vdash F(\{u\}\overline{\mathrm{Acc}}[A](y,z)), \Delta}{\Gamma \vdash \{u\}\overline{\mathrm{Acc}}[A](y,z), \Delta}$$

*Proof.* For simplicity we assume that the only possibility to access an object from another is via an instance field access. Array accesses can be treated in the analogous way.

Let $\Sigma$ be a signature and $P$ be a $\Sigma$-program. Let $s$ be an arbitrary state and $\beta$ a variable assignment. Let $s' = \rho_u(s)$.

We show the equivalence of $\{u\}\overline{\mathrm{Acc}}[A](y,z)$ and $F(\{u\}\overline{\mathrm{Acc}}[A](y,z))$ *for an elementary update* $u = t'.a := t_0$ under the assumption that $a' \notin A$:

$$\begin{aligned}
& s, \beta \models_P^{\emptyset} (t' \doteq \{u\}r_0 \wedge t_0 \doteq \{u\}r_1) \vee \overline{\mathrm{Acc}}[A \cup \{a\}](\{u\}r_0, \{u\}r_1) \\
&\quad \Leftrightarrow (\mathrm{val}_{s,P,\beta}(t') = \mathrm{val}_{s',P,\beta}(r_0) \text{ and } \mathrm{val}_{s,P,\beta}(t_0) = \mathrm{val}_{s',P,\beta}(r_1)) \\
&\qquad \text{or exists } b \notin A \cup \{a\} \text{ with: } b^s(\mathrm{val}_{s',P,\beta}(r_0)) = \mathrm{val}_{s',P,\beta}(r_1) \\
&\quad \Leftrightarrow \text{exists } b \notin A \text{ with:} \\
&\qquad \text{if not } (\mathrm{val}_{s,P,\beta}(t') = \mathrm{val}_{s',P,\beta}(r_0),\ \mathrm{val}_{s,P,\beta}(t_0) = \mathrm{val}_{s',P,\beta}(r_1), \text{ and } a = b) \\
&\qquad \text{then } b^s(\mathrm{val}_{s',P,\beta}(r_0)) = \mathrm{val}_{s',P,\beta}(r_1) \\
&\quad \Leftrightarrow \text{exists } b \notin A \text{ with } b^{s'}(\mathrm{val}_{s',P,\beta}(r_0)) = \mathrm{val}_{s',P,\beta}(r_1) \\
&\quad \Leftrightarrow \mathrm{val}_{s',P,\beta}(r_0) \text{ accesses } \mathrm{val}_{s',P,\beta}(r_1) \text{ by field access not in } A \\
&\quad \Leftrightarrow (\mathrm{val}_{s',P,\beta}(r_0), \mathrm{val}_{s',P,\beta}(r_1)) \in \overline{\mathrm{Acc}}[A]^{s'} \\
&\quad \Leftrightarrow s, \beta \models_P^{\emptyset} \{u\}\overline{\mathrm{Acc}}[A](r_0, r_1) \qquad \square
\end{aligned}$$

## 8.4 Static Analysis Techniques

Sect. 4.1.2 already mentioned static analysis techniques called *alias control policies* and the encapsulation properties they check. Though encapsulation predicates provide a more general framework than these rather specialised properties, the use of deductive verification to prove properties expressed by means of encapsulation predicates has a major disadvantage compared to the static analysis techniques employed for *alias control*: In general, deduction requires user interaction, which is especially in the case of treating Reach non-trivial, while the techniques to prove *alias control* properties are usually fully automated static analyses. Non-trivial automated techniques can nevertheless be used even in the general setting of encapsulation predicates as mentioned in Roth [2005] and worked out in Weiß [2006]. We briefly present the results of the latter here and relate them to our needs.

We introduce yet another encapsulation predicate, Univ, which serves only the purpose of more adequately model the Universe approach. The Universe alias control policy [Müller, 2002, Müller and Poetzsch-Heffter, 2001] has already been discussed in Sect. 4.3.4. Its main characteristics are that it allows to declare variables with three kind of annotations: `rep`, `peer` (which is the default annotation), and `readonly`. The intention is that all objects referenced through a `rep` variable can only be modified by the owner of the object, which is the object which holds the `rep` reference. This restriction extends to objects reachable via `peer`. References through a `readonly` annotated variable are however always allowed. In the original type system it is however not allowed to make modifications by means of such a reference. The check for these conditions, given a complete annotation of all variable declarations, is done completely automatically.

Compared to the other encapsulation predicates the particularity of Univ is that there are three lists of fields needed in this predicate. Each represents one of the Universe modifiers `rep` (the set is called *Rep*), `peer` (*Peer*), and `readonly` (*Friend*). It is defined as follows:

$$\begin{aligned}\mathrm{Univ}[\mathit{Rep};\mathit{Peer};\mathit{Friend}] :\Leftrightarrow\ & \forall g.\ \forall z.\ (\mathrm{Own}[\mathit{Rep};\mathit{Peer}](g,z)( \\ & \quad \to (\ \forall y_0.\ \neg\mathrm{Acc}[\mathit{Rep} \cup \mathit{Peer} \cup \mathit{Friend}](y_0,z) \\ & \qquad \wedge \forall y_1.\ (\mathrm{Acc}[\mathit{Rep}](y_1,z) \to y_1 \doteq g)))\end{aligned}$$

$$\mathrm{Own}[\mathit{Rep};\mathit{Peer}](g,z) :\Leftrightarrow\ \exists u.\ \big(\mathrm{Acc}[\mathit{Rep}](g,u) \wedge \mathrm{Conn}[\mathit{Peer}](u,z)\big)$$

The first line states the situation which is to be described in more detail: $g$ owns $z$; here ownership means that there is an access from $g$ via a `rep` field into the owned context (to an object $u$) and there is a connection from that object via `peer` references to $z$. If there is such an ownership relation between $g$ and $z$ then we require that if there is an access to such a $z$, then this is done via a `rep` or a `readonly` reference; if it is a `rep` reference then it is held by the owner. This is described by the second and third lines: No accesses are allowed via references not described by one of the sets and accesses via `rep` are only allowed from $g$.

The predicate Univ has the following properties:

1. A property like

$$\mathrm{Univ}[\mathit{Rep};\mathit{Peer};\mathit{Friend}] \to [\alpha]\,\mathrm{Univ}[\mathit{Rep};\mathit{Peer};\mathit{Friend}]$$

can be checked automatically with the help of the Universe type system.

2. It formalises an encapsulation property strong enough to protect invariants as detailed in Sect. 9.

Weiß [2006] deals in detail with item 1. The type annotations as partially fixed by the sets *Rep*, *Peer*, and *Friend* are completed such that all variable declarations in the program reachable by $\alpha$ are annotated and these annotations make the program comply with the Universe type rules. The completion works completely automatically by imposing constraints and solving them. Weiß [2006] proves that each program state is well-formed with respect to the annotations if and only if $\mathrm{Univ}[\mathit{Rep}; \mathit{Peer}; \mathit{Friend}]$ holds. This result justifies the soundness of the following rule:

$$\frac{\Gamma, \mathrm{Univ}[\mathit{Rep}; \mathit{Peer}; \mathit{Friend}] \ \vdash \ \mathit{RESULT}, [\alpha]\,\mathrm{Univ}[\mathit{Rep}; \mathit{Peer}; \mathit{Friend}], \Delta}{\Gamma, \mathrm{Univ}[\mathit{Rep}; \mathit{Peer}; \mathit{Friend}] \ \vdash \ [\alpha]\,\mathrm{Univ}[\mathit{Rep}; \mathit{Peer}; \mathit{Friend}], \Delta}$$

where $\mathit{RESULT}$ is

- true if the sketched procedure finds a set of annotation which satisfies the Universe type rules or
- false otherwise.

In the latter case nothing is lost: one can try to discharge the goal with purely deductive means.

So we have to show that this property is really useful for our purposes. While we will see the requirements in the next chapter, we provide some work already here.

Let $G_{\mathit{Rep}}$ and $G_{\mathit{Friend}}$ be two mutually disjoint sets of classes from a program $P$. Let further be *Rep* a subset of the fields of $G_{\mathit{Rep}}$ and *Friend* a subset of the fields in $G_{\mathit{Friend}}$. Let $g$ be a term of a type of $G_{\mathit{Rep}}$. Then the validity of $\mathrm{Univ}[\mathit{Rep}; \mathit{Peer}; \mathit{Friend}]$ implies the validity of

$$\mathrm{Enc}_{y,z}\left[\bigvee_{T \in G_{\mathit{Rep}} \cup G_{\mathit{Friend}}} \mathrm{InstanceOf}_T(y),\ \exists u.(\mathrm{Acc}[\mathit{Rep}](g,u) \wedge \mathrm{Conn}[\mathit{Peer}](u,z))\right]$$

We are later interested in general properties

$$\mathrm{Enc}_{y,z}\left[\bigvee_{T \in G} \mathrm{InstanceOf}_T(y), \quad p(z)\right] \tag{8.5}$$

We have in fact proven this formula (8.5) if

- we can prove $\forall z. \ (p(z) \to \exists u.(\text{Acc}[\mathit{Rep}](g, u) \wedge \text{Conn}[\mathit{Peer}](u, z)))$,
- $G = G_{\mathit{Rep}} \cup G_{\mathit{Friend}}$, and
- $\text{Univ}[\mathit{Rep}; \mathit{Peer}; \mathit{Friend}]$ can be shown for legal choices of *Rep*, *Peer*, and *Friend*.

## 8.5 Summary

In this chapter we have investigated how encapsulation predicates can be verified. Proof obligations needed to be adapted specially to cope with these predicates in order to reflect the fact that callers may reference parameters and return values. Then we looked at how calculi would treat encapsulation predicates. A naive version axiomatised the basic predicates for a closed world assumption. An advanced version took a more modular approach but specified the Acc predicate under state changes, which seems sufficient for our proof obligations. Finally we have discussed how static procedures like alias control policies can be exploited for encapsulation predicates.

In Sect. 9.3.3 we make use of the proof obligation patterns presented here.

# 9 Modular Verification of Call Correctness

Sed quis custodiet ipsos custodes?

*(Juvenal)*

This chapter resumes the discussion of proof obligations from Chapter 7. Still we are only considering observed-state call correctness of closed programs, but are taking a crucial step towards a more modular way of verification. Moreover the system of proof obligations presented now is more precise than the one presented in that chapter because it classifies *more* call correct programs as correct.

In Chapter 7, we needed to take into account *all* pairs of operations and invariants, which led to an explosion of proof obligations. Although we presented a technique which alleviated this by easily discharging many irrelevant invariants, the principal problem was not solved.

Our strategy is now to analyse specifications and exploit additional information we get from this analysis. With them, invariants themselves reveal that *only* certain types are *relevant* to them, we say that they are *guarded* by these classes.

More precisely, our analysis delivers a *depends clause* for an invariant $\varphi$. It specifies those locations for which special care must be taken, so that no invariant-invalidating modifications can be performed. We provide two possibilities of 'taking care' of a depends clause element $d$: Either

- the location described by $d$ is controlled by an object which adheres to $\varphi$, or
- there is a set of objects which are in control of the location described by $d$ and these objects can only be accessed from the outside of this set through *guard* objects. Furthermore, the guard objects adhere to $\varphi$.

**Overview.** We start with the analysis of specifications, with the result of finding depends clauses for the invariants of a specification. Constraints on these depends clauses are discussed in Sects. 9.2 and 9.3; each section is devoted to one of the approaches described above. In Sect. 9.4 these approaches are combined and a system of proof obligations is defined which ensures durable correctness.

## 9.1 Analysis of Dependencies in Specifications

In contrast to other approaches for modular verification, we do not impose any a priori restriction on programs or specifications. Instead we let the developer write arbitrary specifications and programs, and then *analyse* the specification for possible drawbacks on needed encapsulation properties. The analysis gives rise to a number of proof obligations which are then discharged together with the proof obligations for functional correctness and encapsulation. Parts of this analysis are described in Roth and Schmitt [2004].

In this section we develop an analysis instrument (*depends clause*) for invariants which helps us to determine how invariants must be protected against undesired modifications of their values. Depends clauses consist of descriptions of locations using location terms. They specify at least those locations which, if they all remain unchanged by a state change, make an invariant, that is a JavaFOL formula, remain unchanged in its truth value (w.r.t. the state change), too. In the next sections this property is exploited in the sense that these locations are insulated from parts of the system which preservation of invariants is not proven for.

### 9.1.1 Depends Clauses

Depends clauses are the main vehicle to determine how invariants must be protected against undesired modifications. They are finite subsets of $\text{LocTerm}^{\Sigma}$. Remember from Def. 2.9 that these are extended terms with a field or array access as top-level operator. If the evaluations of all these location terms remain unchanged in two different states, then the evaluation of an invariant in these two states remains the same, too. Or the other way round, for any state change in which the evaluation of the invariant changes, one of the elements of the depends clause must be evaluated differently in the two states.

There is also a syntactical condition on the location terms $t$ contained in depends clauses: They must be in prenex normal form. This is to easily transform these extended terms into formulae; the guards and quantified variables can then more easily be read off.

**Definition 9.1.** A *(query-free) depends clause* of a JavaFOL formula $\varphi \in \mathrm{Fma}^\Sigma$ in the context of a $\Sigma$-program $P$ is a finite set $D_\varphi \subseteq \mathrm{LocTerm}^\Sigma$ of extended terms in prenex normal form which do not contain dynamically bound query symbols and for which the following property holds for all states $s_1$ and $s_2$: If, for all $(f,(e_1,\ldots,e_n)) \in \mathrm{Loc}_{s_1,P,\beta}(D_\varphi)$, $f^{s_1,P}(e_1,\ldots,e_n) = f^{s_2,P}(e_1,\ldots,e_n)$ then

$$(s_1 \models_P \varphi \text{ iff } s_2 \models_P \varphi)$$

There are interesting structural similarities to the definition of assignable clauses (Def. 3.5). Both times we are interested in sets of locations described by location terms. While we analysed method bodies in the case of assignable clauses, we are now analysing formulae. While we were in the former case interested in locations which are the only relevant for a piece of program to be evaluated differently in two states, we are now interested in locations which are the only relevant ones for the valuation of a formulae to change in two different interpretations.

*Note:* Until Sect. 10.4 we forbid the occurrence of dynamically bound (that is, non-static and non-private) query symbols in depends clauses. This is why we have added *query-free* to the definition. Queries complicate things as also discussed in Sect. 9.1.4. Anyway, until Sect. 10.4 we refer to query-free depends clauses simply as *depends clauses.*

Arbitrary suffixes of the elements of a depends clause which have the shape $*.a_1.\ldots.a_n$ still form a depends clause.

**Lemma 9.1.** If $D$ is a depends clause for $\varphi$ and $*.a_1.\cdots.a_n \in D$ then

$$D \backslash \{*.a_1.\cdots.a_n\} \cup \{*.a_j.\cdots.a_n\}$$

is a depends clause for $\varphi$ for some $1 < j \leq n$.

*Proof.* We use the abbreviations: $d_1 := *.a_1.\ldots.a_{j-1}$, $d_2 := *.a_j.\cdots.a_n$, and $D' := D\backslash\{*.a_1.\cdots.a_n\} \cup \{d_2\}$. Assume $g^{s_1}(e'_1,\ldots,e'_{n'}) = g^{s_2}(e'_1,\ldots,e'_{n'})$ for all $(g,(e'_1,\ldots,e'_{n'})) \in \mathrm{Loc}_{s_1,\beta}(D')$.

- If $g = a_n$, then in particular

$$a_n^{s_1}(e'_1) = a_n^{s_2}(e'_1) \text{ for all } e'_1 \in \{(a_{n-1}^{s_1}(\cdots(a_j^{s_1}(e))\cdots)) \mid e \in \mathrm{Dom}(\sigma(a_j))\}$$

Hence:

$$a_n^{s_1}(e'_1) = a_n^{s_2}(e'_1) \text{ for all } e'_1 \in \{(a_{n-1}^{s_1}(\cdots(a_1^{s_1}(e))\cdots)) \mid e \in \mathrm{Dom}(\sigma(a_1))\}$$

Thus: $a_n^{s_1}(e'_1) = a_n^{s_2}(e'_1)$ for all $(a_n, (e'_1)) \in \mathrm{Loc}_{s_1,\beta}(D)$
- If $g \neq a_n$ then $(g, (e'_1, \ldots, e'_{n'})) \in \mathrm{Loc}_{s_1,\beta}(D)$.

Since $D$ is a depends clause, $d_1 d_2 \in D$, and $g^{s_1}(e'_1, \ldots, e'_{n'}) = g^{s_2}(e'_1, \ldots, e'_{n'})$ for all $(g, (e'_1, \ldots, e'_{n'})) \in \mathrm{Loc}_{s_1,\beta}(D)$, it follows $\left(s_1 \models_P \varphi \text{ iff } s_2 \models_P \varphi\right)$ □

**Example 9.1.** Coming back to Ex. 1.1, the set

$$D = \left\{ \begin{array}{c} *_{\texttt{Period}}.\texttt{<created>}, *.\texttt{start}, *.\texttt{end}, *.\texttt{start.year}, \\ *.\texttt{end.year}, *.\texttt{start.month}, *.\texttt{end.month}, \\ *.\texttt{start.month.val}, *.\texttt{end.month.val} \end{array} \right\}$$

is a depends clause of $\varphi_{\texttt{Period}}$. Because of Lemma 9.1,

$$D' = \{*_{\texttt{Period}}.\texttt{<created>}, *.\texttt{start}, *.\texttt{end}, *.\texttt{year}, *.\texttt{month}, *.\texttt{val}\}$$

is as well a depends clause of $\varphi_{\texttt{Period}}$. We will see in the rest of this chapter that despite its brevity $D'$ is not a good depends clause; instead we will appreciate depends clauses which have 'chains' that all start in the same type. *

The last example has shown that for the recurring pattern of depends clause elements $*.a_1 \cdots .a_n$ often all 'prefixes' $*.a_1 \cdots .a_j$ $(j = 1, \ldots, n)$ are needed as well. Therefore we aim to introduce a shorthand notation, which for the instance of an extended term $*.a_1 \cdots .a_n$ makes $\mathrm{Exp}(*.a_1 \cdots .a_n)$ designate the set $\{*.a_1 \cdots .a_j \mid j = 2, \ldots, n\}$. Since we want to include array accesses as well, we define slightly more general:

**Definition 9.2.**

1. The subset $\mathrm{WFLocTerm}^\Sigma \subseteq \mathrm{LocTerm}^\Sigma$ of extended terms is defined as

a set containing only extended terms of the following shape:

$$(\text{for } x : T, x_1, \ldots, x_n \; ; \varphi \; ; f_m(f_{m-1}(\cdots(f_1(x), \ldots), \ldots), \ldots)) \tag{9.1}$$

$$(\text{for } x_1, \ldots, x_n \; ; \varphi \; ; f_m(f_{m-1}(\cdots(f_1(t'), \ldots), \ldots), \ldots)) \tag{9.2}$$

$$\begin{aligned}&(\text{for } x : T, x' : T', x_1, \ldots, x_n \; ; \\ &\text{Reach}(g_\ell(g_{\ell-1}(\cdots(g_1(x), \ldots), \ldots), \ldots), x') \wedge \varphi \; ; \\ &\qquad f_m(f_{m-1}(\cdots(f_1(x'), \ldots), \ldots), \ldots))\end{aligned} \tag{9.3}$$

where $x_1, \ldots, x_n$ are logical variables of type INTEGER, $x$ a logical variable of type $T$, $t'$ a static field symbol, and $f_i$ $(i = 1, \ldots, m)$ and $g_j$ $(j = 1, \ldots, \ell)$ instance field or array access symbols.

2. The *start type* $\text{ST}(t)$ of an extended term $t \in \text{WFLocTerm}^\Sigma$ is defined as $T$ if $t$ has shape (9.1) or (9.3). It is the type where the static variable $t'$ is defined if $t$ has shape (9.2).
   For sets $D \subseteq \text{WFLocTerm}^\Sigma$: $\text{ST}(D) = \{ST(t) \mid t \in D\}$
3. Let be $t \in \text{WFLocTerm}^\Sigma$. If $t$ is of the shape (9.1), then we denote with $\text{Exp}(t)$ the set

   $$\{(\text{for } x{:}T, x_1, \ldots, x_n \,; \varphi \,; f_j(f_{j-1}(\cdots(f_1(x), \ldots), \ldots), \ldots)) \mid j = 2, \ldots, m\}$$

   If $t$ is of the shape (9.2), then $\text{Exp}(t)$ is defined as:

   $$\{(\text{for } x_1, \ldots, x_n \; ; \varphi \; ; f_j(f_{j-1}(\cdots(f_1(t'), \ldots), \ldots), \ldots)) \mid j = 2, \ldots, m\}$$

   If $t$ is of the shape (9.3), then $\text{Exp}(t)$ is:

   $$\begin{aligned}&\{(\text{for } x : T, x' : T', x_1, \ldots, x_n \; ; \\ &\qquad \text{Reach}[A](g_\ell(g_{\ell-1}(\cdots(g_1(x), \ldots), \ldots), \ldots), x') \wedge \varphi \; ; \\ &\qquad\quad f_j(f_{j-1}(\cdots(f_1(x'), \ldots), \ldots), \ldots) \mid j = 1, \ldots, m)\} \\ \cup\; &\{(\text{for } x : T, x' : T', x_1, \ldots, x_n \; ; \\ &\quad \text{Reach}[A](g_\ell(g_{\ell-1}(\cdots(g_1(x), \ldots), \ldots), \ldots), x') \wedge \varphi \; ; x'.a \mid a \in A)\} \\ \cup\; &\{(\text{for } x : T, x' : T', x_1, \ldots, x_n \; ; \varphi \; ; g_j(g_{j-1}(\cdots(g_1(x), \ldots), \ldots), \ldots)) \\ &\qquad\qquad \mid j = 2, \ldots \ell\}\end{aligned}$$

   The domain of Exp is extended to sets $D \subseteq \text{WFLocTerm}^\Sigma$ :

   $$\text{Exp}(D) := \bigcup_{d \in D} \text{Exp}(d)$$

For a reason which will be seen in the next section, we sieve out $f_1(t')$ (and $g_1(x)$, resp.).

**Example 9.2.** In Ex. 9.1, $D$ can alternatively be written as

$$\begin{aligned} D = \; & \mathrm{Exp}(\{\, *\texttt{.start.month.val}, *\texttt{.end.month.val}, \\ & \qquad\qquad\qquad *\texttt{.start.year}, *\texttt{.end.year})\} \\ \cup \; & \{*\texttt{.start}, *\texttt{.end}, *_{\texttt{Period}}\texttt{.<created>}\} \end{aligned}$$

$*$

Later (Sect. 9.3.3), we will restrict attention to depends clauses which are finite subsets of $\mathrm{WFLocTerm}^{\Sigma}$ and which are constructed (or can be constructed) via Exp.

Before we investigate how we obtain depends clauses from an invariant, we state the following obvious lemma:

**Lemma 9.2.** Every super set of a depends clause is still a depends clause.

*Proof.* Trivial, since we only specify elements which *must* be elements of a depends clause. □

## 9.1.2 Syntactical Criteria for Depends Clauses

In the majority of cases it is quite easily possible to determine depends clauses of invariants simply by 'reading off' terms. Consider Ex. 9.1. The depends clause of the invariant of `Period` exactly corresponds to the terms of maximal length occurring in the formula representing the invariant. Only the references to the arbitrary `Period` object must be replaced by '$*$'.

For the general case we make use of a function Dep. During the definition we take a set of logical variables $V$ into consideration. This will matter only when we refine the function below. For a first account, $V$ can be considered as the empty set.

**Definition 9.3.** The set $\mathrm{Dep}(\varphi)$ of terms for $\varphi \in \mathrm{Fma}^{\Sigma} \cup \mathrm{Term}^{\Sigma}$ is the set of all subterms of $\varphi$ which are of the shape $f(t_1, \ldots, t_n)$ with terms $t_1, \ldots, t_n$ where $f \in \mathcal{F}^{nr}$.

The following lemma says that the set of location terms delivered by Dep is in fact, after transforming it into prenex normal form, a depends clause.

**Lemma 9.3.** Let $\varphi \in \mathrm{Fma}^{\Sigma}$ be a closed formula without occurrences of other non-rigid function or predicate symbols than field and array access symbols. If $D' = \mathrm{Dep}(\varphi)$ and $D$ is a prenex normal form of $D'$, then $D$ is a depends clause of $\varphi$ in $P$.

*Proof.* Assume two states $s_1$ and $s_2$ with $s_1 \models_P \varphi$ but not $s_2 \models_P$. Furthermore we assume for all $t \in \mathrm{Dep}(\varphi)$: $\mathrm{val}_{s_1,P,\beta}(t) = \mathrm{val}_{s_2,P,\beta}(t)$ for all $\beta$. Since we have disallowed non-rigid predicates, there is a subformula of $\varphi$ of the shape $p(t_1, \ldots, t_n)$ where $p$ is a predicate or the equality symbol and $t_1, \ldots, t_n$ are terms and $\mathrm{val}_{s_1,P,\beta}(t_i) \neq \mathrm{val}_{s_2,P,\beta}(t_i)$ for at least one $i \in \{1, \ldots, n\}$.

In contradiction to this we have (by induction on the construction of terms) for all subterms $t$ of $\varphi$: $\mathrm{val}_{s_1,P,\beta}(t) = \mathrm{val}_{s_2,P,\beta}(t)$ since if the top-level function symbol is rigid this property holds trivially and otherwise our assumptions applies. In case of logical variables we use the fact that we use the same $\beta$. Thus the assumption $s_1 \models_P \varphi$ and not $s_2 \models_P$ cannot be true and the prenex normal form of the set consisting of all subterms with non-rigid function symbols is a depends clause of $\varphi$. □

The depends clauses $\mathrm{Dep}(\varphi)$ satisfy the property $\mathrm{Exp}(D) \subseteq D$.

The following example shows up that depends clauses derived by Dep are not always the best way to go.

**Example 9.3.** Consider the formula

$$\forall x.\ (x = \mathtt{a.b} \rightarrow x\mathtt{.c} > 0)$$

Suppose a is a static variable symbol, and b and c are instance field symbols. Note, that this formula is equivalent to a.b.c $> 0$. Dep from above would find the following depends clause:

$$\{*\mathtt{.c}, \mathtt{a.b}, \mathtt{a}\}$$

In fact $\{\mathtt{a.b.c}, \mathtt{a.b}, \mathtt{a}\}$ is as well a depends clause, which can easily be seen by considering the equivalent formulation. Moreover we will see later that depends clauses with 'longer' elements open up more possibilities to protect the invariant. *

**Example 9.4.** The invariant $\varphi_{\mathtt{Period}}$ of our running example is assigned the following depends clause $\mathrm{Dep}(\varphi_{\mathtt{Period}})$:

$$\begin{aligned}\mathrm{Dep}(\varphi_{\mathtt{Period}}) = \mathrm{Exp}(\{ & *\mathtt{.start.month.val}, *\mathtt{.end.month.val},\\ & *\mathtt{.start.year}, *\mathtt{.end.year}\})\\ \cup \{ & *\mathtt{.start}, *\mathtt{.end}, *_{\mathtt{Period}}\mathtt{.<created>}\}\end{aligned}$$

To improve the performance of Dep we can take into consideration special patterns of formulae. Consider for instance a formula of the shape

$$\forall x{:}T.\ (\mathrm{Reach}[A](t,x) \rightarrow \varphi(x))$$

We claim that the following set is a depends clause:

$$\begin{aligned} &\{(\text{for } x : T\ ;\ \mathrm{Reach}[A](t,x)\ ;\ t') \mid t' \in \mathrm{Dep}_{\{x\}}(\varphi(x))\} \\ \cup\ &\{(\text{for } x : T\ ;\ \mathrm{Reach}[A](t,x)\ ;\ x.a) \mid \text{for instance fields } a \in A\} \\ \cup\ &\{(\text{for } x : T\ ;\ \mathrm{Reach}[A](t,x)\ ;\ x\texttt{[}*\texttt{]}) \mid \text{for all } \texttt{[]} \in A\} \end{aligned} \quad (9.4)$$

Note that we employed Dep parameterised with a set of variables which makes the analysis more thorough. We justify our claim as follows:

$$s_1, \beta \models_P \forall x{:}T.\ (\mathrm{Reach}[A](t,x) \rightarrow \varphi(x)) \quad (9.5)$$

*iff* for all objects $e_n \in \mathrm{Dom}(T)$ and $e_1, \ldots, e_{n-1} \in \mathrm{Dom}(\texttt{Object})$ and $e_1 = \mathrm{val}_{s_1,P,\beta}(t')$ and $(e_i, e_{i+1}) \in \mathrm{Acc}[A]^{s_1,P}$ for all $i = 1, \ldots, n-1$: $s_1, \beta_x^{e_n} \models_P \varphi$. Because of the second and third line of our depends clause, for all $a \in A$ and all suitable objects $e$: $a^{s_1,P}(e) = a^{s_2,P}(e)$. Thus also $\mathrm{Acc}[A]^{s_1,P} = \mathrm{Acc}[A]^{s_2,P}$. Because of the inductive argument as in the proof above and the first line of the depends clause: ($s_1, \beta_x^{e_n} \models_P \varphi$ iff $s_2, \beta_x^{e_n} \models_P \varphi$) and $e_1 = \mathrm{val}_{s_2,P,\beta}(t')$. Thus (9.5) holds if and only if for all objects $e_n \in \mathrm{Dom}(T)$ and $e_1, \ldots, e_{n-1} \in \mathrm{Dom}(\texttt{Object})$ and $e_1 = \mathrm{val}_{s_2,P,\beta}(t')$ and $(e_i, e_{i+1}) \in \mathrm{Acc}[A]^{s_2,P}$ for all $i = 1, \ldots, n-1$: $s_2, \beta_x^{e_n} \models_P \varphi$. And thus it is equivalent to

$$s_2, \beta \models_P \forall x{:}T.\ (\mathrm{Reach}[A](t,x) \rightarrow \varphi(x))$$

The construction of Dep can thus be extended to consider in the case $t = \forall x{:}T.\ \varphi$ the special shape (9.5). It then delivers the depends clause described by (9.4).

It would be possible to identify more specification patterns with special depends clauses as in the example above. This could for instance be coupled with automatically generated specifications for design patterns and idioms [Ahrendt et al., 2005a].

## 9.1.3 Proofs of Depends Clauses

In spite of the syntactical criteria from above, it can be in general a task for a user of our system to find a depends clause, if tricky invariants are investigated as Ex. 9.3 demonstrated.

In this scenario, a user suggests a set of location terms and the system provides a proof obligation to prove the suggestion to be a depends clause. It is the only one throughout this work where no program is involved, instead only the relation between invariant and depends clause is investigated. Roth [2006] contains a number of other such *horizontal* proof obligations.

The idea of the proof obligation for depends clauses is as follows. Given a formula $\varphi$ which $D_\varphi$ is a presumed depends clause for. Let us assume that $\varphi$ is valid. Our goal is to establish the validity of $\varphi$ after a state change of which all but the locations described in $D_\varphi$ are updated to unknown values. The locations described by $D_\varphi$, however, are assigned their original values before the state change. The anonymous state change is expressed by means of an anonymous update (Def. 2.12).

As notational helper we introduce a function $u_{\mathrm{id}}$ which delivers, for an extended term $t$ in prenex normal form, an update which updates the location described by $t$ to the value of $t$. Clearly this update is *per se* effectless. If we however apply the function pre (Def. 7.1) on it, the update updates to previous values. $u_{\mathrm{id}}$ is defined as follows:

$$u_{\mathrm{id}}(\text{for } x_1 : T_1, \ldots, x_n : T_n \; ; \varphi \; ; d') = (\text{for } x_1 : T_1, \ldots, x_n : T_n \; ; \varphi \; ; d' := d')$$

Further on sets $\{d_1, \ldots, d_m\}$ of extended terms in prenex normal form:

$$u_{\mathrm{id}}(\{d_1, \ldots, d_m\}) = u_{\mathrm{id}}(d_1)| \cdots |u_{\mathrm{id}}(d_m)$$

**Proof Obligation Template:** *CorrectDepends*$(\{d_1, \ldots, d_m\}, \varphi)$ .
for $d_1, \ldots, d_m$ extended terms in prenex normal form and $\varphi \in \mathrm{Fma}^\Sigma$

$$\mathrm{Def}(F^{@pre}) \wedge \varphi \rightarrow \{*\}\{u\}\varphi$$

where $\mathrm{pre}(u_{\mathrm{id}}(\{d_1, \ldots, d_m\})) = (u, F^{@pre})$ and $*$ is an anonymous update not occurring in $\varphi$.

**Lemma 9.4.** Let $\Sigma$ be a signature and $P$ a $\Sigma$-program.

$$\models_P \mathit{CorrectDepends}(\{d_1, \ldots, d_m\}, \varphi)$$

implies that $\{d_1, \ldots, d_m\}$ is a depends clause of $\varphi$ in $P$.

*Proof.* Set $u$ as in the lemma. Let $D = \{d_1, \ldots, d_m\} \subseteq \mathrm{ExtTerm}^\Sigma$ be a set of extended terms in prenex normal form. Let $s_1, s_2$ be two states for

which we assume that for all locations $l = (f, (e_1, \ldots, e_n)) \in \mathrm{Loc}_{s_1,\beta}(D)$: $f^{s_1,P}(e_1, \ldots, e_n) = f^{s_2,P}(e_1, \ldots, e_n)$. We can thus characterise $s_2$ as $s_2 = \rho_u(s_1)$. Moreover we may assume $s_1 \models_P \varphi$. Because of the validity of $CorrectDepends(\{d_1, \ldots, d_m\}, \varphi)$: $s_2 \models_P \varphi$.
Because of the symmetry of $s_1$ and $s_2$ in the definition of a depends clause, the opposite direction ($s_2 \models_P \varphi$ implies $s_1 \models_P \varphi$) can be shown the same way. □

**Example 9.5.** With this proof obligation template we can prove that the set $\{\mathtt{a.b.c}, \mathtt{a.b}, \mathtt{a}\}$ is a depends clause of the formula

$$\forall x.\ (x = \mathtt{a.b} \rightarrow x\mathtt{.c} > 0)$$

from Ex. 9.3. It is instantiated to

$$\begin{array}{l} \forall x.\ (x \doteq \mathtt{a.b} \rightarrow x\mathtt{.c} > 0) \land a^{@pre} \doteq \mathtt{a} \\ \land\ \forall x.\ b^{@pre}(x) \doteq x\mathtt{.b} \land \forall x.\ c^{@pre}(x) \doteq x\mathtt{.c} \\ \qquad \rightarrow \{*\}\{\ b^{@pre}(a^{@pre})\mathtt{.c} := c^{@pre}(b^{@pre}(a^{@pre})) \\ \qquad\qquad \mid a^{@pre}\mathtt{.b} := b^{@pre}(a^{@pre}) \mid \mathtt{a} := a^{@pre}\} \\ \qquad\qquad\qquad \forall x.\ (x \doteq \mathtt{a.b} \rightarrow x\mathtt{.c} > 0) \end{array}$$

When loaded into the KeY prover it can be proven correct with a couple of (trivial) quantifier instantiations. *

### 9.1.4 Context-Independent Depends Clauses

We allowed for queries, these are side-effect free methods, being part of an invariant. Queries are dynamically bound unless they are (see Sect. 2.2.2) private or static. They are possibly overridden in other classes if they or their class are not final. Using dynamically bound queries in invariants raises problems of modularity.

The validity of an invariant containing a dynamically bound query depends on the underlying program context. This is even the case in a 'non-local' sense: all concrete locations read by the invoked methods are relevant. Consequently, if a query is overridden which occurs in an invariant, the read concrete locations must additionally be part of the depends clause of the invariant. This leads to non-modular properties of depends clauses as the following example demonstrates.

**Example 9.6.** Finding a depends clause in the following example is difficult:

```
public class A {
  /*@ public instance invariant a.equals(b) */
  private Object a;
  private Object b;
}
```

The query symbol `equals` in the invariant refers to the method `equals` inherited from `Object`, which is by default implemented as the object identity. Assumed the program to consider just consisted of class `A` (and the standard Java types, of course). $\{*.\texttt{a}, *.\texttt{b}\}$ would then be sufficient as depends clause, but as soon as a class would override `equals` in a non-trivial way, the depends clause would have to be extended. Obviously this is an undesired non-modular behaviour. $*$

Depends clauses which do not depend on a context are called *context-independent*. One is particularly interested in context-independence when considering open programs, for obvious reasons: Contexts of open programs have unknown concrete locations, thus it is in general impossible to determine depends clauses of invariants in open programs—unless there is a context-independent one.

**Definition 9.4.** A depends clause $D$ of $\varphi \in \mathrm{Fma}^{\Sigma}$ is *context-independent* if $D$ is a depends clause for every $\Sigma'$-program where $\Sigma'$ is a signature with $\Sigma \subseteq \Sigma'$. All other depends clauses are called *context-dependent.*

Note that in this definition $\varphi \in \mathrm{Fma}^{\Sigma'}$ for all $\Sigma'$ with $\Sigma \subseteq \Sigma'$ according to Lemma 2.1.

A good sufficient criterion for context-independent depends clauses is as follows. If the depends clause $D$ is for an invariant which contains only queries which are declared as private, as static, as final, or in a final class, then $D$ is context-independent. Until Sect. 10.4 we will require that all invariants satisfy this property and that thus all depends clauses are context-independent.

In the next sections, we try to identify sets of classes, called the *guard* or *self-guard*, which is 'responsible' to protect invariants against undesired modifications and which behave in accordance with these invariants. Depends clauses are the basic instrument to analyse invariants and to determine whether a set of types is a suitable guard for them. We have already

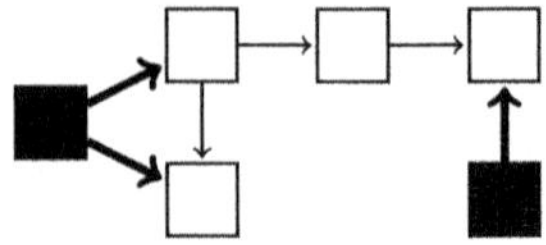

**Figure 9.1:** Instances of self-guards (filled boxes) protecting a set of locations (bold arrows)

mentioned in the introductory notes of this chapter that there are two ways to protect invariants (or the corresponding depends clause), each of them is devoted one of the subsequent sections. Finally we define in Sect. 9.4 that an invariant is guarded if one of these possibilities applies.

## 9.2 Self-Guards

A set $G$ of classes protects a set of locations $L_D$ as a *self-guard* by being in full control of these locations. All modifications of the value assigned to such a location must be done by an operation of an element of $G$ (of which we later can modularly ensure preservation of invariants). In Java, this can only be the case if $L_D$ describes fields of a member of $G$.

Fig. 9.1 illustrates how self-guards work. The rectangles represent objects in a certain state. The arrows represent locations with only one depending object (i.e. of the shape $(f, (e))$), as they occur if we consider only instance fields. The bold arrows represent those locations which must be guarded, that is which are represented by the depends clause. Instances of self-guards (represented by filled rectangles), can only protect locations they are the origin of.

If the fields to be protected have sufficiently restrictive visibilities, as for instance private, the assignment to this field can only be changed by methods of the guard instances. And if these methods satisfy all needed requirements (that is most importantly, preserve invariants), nothing bad can happen to these requirements. In the case of protected fields things get more complicated, since all subclass instances can change the field assignment. In that case we impose the restriction that all subclasses of the field-declaring class must be guards too. Note that the latter has implications for open programs, since there can be an unknown number of subclasses.

**Definition 9.5.** Let $L_D \subseteq L_\Sigma$ be a set of concrete locations. Moreover, let $G$ be a set of types of $\Sigma$.

$G$ is a *self-guard* of $L_D$ in state $s$ if all of the following conditions hold:

1. for all $(f, (e_1, \ldots, e_n)) \in L_D$, $f$ is an instance or static field symbol,
2. for all $(f, (e_1, \ldots, e_n)) \in L_D$ one of the following holds:
   - $f$ is declared private in a class of $G$,
   - $f$ is declared protected in a class $C \in G$ then $\{C\}^{\preceq} \subseteq G$.

A special rule holds for the specification-only field `<created>` which can, though protected, only be written in the constructor of its dynamic type. For this field we do not require that all subclasses $\{C\}^{\preceq}$ are part of the guard $G$.

The notion of self-guards is transferred to the syntax level. We use location terms to describe the locations to be guarded.

**Definition 9.6.** Let $D \subseteq \mathrm{LocTerm}^\Sigma$ be a finite set of location terms (with top($t$) instance or static field) and $G$ a set of types of $\Sigma$. $G$ is a self-guard of $D$ in state $s$ if $G$ is a self-guard of $\mathrm{Loc}_{s,P,\beta}(D)$.
$G$ is a self-guard of $D$ if $G$ is a self-guard of $D$ in all states reached by $P$.

**Example 9.7.** Consider the invariant

$$\varphi_{\texttt{Month}} := \dot{\forall} m{:}\texttt{Month}.\ (1 \leq m.\texttt{val} \land m.\texttt{val} \leq 12)$$

A depends clause of $\varphi_{\texttt{Month}}$ is $\{*.\texttt{val}, *_{\texttt{Month}}.\texttt{<created>}\}$. $\{\texttt{Month}\}$ is a self-guard of $\{*.\texttt{val}\}$ since, for any state $s$,

$$\mathrm{Loc}_{s,P,\beta}(*.\texttt{val}) = \{(\texttt{val}, (e)) \mid e \in \mathrm{Dom}(\texttt{Month})\}$$

and `val` is defined private in `Month`. `Month` is also a self-guard of `<created>`, because of the special rule for this specification-only field. *

**Example 9.8.** Take the (static) invariant

$$\varphi := (\texttt{jan@(Month)} \not\doteq \texttt{null})$$

A depends clause of $\varphi$ is $\{\texttt{jan@(Month)}\}$ with

$$\mathrm{Loc}_{s,P,\beta}(\texttt{jan@(Month)}) = \{(\texttt{jan@(Month)}, ())\}$$

`Month` is a self-guard of this depends clause since `jan` is a private field. *

**Example 9.9.** The (static) invariant

$$\varphi := \texttt{jan@(Month).val} \doteq 1$$

has, as well, `Month` as self-guard, because for any state $s$,

$$\mathrm{Loc}_{s,P,\beta}(\texttt{jan@(Month).val}) = \{(\texttt{val}, (\mathrm{val}_{s,P,\beta}(\texttt{jan@(Month)})))\}$$

and `val` is declared private. *

It is not possible to update locations which have a self-guard in an other way than by calling operations of the self-guard. If the self-guard is proven to adhere to an invariant, and the locations protected by the self-guard are a depends clause of that invariant, the invariant cannot get violated in any way. In Ex. 9.7, if all operations of `Month` preserved the invariant $\forall m{:}\texttt{Month}.\ (1 \leq m.\texttt{val} \wedge m.\texttt{val} \leq 12)$, then this is sufficient to ensure that it holds in all observer states.

There is no need for a proof obligation to find out whether a given set $G$ is a self-guard for another set $D$. Instead a simple syntactic analysis is sufficient: We just need to consider $\{\sigma(\mathrm{top}(d)) \mid d \in D\}$. If this set contains only elements which are a private field symbol declared in a type of $G$ or which are a protected field symbol declared in a type of $G$ and every subtype of $G$ is element of $G$, then $G$ is a self guard for $D$.

## 9.3 Guards

Self-guards are an option only for relatively simple invariants. Consider Ex. 1.1. It is possible to find a self-guard for the depends clause $D$ as found in Ex. 9.1. The smallest self-guard is $\{\texttt{Period}, \texttt{Date}, \texttt{Month}\}$. However (as we will see in detail in the next section), this would require to establish the invariant $\varphi_{\texttt{Period}}$ for all these three classes, which is impossible, since, as already argued in Sect. 1.2, `Date` and `Month` are pretty general and not only intended to be used as helper classes for `Period`.

In this section a new possibility is opened up for invariants with such a wide 'scope'. In our example, we would have solved the problem if only `Period` preserved invariants but were, in addition, responsible not to leak references to the referenced `Date` and `Month` objects. If `Period` behaves this way we call it a *guard*. It is also possible—as for self-guards—that sets of

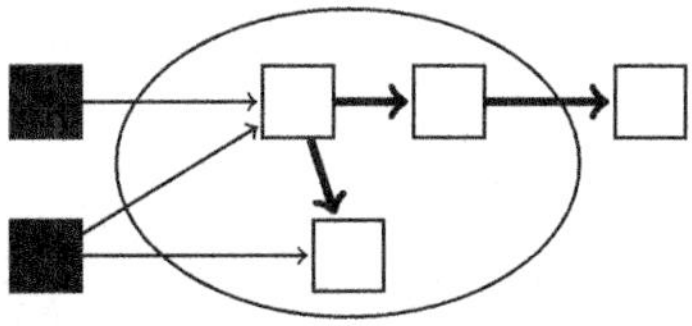

**Figure 9.2:** Instances of guards (filled boxes) protecting a set of locations (bold arrows)

classes play the role of a guard. Note, that guards are the only way how we can cope with array accesses, which were not covered by self-guards, since roughly, the character of an array access is more like a public field access.

## 9.3.1 Motivation

Assume, in a state $s$, a set of types $G$ and a depends clause $D$ are given. Further we have a set $\mathrm{In}^s$ of objects which must be protected. These objects are exactly those from which the locations described by the depends clause emanate, that is, if $(f, (e_1, \ldots, e_n))$ is such a location then $e_1, \ldots, e_n \in \mathrm{In}^s$.

The basic idea that $G$ is a guard for $D$ is, that the types in $G$ are responsible for objects of $\mathrm{In}^s$. In particular, it must be ensured that all accesses to these objects are from instances of $G$, or in other words, if $g^s(e'_1, \ldots, e'_m) \in \mathrm{In}^s$ then $e'_1, \ldots, e'_m$ are instances of an element of $G$. For example, if $g$ is an instance field symbol then $e'_1$ must be an instance of an element of $G$. If, and we will require this in the next section, the operations of the elements of $G$ preserve the invariant belonging to $D$, this invariant holds in all states which can be observed by the observer in our model.

This is however not the complete truth. First of all it does not do any harm if the objects of $\mathrm{In}^s$ have accesses among themselves. In our example, a `Date` object references a `Month` object though both are in the $\mathrm{In}^s$ set and `Date` is not in the guard. However since the `Date` object is itself already protected, this protection naturally extends to `Month`. We can just allow $\mathrm{In}^s$ objects to access each other.

Second, there are not only class instances at work but also arrays. Since we are considering $g$ with $g^s(e_1, \ldots, e_n) \in \mathrm{In}^s$, and impose requirements on $e_1, \ldots, e_n$ it must be taken into account that some of these individuals are of primitive type. For array accesses, $e_2$ is of a primitive type. Primitive values however do not pose any problem since they cannot be the source of an object to leak from $\text{In}^s$.

Finally we need to refine requirements with respect to subtyping and visibilities of the accesses by $g$:

- Assume $g$ is a *private* instance field symbol, but $e_1 \notin \text{In}^s \cup \mathcal{U}^{\text{prim}}$ is a subclass of the class $g$ is defined in. Instead of requiring that the dynamic type $T'$ of $e_1$ is a guard we should rather request that the class $T$ ($T \preceq T'$) which $g$ is defined in is part of the guard. The reason is that operations declared in $T'$ cannot read or write $g$ and so it is not necessary to check for the preservation of invariants in $T'$ nor do we need to check that the operations of $T'$ leak references to the object stored in $g$.

- Furthermore it is not *sufficient* to require that all accesses to an element from $\text{In}^s$ originate from a $G$-instance. Consider the following example. We take Ex. 1.1 but widen visibility of field `start` in `Date` from private to protected:

  ```
  protected Date start;
  ```

  Additionally we imagine a subclass `Period2` of `Period` to exist which contains a method which violates $\varphi_2$, say by allowing to set the start date later than the end date. Still `Period` does not violate $\varphi_2$ and direct instances do not leak references to the depending field `start`. Clearly, by not changing visibility of `start` from private to protected we could not have produced such behaviour. On the other hand, protected fields should not be completely excluded. So we require in such cases that the set of guards is closed under the subtype relation (as we did for self-guards), that is in our example, all subtypes of `Period` must be part of the guard, in particular `Period2`. Then the invariant-violating method would have been disallowed, since guards have to respect invariants.

## 9.3.2 Definitions

As for self-guards we define a guard by means of a set of locations first.

**Definition 9.7** (Guard). Let $L \subseteq L_\Sigma$ be a set of concrete locations. Further, let $G$ be a set of types of $\Sigma$.
Let $\text{In}^s \subseteq \mathcal{U}$ be defined as $\text{In}^s = \{e'_1, \ldots, e'_n \mid (f, (e'_1, \ldots, e'_n)) \in L\} \backslash \mathcal{U}^{\text{prim}}$. $G$ is a *guard* of $L$ in state $s$ if for all $(g, (e_1, \ldots, e_m)) \in L_\Sigma$ with $g^s(e_1, \ldots, e_m) \in \text{In}^s$ one of the following three alternatives holds:

- $g$ is an instance field symbol and $\sigma_1(g) \in G$; if $g$ is declared as protected then additionally: $\{\sigma_1(g)\}^{\preceq} \subseteq G$
- $g$ is a static field symbol and $g$ is declared in a type $T \in G$; if $g$ is declared as protected then additionally: $\{T\}^{\preceq} \subseteq G$
- $e_1, \ldots, e_m \in \mathrm{In}^s \cup \mathcal{U}^{\mathrm{prim}}$

In a closed program there is always a guard for every set of locations, at least the set of all types will do. In open programs this changes however: A program with a class that allows access to a private field via a `get()` method can easily be extended by a class which references the exposed object in a way forbidden by guardedness.

This notion is, as for self-guards, transferred to the syntax level:

**Definition 9.8.** Let $D \subseteq \mathrm{LocTerm}^{\Sigma}$ be a finite set and $G$ a set of types of $\Sigma$. $G$ is a guard of $D$ in state $s$ if $G$ is a guard of $\mathrm{Loc}_{s,P,\beta}(D)$.
$G$ is a guard of $D$ in a program $P$ if $G$ is a guard of $D$ in all states reached by $P$.

**Example 9.10.** Given the program in Ex. 1.1. Let $P$ be the set of classes occurring there. To simplify the invariant a bit, we use, instead of the one presented in Ex. 1.1, the invariant

$$\varphi = \dot{\forall} o{:}\mathtt{Period}.\ o.\mathtt{start.month.val} \not\doteq o.\mathtt{end.month.val}$$

Consider the set of extended terms

$$D := \mathrm{Exp}(\{*.\mathtt{start.month.val}, *.\mathtt{end.month.val}\})$$

$D$ is a depends clause of $\varphi$. We claim that $G_D = \{\mathtt{Period}\}$ is a guard of $D$. To prove our claim the following must be shown for every state $s$ (reached during execution of $P$): With

$$\begin{aligned} L_D = \ & (\mathtt{val}, (\mathrm{val}_{s,P,\beta}(*.\mathtt{start.month}))) \cup (\mathtt{month}, (\mathrm{val}_{s,P,\beta}(*.\mathtt{start}))) \\ & \cup (\mathtt{val}, (\mathrm{val}_{s,P,\beta}(*.\mathtt{end.month}))) \cup (\mathtt{month}, (\mathrm{val}_{s,P,\beta}(*.\mathtt{end}))) \\ \text{and } \mathrm{In}^s = \ & \mathrm{val}_{s,P,\beta}(*.\mathtt{start.month}) \cup \mathrm{val}_{s,P,\beta}(*.\mathtt{start}) \\ & \cup \mathrm{val}_{s,P,\beta}(*.\mathtt{end.month}) \cup \mathrm{val}_{s,P,\beta}(*.\mathtt{end}) \end{aligned}$$

for all non rigid function symbols $g$ and all $e_i \in \sigma_i(g)$ $(i = 1, \ldots, \alpha(g))$ with

$$g^s(e_1, \ldots, e_{\alpha(g)}) \in \mathrm{In}^s$$

either $e_1, \ldots, e_{\alpha(g)} \in \mathrm{In}^s \cup \mathcal{U}^{\mathrm{prim}}$ or $\sigma_i(g) = \texttt{Period}$.
We need to inspect the implementation of the involved classes to show that this property in fact holds. In the next section we see how this is solved completely mechanically. *

The following lemma states a property of guards of depends clauses which are subsets of $\mathrm{WFLocTerm}^\Sigma$ and which are created via $\mathrm{Exp}(D)$: Such a clause always contains the start type of the depends clause. In our running example `Period` is the start type of the depends clause determined for $\varphi_{\texttt{Period}}$ and thus it is necessarily part of a guard.

**Lemma 9.5.** Let $G$ be a guard of a depends clause $D$ of some invariant with $\mathrm{Exp}(D) \subseteq D \subseteq \mathrm{WFLocTerm}^\Sigma$. Then $\mathrm{ST}(\mathrm{Exp}(D)) \subseteq G$.

*Proof.* Let $t$ be an arbitrary extended term with $t \in \mathrm{Exp}(D)$.

- $t$ is of the form (9.1):

$$(\text{for } x : T, x_1, \ldots, x_n \text{ ; } \varphi \text{ ; } f_m(f_{m-1}(\cdots(f_1(x), \ldots), \ldots), \ldots))$$

  for some $m > 1$. Then in an arbitrary state $s$ and for an arbitrary object $e \in \mathrm{Dom}(\sigma(f))$: $f_1^s(e) \in \mathrm{In}^s$. Thus $\sigma(f_1) \in G$. Because of the definition of a start type: $\mathrm{ST}(t) = \sigma(f_1) \in G$.

- $t$ is of the following form (9.2) with a static field symbol $f_0$ declared in class $C$:

$$(\text{for } x_1, \ldots, x_n \text{ ; } \varphi \text{ ; } f_m(f_{m-1}(\cdots(f_1(f_0), \ldots), \ldots), \ldots))$$

  Then for some state $s$, $f_0 \in \mathrm{In}^s$. Thus $\mathrm{ST}(t) = C \in G$.

- The shape (9.3) goes analogously to the first case. □

### 9.3.3 Proof Obligations for Guards

From now on we will only deal with depends clauses which are subsets of $\mathrm{WFLocTerm}^\Sigma$ and which are closed under the Exp operator (that is $\mathrm{Exp}(D) \subseteq D$). This will help us in finding an initial guard since start types of depends clauses $\mathrm{Exp}(D)$ are always part of the guard according to Lemma 9.5.

That a set $G$ of types is a guard of a finite set $D \subseteq \mathrm{WFLocTerm}^{\Sigma}$ of extended terms can (at least partially) be formalised and turned into a proof obligation with the help of the encapsulation predicate Enc [] (see Sect. 4.3.1); for side-conditions concerning the properties of guard sets see below.

**Proof Obligation Template:** *IsGuard*$(D, G)$.
For all $T \in G \cup \mathrm{ST}(D)$, for all non-private operations *op* of $T$:

$$\mathit{PreservesInv}^{*}\left(op, \bigwedge_{k=1,\dots,m} \forall x_1^k : T_1^k. \; \cdots \forall x_{n_k}^k : T_{n_k}^k. \; \mathrm{Enc}_{y,z}\left[\bigvee_{C \in G} \mathrm{InstanceOf}_C(y), \varphi_k \wedge z \doteq d'_k\right]\right)$$

where $D = \{d_1, \dots d_m\}$ and for $k = 1, \dots, m$:

$$(\text{for } x_1^k : T_1^k, \dots, x_{n_k}^k : T_{n_k}^k \; ; \varphi_k \; ; f(d'_k, t_2, \dots, t_n))$$

is a prenex normal form of $d_k$.

On a first glance it might look strange that we only take into consideration the first subterm $d'_k$ of the depends clause elements, but keep in mind that we only have non-rigid function symbols which are of arity $\leq 2$ and that the binary functions are array accesses from which only the first subterm is interesting since the second one is of primitive type.

Justifications and side-conditions for this proof obligation follow in the rest of this chapter. Our goal is to find side-conditions such that *IsGuard*$(D, G)$ implies that $\mathrm{ST}(D) \cup G$ is a guard of $D$.

**Lemma 9.6.** If the following holds:

$$s \models_P \bigwedge_{k=1,\dots,m} \forall x_1^k : T_1^k. \; \cdots \forall x_{n_k}^k : T_{n_k}^k. \; \mathrm{Enc}_{y,z}\left[\bigvee_{C \in G} \mathrm{InstanceOf}_C(y), (\varphi_k \wedge z \doteq d'_k)\right] \tag{9.6}$$

for a set of types $G$ and a depends clause $D = \{d_1, \dots, d_m\}$ in state $s$ then the following implication holds: If $(g, (e_1, \dots, e_m)) \in L_\Sigma$ with $g^s(e_1, \dots, e_m) \in \mathrm{In}^s$ then:

$$e_1, \dots, e_m \in \bigcup_{T \in G} \mathrm{Dom}(T) \cup \mathrm{In}^s \cup \mathcal{U}^{\mathrm{prim}}$$

(with the same designations as in the proof obligation above).

By definition of Enc, the formula in (9.6) is equivalent to:

$$\bigwedge_{k=1,\ldots,m} \forall x_1^k{:}T_1^k. \cdots \forall x_{n_k}^k{:}T_{n_k}^k. \forall y{:}\texttt{Object}. \forall z{:}\texttt{Object}. \\ \big(\mathrm{Acc}(y,z) \land p_k(z) \to p_k(y) \lor \bigvee_{C \in G} \mathrm{InstanceOf}_C(y)\big) \tag{9.6'}$$

with $p_k(z) = \varphi_k \land z \doteq d'_k$

This is 'almost' the desired guard property of Def. 9.7. We just do not know whether, in the case of $e_1, \ldots, e_m \in \bigcup_{T \in G} \mathrm{Dom}(T)$ an instance of $\sigma(g)$ or of a subtype of $\sigma(g)$ is accessing an element of $\mathrm{In}^s$.

*Proof of Lemma 9.6.* It must be shown: If $s \models_P$ (9.6') for $D \subseteq \mathrm{ExtTerm}^\Sigma$ and $G$ a set of types and $(g, (e_1, \ldots, e_m)) \in L_\Sigma$ and $g^s(e_1, \ldots, e_m) \in \mathrm{In}^s$ then $e_1, \ldots, e_m \in \bigcup_{T \in G} \mathrm{Dom}(T) \cup \mathrm{In}^s \cup \mathcal{U}^{\mathrm{prim}}$.
We set $L_D = \mathrm{Loc}_{s,P,\beta}(D)$, $(f, (e'_1, \ldots, e'_n)) \in L_D$, $(g, (e_1, \ldots, e_m)) \in L_\Sigma$, and $g^s(e_1, \ldots, e_m) = e'_i$ for some $i$. That is each $e_j$ accesses $e'_i$.
Set $\beta(y) = e_j$ and $\beta(z) = e'_i$. Because of $(f, (e'_1, \ldots, e'_n)) \in L_D = \mathrm{Loc}_{s,P,\beta}(D)$, there is $d_k \in D$ with $f^s(e'_1, \ldots, e'_n) \in \mathrm{val}_{s,P,\beta}(d_k)$. $f$ is no static field symbol since otherwise there would be no $e'_i$.

- Let $f$ be an instance field symbol. $i = n = 1$ and $e'_i = e'_1$.

$$\begin{aligned} f^s(e'_1) \in \mathrm{val}_{s,P,\beta}(d_k) &\Leftrightarrow f^s(\beta(z)) \in \mathrm{val}_{s,P,\beta}(d_k) \\ &\Leftrightarrow \beta(z) \in \mathrm{val}_{s,P,\beta}(\mathrm{for}\ x_1^k{:}T_1^k, \ldots, x_{n_k}^k{:}T_{n_k}^k\ ;\ \varphi_k\ ;\ d'_k) \\ &\Leftrightarrow s, \beta \models_P p_k(z) \end{aligned}$$

  So we have $s, \beta \models_P p_k(z)$. Thus because of $s, \beta \models_P$ (9.6'):

$$s, \beta \models_p p_k(y) \lor \bigvee_{C \in G} \mathrm{InstanceOf}_C(y)$$

  In the case that $s, \beta \models_P p_k(y)$ then (as above) $h^s(\beta(y)) \in \mathrm{val}_{s,P,\beta}(d)$ for some function symbol $h$ and some $d \in D$. Thus $(h, \beta(y)) \in L_D$ and $\beta(y) \in \mathrm{In}^s$. Thus $e_j \in \mathrm{In}^s$.
  In the case that $s, \beta \models_P \bigvee_{C \in G} \mathrm{InstanceOf}_C(y)$ then there is $C \in G$ with $\beta(y) \in \mathrm{Dom}(C)$. Thus $e_j \in \mathrm{Dom}(C)$.

- Let $f$ be an array access symbol. $e'_i = e'_1$ since $e'_2 \in \mathcal{U}^{\text{prim}}$.

$$\begin{aligned} f^s(e'_1, e'_2) \in \text{val}_{s,P,\beta}(d_k) &\Leftrightarrow f^s(\beta(z), e'_2) \in \text{val}_{s,P,\beta}(d_k) \\ &\Leftrightarrow \beta(z) \in \text{val}_{s,P,\beta}(\text{for } x_1^k : T_1^k, \ldots, x_{n_k}^k : T_{n_k}^k \, ; \varphi_k \, ; d'_k) \\ &\Leftrightarrow s, \beta \models_P p_k(z) \end{aligned}$$

And further as in the last case. □

If we had no inheritance then we could stop here as already mentioned. With inheritance though, we have to impose additional obligations on guards. To cope with the case that a super class declares the reference which points into $\text{In}^s$ we require that super classes with reference fields must be part of the guard. This is captured by the notion of an *admissible* set of types.

In the case of protected fields also subclasses must be checked to preserve invariants and not to leak references to the objects stored in these fields. Thus all subclasses of classes with protected fields must be part of a guard. To deal with this issue we define the subset of *subclass-vulnerable* classes. Subclasses of them must be part of a guard, too, so that they are also checked for preservation of invariants and non-leakage.

These two notion are defined as follows and used as indicated above in the subsequent lemma.

**Definition 9.9.** Let $G$ be a set of types (in a signature $\Sigma$).

1. Let $\bar{G}$ be all super types of $G$ which declare at least one field which is of a reference type. $G$ is *admissible* if $\bar{G} \subseteq G$.

2. We call the subset of classes in $G$ with at least one protected field the *subclass-vulnerable* classes $\text{SCV}(G)$.

**Lemma 9.7.** $G$ is a guard for $D$ in $s$ if

- $G$ is admissible,
- $\text{SCV}(G)^{\preceq} \subseteq G$, and
- $s \models_P$ (9.6').

*Proof.* Let $(g, (e_1, \ldots, e_m)) \in L_\Sigma$ with $g^s(e_1, \ldots, e_m) \in \text{In}^s$. According to Lemma 9.6:

$$e_1, \ldots, e_m \in \bigcup_{T \in G} \text{Dom}(T) \cup \text{In}^s \cup \mathcal{U}^{\text{prim}}$$

The class which declares $g$ is contained in Dom($T$) for some $T \in \bar{G} \subseteq G$ because of the admissibility of $G$. If $g$ is a protected field then the conditions are met because $\mathrm{SCV}(G)^{\preceq} \subseteq G$. □

With this, we can state the final statement on guards: If the provisons of the last lemma are met and we have a depends clause $D$ which is constructed via Exp and the start type is contained in $D$, then $G$ is in fact a guard of $D$.

**Lemma 9.8.** If

- $G$ is admissible,
- $\mathrm{SCV}(G)^{\preceq} \subseteq G$,
- $\mathrm{Exp}(D) \subseteq D$, and
- $\mathrm{ST}(D) \subseteq G$

then: $\models_P \mathit{IsGuard}(D, G)$ implies that $G$ is a guard for $D$.

*Proof.* We consider an arbitrary sequence $(s_0, s_1, \ldots, s_n)$ of states which are reached by calling operations on $P$. $s_0$ is the initial state of the program. We further require that the sequence contains all such reached states but does not contain intermediate states in operations of classes of $G$ and the dynamic types of the $\mathrm{In}^s$ objects. By induction on the length of this sequence we show: If $\models_P \mathit{IsGuard}(D, G)$ then for all states $s$ in the sequence, $G$ is a guard of $D$ in $s$.
$n = 0$. Trivial, since in initial states there are no references.
*Step from $n$ to $n+1$:* Consider an arbitrary semantic update $U : L_\Sigma \to \mathcal{U}$ and states $s_n$, $s_{n+1}$ with $s_{n+1} = s_n^U$. We consider a semantic update $U$ consisting w.l.o.g. of pairs $((g, (e_1, \ldots e_m)) \mapsto e)$.
Consider an arbitrary such pair in $U$. If $e \notin \mathrm{In}^{s_{n+1}}$ the induction hypothesis remains trivially true.

Otherwise $e \in \mathrm{In}^{s_{n+1}}$. Assume $e \in \mathrm{In}^{s_n}$. For all $h$ with $h^{s_n}(e'_1, \ldots, e'_k) = e$: $e'_1, \ldots, e'_k \in \mathrm{In}^{s_n} \cup \mathcal{U}^{\mathrm{prim}}$ or $h$ is a private field declared in $G$ by the induction hypothesis. The operation which performs the update $U$ must have a direct reference to $e$. Thus the update must be executed during a call to an instance of a class of $G$ or during a call to an object of $\mathrm{In}^{s_n}$.

- Assume first that $U$ is executed during an operation call of a class of $G$ (This includes the case that the execution is put on the stack during call to a subroutine). Then, because of $\models_P \mathit{IsGuard}(D, G)$: $s_{n+1} \models_P$ (9.6'). By Lemma 9.7 the desired property follows for $s_{n+1}$.

- Assume now that $U$ takes place in a class of $\mathrm{In}^{s_n}$. Then since $\mathrm{In}^{s_n}$ objects are in $s_n$ only referenced from instances of $G$ or among themselves, the update happens as well during an operation call to $G$ and we can go on as before.

Consider now the case $e \in \mathrm{In}^{s_{n+1}} \setminus \mathrm{In}^{s_n}$. Then either $g \in \mathrm{top}(D)$ or $\sigma(g) = \mathrm{ST}(D)$. Thus the state change $U$ takes place in a method of $\mathrm{In}^{s_n}$ or $\mathrm{ST}(D) \subseteq G$. As before we can conclude that $G$ is a guard for $D$ in $s_{n+1}$. □

**Example 9.11.** In Ex. 9.10, we discovered the part of a depends clause

$$D' := \{\ *\texttt{.start.month.val}, *\texttt{.end.month.val}, \\ *\texttt{.start.month}, *\texttt{.end.month}\}$$

In that example it was concluded that {`Period`} could be a candidate for a guard; an inspection of the implementation was considered necessary to confirm this. With the above proof obligation we have the right instrument in our hands.

First of all we note that $D' = \mathrm{Exp}(D')$. Furthermore all fields are private, so that $\mathrm{SCV}(G)^{\preceq} \subseteq G$ is satisfied. But even if all fields in `Period` were protected no problem would occur since $\{\texttt{Period}\}^{\preceq} = \{\texttt{Period}\}$. Moreover the start type of $D'$ is `Period` and included in $G$.

It is thus sufficient to show proof obligation *IsGuard*. It produces for each operation *op* of `Period` a formula, for which validity must be proven. As example we take the constructor of `Period` (unqualified logical variables in junctors are of type `Object`):

$$\begin{aligned} &\mathit{IsGuard}(D', G) \\ =&\forall x : \texttt{Period}.\ \mathit{PreservesInv}^*(op, \{\mathrm{Enc}_{y,z}\,[\mathrm{InstanceOf}_{\texttt{Period}}(y), p(x,z)]\} \\ &\text{with } p(x,z) = (\ z \doteq x\texttt{.start} \vee z \doteq x\texttt{.start.month} \\ &\qquad\qquad \vee z \doteq x\texttt{.end} \vee z \doteq x\texttt{.end.month}) \end{aligned}$$

This is further expanded to:

$$\begin{aligned} &\exists v.\ \mathrm{Acc}(v, \mathtt{s}) \wedge \exists v.\ \mathrm{Acc}(v, \mathtt{e}) \wedge \\ &\forall x{:}\texttt{Period}.\ \forall y.\ \forall z.\ \Big(\big(\mathrm{Acc}(y,z) \wedge p(x,z) \rightarrow p(x,y) \vee \mathrm{InstanceOf}_{\texttt{Period}}(y)\big)\Big) \\ &\rightarrow [\texttt{r=new Period(s, e);}] \\ &\quad (\exists v.\ \mathrm{Acc}(v, \mathtt{r}) \\ &\quad \rightarrow \forall x{:}\texttt{Period}.\ \forall y.\ \forall z.\ (\ \mathrm{Acc}(y,z) \wedge p(x,z) \\ &\qquad\qquad \rightarrow p(x,y) \vee \mathrm{InstanceOf}_{\texttt{Period}}(y))) \end{aligned}$$

for fresh program variables `s` and `e` of type `Date`. This formula is provably valid in $P$. We can prove the corresponding formulae for the other operations of `Period`, too. `Period` is thus a guard for $D'$ according to Lemma 9.8. $*$

## 9.4 Modular Verification of Invariants

So far, this chapter provided instruments to ensure that there is a sufficient degree of encapsulation for modularly checking invariants. This section will compile these techniques into an approach which ensures call correctness of programs.

First we state that both, guards and self-guards, can be used to protect or, as we will call it, *guard* invariants. This is just a matter of dividing the depends clause of an invariant into two subsets. If $G$ is a set of types then, for one of these sets of location terms, $G$ is a self-guard and for the other it is a guard.

**Definition 9.10** (Guarded Invariants)**.** An invariant, represented as formula $\varphi \in \mathrm{Fma}^{\Sigma}$, is *guarded* by a set of types $G$, if

- there is a depends clause $D \subseteq \mathrm{LocTerm}^{\Sigma}$ of $\varphi$,
- there are sets $D_1 \subseteq \mathrm{LocTerm}^{\Sigma}$ and $D_2 \subseteq \mathrm{LocTerm}^{\Sigma}$ with $D = D_1 \uplus D_2$,
- $G$ is a self-guard for $D_1$, and
- $G$ is a guard for $D_2$.

**Example 9.12.** Following Ex. 9.7, {`Month`} is a self-guard for $\varphi_{\texttt{Month}}$. $\varphi_{\texttt{Month}}$ is thus guarded by {`Month`}.

Resuming Ex. 9.10, assume we had shown that {`Period`} is a guard of $D'$. Then $D_1 = \{*\texttt{.start}, *\texttt{.end}\}$ complement $D'$ to a depends clause of the invariant $\varphi$ in that example. Since `Period` is a self-guard for $D_1$, $\varphi$ is guarded by {`Period`}. $*$

With the tools developed so far, (7.7) can be refined modularly. We may find guards or self-guards $G$ and have to show for all invariants $\varphi \in \mathrm{Inv}$:

1. if $\varphi$ is guarded by a set of types $G$:

$$\text{for all } op \text{ declared in } G\text{:} \quad \mathit{PreservesInv}(op, \{\varphi\}) \qquad (7.7')$$

2. otherwise:

$$\text{for all } op \text{ in } P: \quad PreservesInv(op, \{\varphi\}) \qquad (7.7'')$$

The following lemma states, that this condition is in fact sufficient to replace (7.7), which required *PreservesInv* to hold for all operations of $P$. The lemma and the proof aim at *durable* correctness of a closed program as defined in Def. 3.11. Though we are currently only aiming at call correctness for closed programs we are showing the stronger (Lemma 3.5) notion of durable correctness. In the next chapter, when dealing with open programs, we can 'replay' the proof, so that we take the more difficult way here.

**Lemma 9.9.** If the above proof obligations are valid in a closed program $P$ for a specification $S$ then $P$ is durable invariant correct w.r.t. $S$.

*Proof.* Let $P^{cl}$ be a closure of $P$ and $Obs := P^{cl} \backslash P$ the observer of $P$. We consider an arbitrary path as a sequence $(s_0, s_1, \ldots, s_k)$ of states through the graph of states reachable during the execution of a program $P^{cl}$. In this sequence, intermediate states which occur during operation calls to $G$ (including states during subroutines of such operations) are filtered out. Furthermore $s_0$ is the initial state. By induction on the length of such a sequence we show for all states $s_n$: $s_n \models_P \varphi$ for all $\varphi \in \text{Inv}$.

- *Base case $n = 0$:* $s_0$ is the initial state. $s_0 \models_P \varphi_{\text{init}}$ by definition of the initial state. Because of $InitInv(\{\varphi\})$ for all $\varphi \in \text{Inv}$, as well $s_0 \models_P \varphi$ for all invariants $\varphi$.
- *Step case from $n$ to $n+1$:* Pick one arbitrary $\varphi \in \text{Inv}$. Then by the induction hypothesis: $s_n \models_P \varphi$.
  For some $D_1$, $D_2$ and a depends clause $D = D_1 \uplus D_2$ of $\varphi$, either $G$ is a self-guard of $D_1$ or a guard of $D_2$. If $s_n$ is a start state of an operation *op* of $P$ and $\varphi$ is not guarded by a set of classes $G$ then, by $\models_P PreservesInv(op, \varphi)$, $s_{n+1} \models_P \varphi$. If $s_n$ is a start state of *op* but $\varphi$ is guarded by a set of classes $G$, then, if *op* is declared in $G$, we continue to reason as above.
  In all other cases we aim to show for all $(f, (e_1, \ldots, e_{\alpha(f)})) \in \text{Loc}_{s_n}(D)$:
  $$f^{s_n}(e_1, \ldots, e_{\alpha(f)}) = f^{s_{n+1}}(e_1, \ldots, e_{\alpha(f)})$$
  Then by the definition of a depends clause $s_{n+1} \models_P \varphi$.
  Suppose $d = (f, (e_1, \ldots, e_{\alpha(f)})) \in \text{Loc}_{s_n}(D)$, $s_{n+1} = {s_n}^U$ for a semantic update $U$ and $((f, (e_1, \ldots, e_{\alpha(f)})) \mapsto e) \in U$ (If there is no such pair in $U$ then our goal is trivially achieved.)

- As the first case we assume that $d \in \mathrm{Loc}_{s_n}(D_1)$. Because $G$ is a self-guard for $D_1$, $f$ is an instance or static field symbol declared in a type of $G$. If $f$ is a private field symbol, then an assignment to it must occur in a type of $G$, thus an operation call to a class of $G$ is in progress in contradiction to our assumptions. Otherwise $f$ is a protected field symbol. Then an assignment to it must occur in a type of $\mathrm{SCV}(G)^{\preceq} \subseteq G$ which yields again a contradiction.
- Consider the case $d \in \mathrm{Loc}_{s_n}(D_2)$. For all field symbols or array access symbols $g$ and all $e'_1, \ldots, e'_{\alpha(g)} \in \mathcal{U}$ with $g(e'_1, \ldots, e'_{\alpha(g)}) = e_j$ for some $j$: Either $g$ is an instance field symbol and $\sigma_1(g) \in G$. Then however by performing $U$, an instance method of a class in $G$ must be in progress in contradiction to our assumptions. The same holds for static fields. The third possibility is that $e'_1 \in \mathrm{In}^{s_n}$. Then again a method of a class in $G$ must be in progress, since only through them access to $\mathrm{In}^{s_n}$ is possible in $s_n$; this yields again a contradiction. Finally $e'_j \in \mathrm{In}^{s}$ $(j > 1)$ is not possible because of the considered non-rigid functions. □

With the following lemma the results so far are summarised.

**Lemma 9.10.** Suppose $P$ is a program and $S$ a specification of $P$. If the following conditions hold then $P$ is call correct w.r.t. $S$:

- For all non-private operations *op* of $P$ and all operation contracts *opct* on *op*:
  - $\models_P \mathit{EnsuresPost}(\mathit{opct})$ (7.5)
  - $\models_P \mathit{RespectsModifies}(\mathit{opct})$ (7.6)
- For all invariants $\varphi \in \mathrm{Inv}$, $\models_P \mathit{InitInv}$ and one of the following conditions holds:
  - (Guard, as (7.7′)) There is a depends clause $D \subseteq \mathrm{LocTerm}^{\Sigma}$ of $\varphi$ and a set $G \subseteq P$ of types such that for all operations *op* of all classes of $G$:

    $$\models_P \mathit{PreservesInv}(op, \{\varphi\})$$

    and there are sets $D_1, D_2$ with $D = D_1 \uplus D_2$ with the following properties

  * $G$ is a self-guard of $D_1$, that is, there exists $t \in D$ such that $\mathrm{top}(t)$ is a field symbol and $\sigma(\mathrm{top}(t)) \in G$; if $\mathrm{top}(t)$ is declared protected in $C$ then $\{C\}^{\preceq} \subseteq G$.
  * $G$ is a guard for $D_2$, that is (e.g.) $\mathrm{Exp}(D_2) \subseteq D_2$, $G$ is admissible, $\mathrm{SCV}(G)^{\preceq} \subseteq G$, $\mathrm{ST}(D_2) \subseteq G$, and $\models_P \mathit{IsGuard}(D_2, G)$

- (No Guard, as (7.7″)) For all operations $op$ in $P$:

$$\models_P \mathit{PreservesInv}(op, \{\varphi\})$$

*Proof.* Because of (7.5) and (7.6) all operations fulfil the operation contracts of $S$ which are for $op$ as in the proof of Lemma 7.5. Because of Lemma 9.9, $P$ is durable invariant correct. This yields durable correctness. With Lemma 3.5 call correctness follows. □

The following example demonstrates that this system of proof obligations is stronger than that presented in Chapter 7.

**Example 9.13.** Consider, once more, Ex. 1.1. It was impossible to show the call correctness of {`Period`, `Date`, `Month`} with the proof obligations of Chapter 7. The reason was that `setYear(int)` in `Date` did not preserve the invariant of `Period`. We could not exploit the fact that a state in which an object assigned to `start` or `end` of `Period` was modified by that method could never be reached.

With our new system of proof obligations, this is changed. The reachable states are more adequately reflected if `Period`'s invariant is guarded.

On a more detailed level, the following steps must be performed to prove call correctness:

- First a depends clause for $\varphi_{\texttt{Period}}$ must be determined. Like in Ex. 9.1, the clause

$$\begin{aligned} D = \mathrm{Exp}(\{\ & *.\texttt{start.month.val}, *.\texttt{end.month.val}, \\ & *.\texttt{start.year}, *.\texttt{end.year}\}) \\ \cup\ & \{*.\texttt{start}, *.\texttt{end}\} \end{aligned}$$

  results as application of Dep.

  For the invariant $\varphi_{\texttt{Month}}$ of `Month` the depends clause $\{*.\texttt{val}\}$ results.

- Then we investigate guardedness of $D$. We can split $D$ into

$$\begin{aligned} D_1 &= \{*.\texttt{start}, *.\texttt{end}\} \\ \text{and } D_2 &= \mathrm{Exp}(\{\ *.\texttt{start.month.val}, *.\texttt{end.month.val}, \\ &\qquad\qquad *.\texttt{start.year}, *.\texttt{end.year}\}) \end{aligned}$$

  {`Period`} is a self-guard of $D_1$ since `start` and `end` are declared private in that class. Moreover {`Period`} is a guard of $D_2$. The proof is done similarly to Ex. 9.11.

  All operations *op* of `Period` preserve $\varphi_{\texttt{Period}}$, that is, we can show

$$\models_P \mathit{PreservesInv}(op, \{\varphi_{\texttt{Period}}\})$$

  for all of them. Also $\models_P \mathit{InitInv}$ can be established trivially, since $\varphi_{\texttt{Period}}$ is an instance invariant.

  In Ex. 9.7 we have discussed that $\varphi_{\texttt{Month}}$ is guarded by the self-guard `Month`. All operations of `Month` preserve this invariant.

- Of course, the fulfilment of all attached operation contracts must be shown. *

## 9.5 Summary

In this section we have done a main step towards verification of open programs though, for now, only closed programs have been considered. We have found a technique which allows for a modular verification of invariants. It includes an analysis the invariants which results in the extraction of depends clauses. These are descriptions of locations the evaluation of an invariant depends on. These locations must be protected from uncontrolled modifications with one of two techniques: either self-guard classes are found which control the locations, or guard classes are found which do not leak references to those objects which are allowed to modify a depends location. Based on these approaches we could find a new more powerful system of proof obligations which ensures durable correctness of a closed programs.

In the next chapter we make use of the results of this chapter in the context of open programs.

# 10 Verification of Durable Correctness of Open Programs

Gutta cavat lapidem.

*(Ovid)*

In the last chapter we provided a system of proof obligations to verify a program modularly (in the sense of call correctness), in particular, allowing for the modular verification of invariants. Modular verification of invariants is, apart from modular program proofs (Chapter 6), the main step towards durable correctness of open programs.

So the proof obligation system from Chapter 9 'almost' establishes durable correctness for open programs $P$. In the following we list the items that prevent it to be a proof obligation system for durable correctness:

- Subclasses are in general not known when dealing with open programs. So invariants without guards can only be supported by a system that establishes durable correctness of open programs if the context behaves sufficiently well.
- The needed proof obligations (7.5), (7.6), and (7.7′), were defined to be valid in a fixed context where all additional subclasses comply to certain criteria. Since a context can have subclasses which do not fulfil this criteria, obligations on the context must be imposed.

There are the following instruments discussed in the previous chapters to solve these problems:

1. We completely rely on guarded invariants.
2. The context is constrained, i.e. extension contracts are imposed as described in Chapter 5 if there are no guards available.
3. Modular proof strategies are applied as discussed in Chapter 6, possibly extension contracts are to be imposed here as well.

This chapter thus re-arranges these instruments with the goal to prove durable correctness of open programs.

**Overview.** We start with the strictest form of modularity, resulting in the guarantee that after proving a system of proof obligations the program behaves correct in every context. Sect. 10.2 presents a weakened version of the proof obligation system which only ensures relative durable correctness. Then in Section 10.3 two examples are extensively discussed. An issue omitted so far is discussed in Sect. 10.4, namely how dynamically bound queries occurring in invariants are treated. Finally we take the (small) step to transfer all this to component contracts.

## 10.1 Strict Durable Correctness

With durable correctness we can treat *open programs*. So our verified program is not self-contained anymore, but refers to other components which are not accessible to verification. Moreover the program is used in an unknown context, so it will be part of a larger program. As noted earlier (Sect. 3.2), it is not sufficient to establish call correctness, since for open programs, this notion is not equivalent to durable correctness.

We define proof obligations which ensure durable correctness of open programs. When it is possible to establish all the indicated conditions, the verified program can be put in *any* context and works as the specification requires. There are three changes to the proof obligation system presented in the last chapter.

- All proof obligations must be valid in every extending context. Thus *modular* validity as introduced in Chapter 6 is necessary.
- In the former proof obligation system we allowed, in addition to the modular ways, for the traditional way of showing a particular invariant for *all* operations independent from its shape. This was appropriate if the relevant locations were not sufficiently encapsulated. In an open world, there is no handle on *all* operations. So we cannot get away with this non-modular approach.
- We must be stricter concerning fields declared as protected. Such fields were allowed in the definition of self-guards (Def. 9.5) under the pro-

vision that the guard set was closed under subtypes. The latter is not possible in an open program where closures can subclass existing classes. So we must exclude protected fields. The analogous case holds for guards.

We thus modify Lemma 9.10 as follows:

**Lemma 10.1** (Proof Obligations for Durable Correctness). Suppose $P$ is a program and $S$ a specification of $P$. If the following conditions hold then $P$ is durable correct w.r.t. $S$:

- For all non-private operations *op* of $P$ and all operation contracts *opct* for *op*:
  - $\models^{\emptyset}_{P}$ *EnsuresPost*(*opct*) (7.5)
  - $\models^{\emptyset}_{P}$ *RespectsModifies*(*opct*) (7.6)
- For all invariants $\varphi \in \mathrm{Inv}$, $\models^{\emptyset}_{P}$ *InitInv* holds and there is a context-independent depends clause $D \subseteq \mathrm{LocTerm}^{\Sigma}$ of $\varphi$ and a set $G \subseteq P$ of types such that for all operations *op* of all classes of $G$:

  $$\models^{\emptyset}_{P} \mathit{PreservesInv}(op, \{\varphi\})$$

  and there are sets $D_1, D_2$ with $D = D_1 \uplus D_2$ with the following properties:
  - $G$ is a self-guard of $D_1$, that is, there exists $t \in D$ such that $\mathrm{top}(t)$ is a private field symbol and $\sigma(\mathrm{top}(t)) \in G$.
  - $G$ is a guard for $D_2$, that is, $\mathrm{Exp}(D_2) \subseteq D_2$, $G$ is admissible, all fields in $G$ are private, $\mathrm{ST}(D_2) \subseteq G$, and $\models^{\emptyset}_{P}$ *IsGuard*$(D_2, G)$

*Proof.* Follows from the more general Lemma 10.2 about relative-modular correctness and Lemma 6.1. □

Remember (from Sect. 6.4.3) that modular validity is only possible if we are avoiding dynamic dispatching by declaring methods `final` and the like. Moreover with this proof obligation system we have restrictive encapsulation. To avoid severe restrictions on extensibility of our program—which is definitely a design goal of object-oriented systems—, generic extension contracts are imposed on the context. By making use of this possibility we can liberalise the proof obligations. See Sect. 10.2 for how this works.

**Example 10.1.** The open program {Period} in our running example Ex. 1.1 *cannot* be proven to be durable correct. The problem is the following: We cannot prove modularly properties like the preservation of invariants for Period's methods without referring to methods in Date. Since Date is however outside the scope of the open program {Period} we have no means to prove that methods of potential subclasses of Date adhere to their specification. We would need to require this by employing generic extension contracts, but this is not possible with the strict notion of durable correctness presented here. An alternative is to modify Date and declare the called methods `earlierOrEqual(Date)` and `copy()` as `final`.

Then durable correctness can be shown with the help of the new proof obligation system. Most is the same as in Ex. 9.13.

- No operation contract is attached to Period so nothing must be proven here with *EnsuresPost* and *RespectsModifies*.
- For the invariant $\varphi_{\texttt{Period}}$ the following is required:
  - A depends clause $D_1$ is extracted automatically (as in Ex. 9.13) with the help of the procedure in Sect. 9.1.2:

$$\begin{aligned} D_1 = \; & \mathrm{Exp}(\{*\texttt{.start.month.val}, *\texttt{.end.month.val}, \\ & \quad *\texttt{.start.year}, *\texttt{.end.year}\}) \\ & \cup\{*\texttt{.start}, *\texttt{.end}\} \end{aligned}$$

  - For $D_1$ we find a guard {Period}. For this the following must be proven

$$\models^{\emptyset}_{P} \mathit{IsGuard}(D_1, \{\texttt{Period}\})$$

    Therefore we need to take into account all operations *op* of Period. We have elaborated on one of these proof obligations in Ex. 9.11. Since we are now aiming at a modular proof we must not use the non-modular method call rules (Rules (6.3) and (6.4)). Instead we use the rules from JavaDL$^{m}$ containing Rule (6.8). When this rule is applied in the proof of the above proof obligation (for instance for the constructor of Period), no generic contract is generated since `earlierOrEqual(Date)` is `final`. The same holds for `copy()`.

– Then all operations *op* of the guard `Period` must preserve $\varphi_{\texttt{Period}}$. It must be shown:

$$\models^{\emptyset}_{P} \mathit{PreservesInv}(op, \{\varphi_{\texttt{Period}}\})$$

In the proofs for the constructor again no generic contract is generated because of the `final` modifier. *

## 10.2 Durable Correctness with Extension Contracts

As we have seen, *strict* modular validity and complete encapsulation is not always feasible. After all it is a goal of object-orientation to foster re-usability and one of the vehicles to do this is to override dynamically bound methods. Overriding of relevant methods would however be forbidden when establishing strict modular validity.

Thus we provide a system of proof obligations to establish relative-durable correctness as defined in Def. 5.5. It contains elements of the proof obligations of Lemma 9.10 and those of Lemma 10.1. The two main characteristics compared to these other proof obligation systems are:

- We can allow again for the non-modular way (that is, *all* operations preserve the invariant) of establishing invariants as in Lemma 9.10, but not entirely. It must be ensured in this case that the classes of the context preserve this invariant. This requirement is met by generating a suitable extension contract.

- Moreover we must use the relativised validity relation $\models^{GCt}_{P}$ for programs $P$ and sets $GCt$ of extension contracts as defined in Def. 6.3.

- Protected fields can be allowed again for use in self-guards and guards. Compared to the case of closed programs, we must take care of the classes SCV($G$) in a different way. There it was sufficient to require that all subtypes are part of the guard $G$, too. Now we must ensure that subtypes in the context behave in the desired way by means of extension contracts.

**Lemma 10.2** (Proof Obligations for Relative-Durable Correctness). Suppose $P$ is a program, $S$ a specification of $P$, and $GCt$ a set of generic contracts. If the following conditions hold then $P$ is durable correct relative to $GCt$ and w.r.t. $S$:

- For all non-private operations *op* of $P$ and all operation contracts *opct* on *op*:
  - $\models_P^{GCt}$ *EnsuresPost*(*opct*) (7.5)
  - $\models_P^{GCt}$ *RespectsModifies*(*opct*) (7.6)
- For all invariants $\varphi \in \text{Inv}$: $\models_P^{GCt}$ *InitInv* and one of the following conditions holds:
  - (Guard) There are a context-independent depends clause $D \subseteq \text{LocTerm}^\Sigma$ of $\varphi$ and a set $G \subseteq P$ of types such that for all operations *op* of all classes of $G$:

    $$\models_P^{GCt} \mathit{PreservesInv}(op, \{\varphi\})$$

    and there are sets $D_1, D_2$ with $D = D_1 \uplus D_2$ with the following properties
    * $G$ is a self-guard of $D_1$, that is, there exists $t \in D$ such that $\text{top}(t)$ is a field symbol with $\sigma(\text{top}(t)) \in G$ and if $f$ is declared as protected then $GCt$ contains the following generic contract:

      ```
      generic contract {
        T extends* σ(top(t));
        (∅, {φ})
      }
      ```
    * $G$ is a guard for $D_2$, that is, $\text{Exp}(D_2) \subseteq D_2$, $G$ is admissible, $\text{ST}(D_2) \subseteq G$, $\models_P^{GCt}$ *IsGuard*$(D_2, G)$, and for all $C \in \text{SCV}(G)^{\preceq}$ as well as for all super types of $G$ declaring at least one field which is of a reference type the following extension contract, capturing the guard property (9.6'), is contained in $GCt$:

      ```
      generic contract {
        T extends* C;
        (∅, {φ, (9.6')})
      }
      ```

– (No Guard) For all operations *op*: $\models_P^{GCt}$ *PreservesInv*$(op, \{\varphi\})$ and *GCt* contains the generic contract

```
generic contract {
  T unconstrained;
  (∅, {φ})
}
```

*Proof.* The proof is done as before for Lemma 9.10 but with the validity relation $\models_P^{GCt}$ instead of $\models_P$. For it we need a claim corresponding to Lemma 9.9. Since we did not exploit the fact that the program was closed and we proved durable correctness directly, we can replay this proof exactly for the case of open programs with the following exceptions: Whenever we used the fact that $\mathrm{SCV}(G)^{\preceq} \subseteq G$, we must now use that this condition is satisfied in all closures of $P$ since the

```
generic contract {
  T extends* σ(top(t));
  (∅, {φ})
}
```

must be fulfilled by the classes which are complemented for such a closure. When we argue for the case that $\varphi$ is not guarded by some classes $G$ we have to take into account that we have an extension contract which requires the preservation for all suiting context methods.

Our lemma here also makes claims about proving guardedness. These are based on the Lemmas 9.6, 9.7, and 9.8, for which we can as well use the proofs made there, but for modular validity relative to *GCt*. The completion for claiming, in the arbitrary closure, that all subtypes of a class declaring a protected field are in $G$, is that we have the extension contract requiring that the relevant subclasses satisfy guardedness and preserve invariants. The same holds for super types in the context with a reference field. □

**Example 10.2.** We apply the new proof obligation system to our running example. Unlike in the last example we assume again that the methods `earlierOrEqual(Date)` and `copy()` are not declared as final. This will necessitate to prove *relative* modular correctness of {`Period`}. Most is the same as in Examples 9.13 and 10.1: The same depends clause and the same treatment with self-guards and guards is applied. For the proofs we must use the calculus JavaDL$^m$ and the generation of extension contracts. Extension contracts are generated whenever a method reference is symbolically executed which is referring to a non-final dynamically bound method in a class not in {Period}. Since the two mentioned methods are no more final, we get the generic extension contracts $GCt = \{gct_{\texttt{earlierOrEqual(Date)}}, gct_{\texttt{copy()}}\}$ with the extension contracts as defined in Ex. 5.8, that is $gct_{\texttt{earlierOrEqual(Date)}}$:

```
generic contract {
  T extends* Date;
  class T {
    /*@ normal_behavior
      @ requires cmp !=null;
      @ ensures \result == (year<cmp.year || (year==cmp.year
      @                          && month.val<=cmp.month.val));
      @*/
    /*@pure@*/ boolean earlierOrEqual(Date cmp);
  }
}
```

and $gct_{\texttt{copy()}}$:

```
generic contract {
  T extends* Date;
  class T {
    /*@ normal_behavior
      @ ensures ( \result.month.val==month.val
      @         & \result.year==year
      @         & \fresh(\result) & \fresh(\result.month);
      @*/
    /*@pure@*/ Date copy();
  }
}
```

We must show that all operations of Period preserve $\varphi_{\texttt{Period}}$. This is shown with $\mathit{PreservesInv}(op, \varphi_{\texttt{Period}})$ and a relative modular proof. Because the same operation calls as in the proof for guardedness are symbolically executed the same generic contracts would be generated here, too. There is no operation contract attached to Period, so nothing must be proven with the proof obligation templates *EnsuresPost* or *RespectsModifies*. Altogether this proves that Period is durable modular correct relative to $GCt$.

In Ex. 1.1 we used the class Main to show how to violate $\varphi_{\texttt{Period}}$ in a modified variant of the example. It is now indeed *allowed* to write Main but it cannot do any harm because `Period` is sufficiently encapsulated. The class `Main2` which exploited non-conforming overriding of methods is still disallowed because of the imposed generic extension contract. *

**Example 10.3.** We take again our running example but now in the modified version of Ex. 1.2. Though the invariant is fragile we can establish relative-durable correctness of the program {`Period`}. Because references to the representation of a `Period` may leak, `Period` cannot establish the guardedness property. We must thus show the second of the alternatives ('No Guard') in the above lemma. Again we have to prove the preservation of invariants of all operations of `Period`. During the proof, the same generic contract as in the last example is generated. We must include it in *GCt* to prove

$$\models_P^{GCt} \mathit{PreservesInv}(\texttt{Period(Date, Date)}, \{\varphi_{\texttt{Period}}\})$$

We are however not finished yet, since *GCt* must include the extension contract required by Lemma 10.2. In our case this is:

```
generic contract {
  T unconstrained;
  class T {
    /*@ static invariant (\forall Period p;
      @                      start.year<end.year ||
      @                     (   start.year==end.year
      @                     && start.month.val<=end.month.val));
      @*/
  }
}
```

With these three extension contracts forming the set *GCt*, {`Period`} is modularly correct relative to *GCt* and w.r.t the specification consisting of $\varphi_{\texttt{Period}}$. Contexts like `Main` or `Main2` as described in Sect. 1.2 are thus not allowed and violations of $\varphi_{\texttt{Period}}$ cannot occur. *

## 10.3 Examples

In this chapter we present some examples demonstrating our system of proof obligations. The examples are taken from literature on other approaches. In some places we have made the scenario more difficult. We will always show first a way to establish *strict* durable correctness and then a way to establish relative durable correctness.

All proofs mentioned in the examples have been conducted with the KeY system. The proofs can often be done with large automatic support, on the other hand often human input is needed almost always in order to instantiate quantifiers. Almost all instantiations are however fairly trivial, and can be expected to be discharged automatically while the automated deduction engine of KeY is being improved.

### 10.3.1 Producer and Consumer with Shared Array

Consider the example program depicted in Figs. 10.1 to 10.2 adapted from Dietl and Müller [2005].

The depicted program implements a producer/consumer scenario in Java and specifies the functional behaviour with JML. In the original version [Dietl and Müller, 2005], protection against undesired modifications did only work if the context adhered to the universe type system. In contrast to Dietl and Müller [2005] our version includes sensible invariants of classes which necessitate such protection.

The particularity of the example is that buffers, implemented as an array of `Product` elements, of the classes `Producer` and `Consumer` are shared. The (added) invariant of `Producer` specifies that there are no duplicates in the buffer of a `Producer`, though multiple occurrences of `null` are allowed. The obvious danger is that the buffer array object could as well leak to an unknown object which could manipulate array entries and thus violate `Producer`'s invariant.

The program in Figs. 10.1 to 10.2 reimplements the classes and ensures modular correctness by *standard* Java means. That is, we must not rely on programming language extensions like Universes. This requires however a more sophisticated initialisation procedure: First a `Producer` instance is created, then a `Consumer` instance. As argument of the constructor call of the latter, a `Producer` instance is passed. This should trigger that `Producer` holds a reference to `Consumer` and that the buffer array is shared among `Producer` and `Consumer`. Since that array is represented as a private field in `Consumer`, it must necessarily be set via an operation like `setBuffer(Product[])`. This method must however not be arbitrarily called by an observer, since otherwise there could be references in the observer to the array and the observer can violate invariants. Thus we require in the

```
public class Producer {
  private /*@ spec_public @*/ Product[] buf;
  private /*@ spec_public @*/ int n;
  private /*@ spec_public @*/ Consumer con;

  /*@ public instance invariant buf!=null && buf.length>0
    @        && 0<=n && n<buf.length
    @        && (\forall int i,j;
    @            buf[i]==buf[j] && 0<=i && i<buf.length && 0<=j
    @                                              && j<buf.length;
    @            i==j || buf[i]==null);
    @*/
  public Producer() {
    buf = new Product[10];
  }

  /*@ requires p!=null;
    @ ensures \result <==> (\exists int i;
    @                     0<=i && i<buf.length; buf[i]==p);
    @*/
  public final /*@ pure @*/ boolean produced(Product p) {
    int i=0;
    /*@ loop_invariant (i>=0 && i<=buf.length
      @               && !(\exists int j;
      @                     j>=0 && j<i && j<buf.length;
      @                     buf[j]==p));
      @ assignable i;
      @*/
    while (i<buf.length) {
      if (buf[i]==p) return true;
      i++;
    }
    return false;
  }

  /*@ requires c.pro==this && c!=null;
    @ ensures this.con==c && c.buf==buf;
    @ assignable this.con, c.buf;
    @*/
  public final void setConsumer(Consumer c) {
    this.con = c;
    c.setBuffer(buf);
  }
```

**Figure 10.1:** Producer class of consumer/producer scenario (Part 1)

```
  /*@ requires con!=null && con.n!=n && p!=null;
    @ ensures (\forall int i; 0<=i && i<buf.length;
    @          \old(buf[i])!=p) ==> ((buf.length-1==n ==> n==0)
    @          && ((buf.length-1>n) ==> n==\old((n+1))));
    @ assignable buf[n], n;
    @*/
  public void produce(Product p) {
    if (!produced(p)) {
      buf[n] = p;
      if (n==buf.length-1) {
        n=0;
      } else {
        n=(n+1);
      }
    }
  }
}

public class Consumer {
  private /*@ spec_public @*/ Product[] buf;
  private /*@ spec_public @*/ int n;
  private /*@ spec_public @*/ Producer pro;

  /*@ invariant buf!=null && 0<=n
    @          && n<buf.length && pro!=null
    @          && pro.con==this && pro.buf==buf;
    @*/

  /*@ requires p!=null && p.con==null;
    @*/
  public Consumer(Producer p) {
    pro = p;
    pro.setConsumer(this);
  }

  /*@ requires b==pro.buf;
    @ ensures b==this.buf;
    @ assignable this.buf;
    @*/
  public final void setBuffer(Product[] b) { this.buf = b; }
}

public class Product {}
```

**Figure 10.2:** Producer class (Part 2) and consumer class of consumer/producer scenario precondition that the array to set is the same as that of the corresponding `Producer`. Calling the method `setConsumer(Consumer)` in `Producer` then cares for safely initialising the sharing between `Consumer` and `Producer`. As a result (of this implementation) no Java context (which obeys the annotated preconditions) will be able to violate the class invariants of `Producer` and `Consumer`. But this is still to be proven, as detailed in the following.

### Durable Correctness

What has to be done to prove (not relativised) durable correctness of the open program $P = \{\texttt{Producer}, \texttt{Consumer}\}$ with respect to the annotated JML specification $S$ as defined in Sect. 10.1? We proceed step by step:

1. The invariants are translated from JML to JavaFOL as follows:

$$\begin{aligned}\varphi_{\texttt{Producer}} = \dot{\forall} o{:}\texttt{Producer}.\ & o.\texttt{buf} \not\doteq \texttt{null} \\ & \wedge 0 \leq o.\texttt{n} \wedge o.\texttt{n} < o.\texttt{buf.length} \\ & \wedge \forall i{:}\textsc{Integer}.\,\forall j{:}\textsc{Integer}.\,(o.\texttt{buf}[i] \doteq o.\texttt{buf}[j] \\ & \qquad \wedge 0 \leq i \wedge i < o.\texttt{buf.length} \\ & \qquad \wedge 0 \leq j \wedge j < o.\texttt{buf.length} \\ & \qquad \rightarrow i \doteq j \vee o.\texttt{buf}[i] \doteq \texttt{null})\end{aligned}$$

$$\begin{aligned}\varphi_{\texttt{Consumer}} = \dot{\forall} o{:}\texttt{Consumer}.\ & o.\texttt{buf} \not\doteq \texttt{null} \\ & \wedge 0 \leq o.\texttt{n} \wedge o.\texttt{n} < o.\texttt{buf.length} \\ & \wedge o.\texttt{pro} \not\doteq \texttt{null} \wedge o.\texttt{pro.con} \doteq o \wedge o.\texttt{pro.buf} \doteq o.\texttt{buf}\end{aligned}$$

2. First of all we have to identify depends clauses for both invariants. We restrict our attention to `Producer`. We have two possibilities of finding a depends clause for $\varphi_{\texttt{Producer}}$:

   - The user finds a set of extended terms and proves that it is in fact a depends clause. A natural choice for $\varphi_{\texttt{Producer}}$ is

$$D = \left\{\begin{array}{l} *_{\texttt{Producer}}.\texttt{<created>}, *.\texttt{buf}, *.\texttt{buf.length}, *.\texttt{n}, \\ (\text{for } x : \texttt{Producer}, i : \textsc{Integer}\ ; \\ \qquad\qquad 0 \leq i \wedge i < x.\texttt{buf.length}\ ;\ x.\texttt{buf}[i]) \end{array}\right\}$$

   The found set of extended terms must be proven to be a depends clause for $\varphi_{\texttt{Producer}}$. We use Proof Obligation Template

*CorrectDepends* in the following instantiation:

$$\begin{aligned}
&\text{Def} \wedge \varphi_{\texttt{Producer}} \\
&\quad \rightarrow \{*\}\{\ (\text{for } o : \texttt{Producer}\ ;\ ;\ (o.\texttt{buf} := \text{buf}^{@pre}(o) \\
&\qquad\qquad\qquad \mid \text{buf}^{@pre}(o).\texttt{length} := \text{length}^{@pre}(\text{buf}^{@pre}(o)) \\
&\qquad\qquad\qquad \mid o.\texttt{n} := \text{n}^{@pre}(o) \\
&\qquad\qquad\qquad \mid (\text{for } k : \text{INTEGER}\ ; \\
&\qquad\qquad\qquad\quad 0 \leq k \wedge k < \text{length}^{@pre}(\text{buf}^{@pre}(o))\ ; \\
&\qquad\qquad\qquad\quad \text{buf}^{@pre}(o)[k] := \text{arr}^{@pre}(\text{buf}^{@pre}(o), k)))))\} \\
&\qquad\qquad\qquad\qquad\qquad\qquad\qquad\qquad\qquad\qquad\qquad \varphi_{\texttt{Producer}}
\end{aligned}$$

with

$$\begin{aligned}
\text{Def} = \ & \forall x{:}\texttt{Producer}.\ \text{buf}^{@pre}(x) \doteq x.\texttt{buf} \\
& \wedge \forall x{:}\texttt{Producer}.\ \text{n}^{@pre}(x) \doteq x.\texttt{n} \\
& \wedge \forall x{:}\texttt{Product[]}.\ \text{length}^{@pre}(x) \doteq x.\texttt{length} \\
& \wedge \forall x{:}\texttt{Product[]}.\ \forall i{:}\text{INTEGER}.\ \text{arr}^{@pre}(x, i) \doteq x[i]
\end{aligned}$$

- Alternatively we may use the function Dep which delivers the following depends clause. It does not need to be verified by a proof obligation according to Lemma 9.3.

$$\text{Dep}(\varphi_{\texttt{Producer}}) = \left\{ \begin{array}{l} *_{\texttt{Producer}}.\texttt{<created>}, *.\texttt{buf}, \\ *.\texttt{buf.length}, *.\texttt{n}, \\ (\text{for } x{:}\texttt{Producer}, i{:}\text{INTEGER}\ ;\ ;\ x.\texttt{buf}[i]) \end{array} \right\}$$

In this case it does not play a role with which of both depends clauses we continue our investigations.

3. For the subset of $D$ consisting of the first, second, and the fourth depends clause element ($*_{\texttt{Producer}}$.`<created>`, $*$.`buf` and $*$.`n`), `Producer` is a self-guard. This is because `buf` and `n` are private fields in `Producer`, and because of the special rule for `<created>`.

4. The type of the `buf` field, `Producer[]`, is an array type. So there cannot be a self-guard for the remaining items of $D$. We must thus search for guards: Since both, `Producer` and `Consumer` reference `.buf`, we define the guard to be $G = \{\texttt{Producer}, \texttt{Consumer}\}$.

   Now it must be proven that $G$ is in fact a guard. We can easily see that $\text{Exp}(D) \subseteq D$. Moreover, $ST(D) = \{\texttt{Producer}\} \subseteq G$ and all fields in `Producer` and `Consumer` are private.

Guardedness can thus be shown with the proof obligation

$$IsGuard(D', \{\texttt{Producer}, \texttt{Consumer}\})$$

with

$$D' = \left\{ \begin{array}{l} *\texttt{.buf.length}, \\ (\text{for } x : \texttt{Producer}, i : \text{INTEGER} \; ; \\ \quad 0 \leq i \wedge i < x\texttt{.buf.length} \; ; \; x\texttt{.buf[}i\texttt{]}) \end{array} \right\}$$

This requires to show the validity of a formula for every applicable operation of the guard elements. As example we pick the method `setConsumer(Consumer)` in `Producer`. With $\varphi_{enc}$ defined as

$$\forall x\texttt{:Producer}.\ \text{Enc}_{y,z}\ [\text{InstanceOf}_{\texttt{Consumer}}(y) \vee \text{InstanceOf}_{\texttt{Producer}}(y), \\ z \doteq x\texttt{.buf}]$$

which is equivalent to

$$\forall y.\ \forall x\texttt{:Producer}.\ (\text{Acc}(y, x\texttt{.buf}) \\ \rightarrow \text{InstanceOf}_{\texttt{Consumer}}(y) \vee \text{InstanceOf}_{\texttt{Producer}}(y))$$

we get:

$$PreservesInv^*(\texttt{setConsumer(Consumer)}, \varphi_{enc}, \texttt{self}, \texttt{c})$$

which is equivalent to

$$\begin{array}{c} \exists x.\ \text{Acc}(x, \texttt{self}) \wedge \exists x.\ \text{Acc}(x, \texttt{c}) \wedge \varphi_{enc} \\ \wedge \varphi_{\texttt{Consumer}} \wedge \varphi_{\texttt{Producer}} \wedge \texttt{c.pro} \doteq \texttt{self} \\ \rightarrow \left[ \begin{array}{l} \texttt{try\{ self.setConsumer(c0=c)@Consumer; \}} \\ \texttt{catch (Throwable e) \{\}} \end{array} \right] \varphi_{enc} \end{array}$$

This formula must be modularly valid. With the help of Lemma 6.3 a closed proof with an empty set of generated contracts suffices for modular validity. Since the called method `setBuffer(Product[])` in `Consumer` is `final` this is possible.

5. In order to complete all the requirements of Lemma 10.1 there is one step left: It must be modularly shown that all operations in `Consumer`

and Producer preserve $\varphi_{\texttt{Producer}}$. This is possible as all public methods called by some method in these two classes are `final`. In the example of `setConsumer(Consumer)` it must be shown that the following formula holds modularly:

$$\mathit{PreservesInv}(\texttt{setConsumer(Consumer)}, \varphi_{\texttt{Producer}})$$

which is equivalent to

$$\begin{array}{c} \varphi_{\texttt{Producer}} \wedge \varphi_{\texttt{Consumer}} \wedge \texttt{c.pro} \doteq o \\ \rightarrow \left[ \begin{array}{l} \texttt{try\{ self.setConsumer(c0=c)@Consumer; \}} \\ \texttt{catch (Throwable e) \{\}} \end{array} \right] \varphi_{\texttt{Producer}} \end{array}$$

6. Finally the other two requirements of Lemma 10.1 must be fulfilled. We show

$$\mathit{EnsuresPost}(\mathit{opct})$$
$$\mathit{RespectsModifies}(\mathit{opct})$$

for all operation contracts *opct* attached as JML specifications in the above program. The modularity of proofs poses no problem since methods are declared `final` as necessary.

#### Relative Durable Correctness

We are now aiming at a more extensible program. So we get rid of all `final` modifiers, say only those in `Producer`. Moreover we declare the `buf` field in `Producer` as protected.

The first two steps are identical to before: The invariants representation in JavaFOL is the same as before and also the depends clauses do not change.

In step 3 we needed, before, the requirement that `Producer`'s `buf` field is private. Since this is not the case now, a generic extension contract is needed here. According to Lemma 10.2 all subclasses of `Producer` must preserve $\varphi_{\texttt{Producer}}$, which is formalised as the following extension contract:

```
generic contract {
  T extends* Producer;
  (∅, {φProducer})
}
```

Likewise, with the guards for the array access, the reasoning above suffices, but we have to take care that classes which are subclassing a guard class declaring a protected field satisfies the guard properties. Again we do this with the help of generic extension contracts:

```
generic contract {
  T extends* Producer;
  (∅, {φProducer, φenc})
}
```

with $\varphi_{enc}$ as defined in (4).

Moreover we need to prove $IsGuard(D', \{\texttt{Producer}, \texttt{Consumer}\})$ for the program consisting of `Producer` and `Consumer` itself. This is done as before, with one exception: the missing `final` modifiers of `produced(Product)` and `setConsumer(Consumer)` trigger the generation of extension contracts when the contracts of these methods are used during the proof. So we obtain as extension contracts (written in the JML extension):

```
generic contract {
  T extends* Producer;

  /*@ ensures \result <==> (\exists int i; buf[i]==p);
    @ assignable \nothing
    @*/
  public boolean produced(Product p);
}

generic contract {
  T extends* Producer;

  /*@ requires c.pro==this;
    @ ensures this.con==c;
    @ assignable this.con;
    @*/
  public void setConsumer(Consumer c);
}
```

All other proofs, for showing that invariants are preserved and operation contracts are fulfilled, are done as before. Here extension contracts are generated as well but they are subsumed by the ones obtained during the proofs above.

Altogether, we have achieved durable correctness of $\{\texttt{Producer}, \texttt{Consumer}\}$ relative to the (four) generic contracts denoted above.

### 10.3.2 Linked List with Iterator

Doubly linked lists are an omnipresent example when ownership based systems are discussed. Ownership systems often run into problems with this example since both the linked list and their iterators access the internals of the list. Thus, with strict ownership, no iterators are allowed. The Universe type system [Müller, 2002] attacks this issue by providing *readonly* references which are used by iterators for their access to the internals. Then iterators must not change anything directly. If they however do not violate invariants, we can argue that nothing bad can happen. With our technique it is no problem to allow for such modifying iterators.

Our linked list example is depicted in Figures 10.3 and 10.4. It is inspired by the class `java.util.LinkedList` from the standard Java Collections Framework as included in the Java 2 Platform, Standard Edition. That version uses *inner classes* for entries and iterators. We have not used inner classes since KeY cannot treat them presently. Whenever fields were accessed exploiting the special visibility rules for inner classes we have used getter and setter methods instead.

#### Durable Correctness

1. We are interested in the invariant $\varphi_{\mathtt{DLList}}$ defined as follows:

   $$\dot{\forall} l{:}\mathtt{DLList}.\ \forall e{:}\mathtt{Entry}.\ (\mathrm{Reach}[\{\mathtt{next}\}](l\mathtt{.header}, e) \\ \rightarrow e \doteq e\mathtt{.next.previous})$$

   It states that the linked list has correct links. So for all entries $e$ reached from the list header: $e$`.next` references via `previous` the entry $e$.

2. A depends clause for this invariant is

   $$D = \{(\text{for } l : \mathtt{DLList}, e : \mathtt{Entry}\ ;\ \mathrm{Reach}[\{\mathtt{next}\}](l\mathtt{.header}, e)\ ; \\ e\mathtt{.next.previous}), \\ (\text{for } l : \mathtt{DList}, e : \mathtt{Entry}\ ;\ \mathrm{Reach}[\{\mathtt{next}\}](l\mathtt{.header}, e)\ ;\ e\mathtt{.next}), \\ *\mathtt{.header}, *_{\mathtt{DLList}}\mathtt{.<created>}\}$$

   This is obtained by the extended procedure Dep from Sect. 9.1.2.

3. For the third and the fourth element of this clause, `DLList` is a self-guard because `header` is a private field in that class, and for `<created>` the special rule applies.

```
public class DLList {
  private DLEntry head;
  private int size;
  public DLList() {
    head=new DLEntry(null, null, null);
    head.setNext(head);
    head.setPrevious(head);
  }
  public DLItr listIterator(int index) {
    return new DLItr(head, index, size);
  }
  public boolean add(Object o) {
    DLEntry newDLEntry = new DLEntry(o, head, head.getPrevious());
    newDLEntry.getPrevious().setNext(newDLEntry);
    newDLEntry.getNext().setPrevious(newDLEntry);
    size++;
    return true;
  }
}

final class DLEntry {
  private Object element;
  private DLEntry next, previous;
  public DLEntry(Object element, DLEntry next, DLEntry previous) {
    this.element = element;
    this.next = next;
    this.previous = previous;
  }
  public Object getElement() { return element; }
  public void setElement(Object o) { element=o; }
  public DLEntry getNext() { return next; }
  public void setNext(DLEntry e) { next=e; }
  public DLEntry getPrevious() { return previous; }
  public void setPrevious(DLEntry e) { previous=e; }
}
```

**Figure 10.3:** Main class and entry class of the linked list

```
class DLItr {
  private DLEntry last, next, head;
  private int nextIndex, size;
  DLItr(DLEntry head, int index, int size) {
    this.head = head;
    last = head;
    if (index < 0 || index > size) throw new RuntimeException();
    next = head.getNext();
    for (nextIndex=0; nextIndex<index; nextIndex++) {
      next = next.getNext();
    }
  }
  public boolean hasNext() {
    return nextIndex != size;
  }
  public Object next() {
    if (nextIndex == size) throw new RuntimeException();
    last = next;
    next = next.getNext();
    nextIndex++;
    return last.getElement();
  }
  public void set(Object o) {
    if (last == head) throw new RuntimeException();
    last.setElement(o);
  }
}
```

**Figure 10.4:** Iterator of the linked list

4. **Entry** cannot serve as a self-guard for the remaining depends clause items since `setNext(Entry)` and `setPrevious(Entry)` do not preserve $\varphi_{\texttt{DLList}}$. So a guard is needed. A suitable candidate is the set $G := \{\texttt{DLList}, \texttt{DLItr}\}$ since both access the relevant objects induced by the depends clause and preserve $\varphi_{\texttt{DLList}}$.

   We see that $\mathrm{Exp}(D) \subseteq D$ and that the start type of $D$, which is $\{\texttt{DLList}\}$, is part of $G$. We need to prove guardedness though.

   The property $\varphi_{enc}$ to be preserved by all operations of $G$ is

$$\forall l{:}\texttt{DLList}.\, \forall e{:}\texttt{Entry}.\, \mathrm{Enc}_{y,z}\left[\mathrm{InstanceOf}_{\texttt{DLList}}(y) \vee \mathrm{InstanceOf}_{\texttt{DLItr}}(y), \mathrm{Reach}[\{\texttt{next}\}](l\texttt{.header}, e)\right]$$

   which is equivalent to

$$\begin{aligned}\forall l{:}\texttt{DLList}.\ \forall y.\ \forall z{:}\texttt{Entry}.\ &(\mathrm{Acc}(y,z) \wedge \mathrm{Reach}[\texttt{next}](l\texttt{.header}, z)\\ &\to \mathrm{InstanceOf}_{\texttt{DLList}}(y) \vee \mathrm{InstanceOf}_{\texttt{DLItr}}(y)\\ &\vee \mathrm{Reach}[\texttt{next}](l\texttt{.header}, y))\end{aligned}$$

   It must be shown that this property is preserved by all operations of the guards (which include the start type of $D$). We present as example the case of the `next()` method in `DLItr`.

$$\mathit{PreservesInv}^{*}(\texttt{next()}, \varphi_{enc}, \texttt{self})$$

   which is equivalent to

$$\exists x.\ \mathrm{Acc}(x, \texttt{self}) \wedge \varphi_{enc} \wedge \varphi_{\texttt{DLList}} \to \left[\begin{array}{l}\texttt{try\{ self.next()@DLItr; \}}\\ \texttt{catch (Throwable e) \{\}}\end{array}\right]\varphi_{enc}$$

   Again we have to show modular validity by finding a closed proof with an empty set of generated contracts. Since `getNext()` in `DLItr` is final no extension contracts need to be generated.

5. Finally all methods of $G$ must be modularly proven to preserve $\varphi_{\texttt{DLList}}$. We must, for instance, prove

$$\mathit{PreservesInv}(\texttt{next()@DLItr}, \varphi_{\texttt{DLList}})$$

equivalent to $\varphi_{\texttt{DLList}} \rightarrow \left[\begin{array}{l}\texttt{try\{ self.next()@DLItr; \}} \\ \texttt{catch (Throwable e) \{\}}\end{array}\right] \varphi_{\texttt{DLList}}$.

Again the invocation to `getNext()` does not produce generic contracts for the same reason as above.

6. Since there are no operation contracts we are done.

### Relative Durable Correctness

In order to improve extensibility we could remove the final modifier in the class declaration of `DLEntry`. This would, as in the last example, trigger the generation of generic extension contracts. Also, we would need operation contracts for the methods in `DLEntry`. So, for example, the method `getNext()` would get the following JML contract:

```
/*@ ensures \result = next;
  @ assignable \nothing;
  @*/
public DLEntry getNext();
```

Used in one of the relative-modular proofs, we obtain the extension contract:

```
generic contract {
  T extends* DLEntry;

  /*@ ensures result = next;
    @ assignable \nothing;
    @*/
  public DLEntry getNext();
}
```

With the exception that during the proofs extension contracts emerge, the steps equal the treatment for un-relativised durable correctness from above.

## 10.4 Durable Correctness in the Presence of Abstraction in Invariants

So far we have ruled out (in Sect. 9.1.4 and with Def. 9.1) occurrences of dynamically bound queries in invariants. This guaranteed context-independent query-free depends clauses. We have seen in Ex. 1.3 an example where a query (`equals(Object)`) occurs in an invariant. In closed programs, it was possible to rewrite the invariant without using queries. In Ex. 9.6 we could for instance use the fact that the default implementation of `equals` is the object identity. If classes had overridden `equals` then we would have incorporated the concrete locations read in these implementations.

The same issue holds for abstract (that is, specification-only) fields in specifications. Such fields are called *model fields* in JML. Every concrete subclass may interpret abstract fields differently. We can simulate abstract fields by employing queries. The binding to concrete fields corresponds to overriding the query. We will thus only treat the case of queries. An explicit treatment of abstract fields would be done analogously.

In this section we can only sketch at an example what needs to be done to extend our approach. There are no formal proofs, which need to be done as future work.

First of all we can state that it is necessary for dynamically bound queries used in specifications of open programs that all overridings of these queries in the context fulfil the same operation contract as the original query. Otherwise it would be impossible to reason about this query, without knowledge of a concrete context, at all.

**Example 10.4.** Assume the `Period` class of our running example contained an invariant $\varphi'_{\texttt{Period}}$:

$$\dot{\forall} p{:}\texttt{Period}.\ \texttt{earlierOrEqual}(p\texttt{.start}, p\texttt{.end}) \doteq \text{TRUE}$$

The specification of `earlierOrEqual(Date)` is as before. By the invariant the already known generic extension $gct_{\texttt{earlierOrEqual(Date)}}$ contract must be created when durable correctness is proven:

```
generic contract {
  T extends* Date;
  class T {
    /*@ normal_behavior
      @ requires cmp !=null;
      @ ensures \result == (year<cmp.year || (year==cmp.year
      @                            && month.val<=cmp.month.val));
      @*/
    /*@pure@*/ boolean earlierOrEqual(Date cmp);
  }
}
```

*

If the specification of the used query is complete, that is, the functional behaviour is completely determined by the method contract, and moreover the contract does not contain query symbols, then it is always possible to obtain a query-free invariant and thus a query-free depends clause. In our example we would just need to replace the occurrence of the query with the right hand side of the specification `\result == ...` and substitute parameters appropriately. We would then obtain the original invariant $\varphi_{\texttt{Period}}$.

Some query specifications are incomplete however, as for instance the following contract of `earlierOrEqual(Date)`:

```
public class Date {
 /*@ normal_behavior
   @ requires cmp !=null;
   @ ensures \result ==> (year<cmp.year || (year==cmp.year
   @                         && month.val<=cmp.month.val));
   @*/
 /*@pure@*/ boolean earlierOrEqual(Date cmp);
}
```

where the equivalence is replaced by an implication. A correct overriding of this method satisfying the corresponding generic contract could be specified as follows:

```
public class Date3 extends Date {
  private Day day;
 /*@ normal_behavior
   @ requires cmp !=null;
   @ ensures \result ==>
   @            (year<cmp.year ||
   @            (year==cmp.year && month.val<cmp.month.val) ||
   @            (year==cmp.year && month.val==cmp.month.val &&
   @              ((cmp instanceof Date3)
   @                    ==> day.val<=((Date3)cmp).day.val)));
   @*/
 /*@pure@*/ boolean earlierOrEqual(Date cmp);
}
```

This method however introduces a new dependency, namely to a new field `day` and the integer value in `day.val`. At a first glance this has no implications for correctness, but imagine `Period` contained a method `getObject()`

specified not to leak references to the usually protectable objects; this method delegates to `Date` instance `start` and its implementation in `Date3` returns the `Day` instance stored in `date`. Then it would be possible for an observer to get in control of such a reference and manipulate it such that the new invariant is violated. All this would not be prevented by the guard mechanism, since the new location is not proven to be protected.

This is why we introduce additional requirements on newly added locations. All locations which are additional dependencies must

- either be a private field in a class which preserves the invariant of question; this is clearly not the case for the `Day` instance, which is again a quite general class and not specific for `Period`, or

- origin from a private field $a$ and from $a$ quite a strict encapsulation must start: Let $e$ be an instance of the class which declares $a$. Then the locations to protect can be described by terms with a field as top operator[1] as $e.a$, $e.a.a_1$, $e.a.a_1, \ldots a_n$ and so on. Let $D$ be this set of location terms. In terms of encapsulation predicates we require the following property:

$$\mathrm{Enc}_{y,z}\left[y \doteq e, \quad \bigvee_{d \in D} z \doteq d\right]$$

  In the example of `day`, we would require from a `Date3` instance `d3`:

$$\mathrm{Enc}_{y,z}\left[y \doteq \texttt{d3}, z \doteq \texttt{d3.day}\right]$$

  This means, only `d3` is allowed to access `d3.day`.

There are two issues still to clarify:

- How do we determine dependencies of queries?

- How do we impose the mentioned restrictions on unknown subclasses?

The first question is answered by the following definition which follows quite closely the depends clauses of formulae:

[1] This can easily be extended to full location terms.

**Definition 10.1.** Let $q$ be a query symbol with $\sigma(q) = (T_1, \ldots, T_n)$ occurring in a program $P$. A *depends clause of the query symbol* $q$ in $P$ is a finite set $D_q(p_1, \ldots, p_n)$ of extended terms with possible free occurrences of logical variables $p_1, \ldots, p_n$ of types $T_1, \ldots, T_n$; $D_q(p_1, \ldots, p_n)$ which does not contain query symbols but satisfies the following property in all states $s_1$ and $s_2$ and for all $\beta$: If $f^{s_1}(e_1, \ldots, e_m) = f^{s_2}(e_1, \ldots, e_m)$ for all $(f, (e_1, \ldots, e_m)) \in \mathrm{Loc}_{s_1,P,\beta}(D_q(p_1, \ldots, p_n))$ then

$$\mathrm{val}_{s_1,P,\beta}(q(p_1, \ldots, p_n)) = \mathrm{val}_{s_2,P,\beta}(q(p_1, \ldots, p_n))$$

**Example 10.5.** The method declaration `earlierOrEqual(Date)` in `Date` of our running example has the following depends clause with free occurrences of the logical variable $d$ of type `Date`:

$$\{d.\mathtt{year}, d.\mathtt{month}, d.\mathtt{month.val}\}$$

The overridden version in class `Date3` additionally contains

$$\{d.\mathtt{day}, d.\mathtt{day.val}\}$$

*

We need to impose restrictions on the context in which our program is used. And as we have done earlier, we employ generic extension contracts to formalise these constraints. The needed property requires to talk about the depends clause of a query on the object level. Clearly this is not expressible by means of JavaFOL or our specification languages and thus also not by generic contracts as defined in Sect. 5.1. In the sequel a quite specialised extension to the specification machinery is thus introduced. Since we need the extension only in generic contracts (Sect. 5.1), the extension is added on that level. Note that this is only our second (after the basic encapsulation predicates) and last extension to specification languages keeping our invasions into existing languages as small as possible.

If the query $q$ in question was declared in class $C$ as

```
R q(p1, ..., pn)
```

we write that property as follows as generic contract

```
generic contract {
  T extends* C;
  (qpt(q), ∅)
}
```

where $qpt(q)$ is the special *query protection contract* of $q$ with the semantics as discussed above.

For the invariant $\varphi'_{\texttt{Period}}$ we would need to impose the following generic contract:

```
generic contract {
  T extends* C;
  (qpt(earlierOrEqual), ∅)
}
```

which would be instantiated for `Date3` as

$$\mathrm{Enc}_{y,z}\,[y \doteq \texttt{d3}, \texttt{d3}, z \doteq \texttt{d3.day}]$$

If this invariant property is preserved (naively) by the methods of `Date3`, $\varphi'_{\texttt{Period}}$ with its dependency from the dynamically bound `earlierOrEqual()` can be durably verified.

## 10.5 Verification of Components

We are now referring to component contracts as introduced in Sect. 5.2. Component contracts were defined as pairs of a set $GCt$ of generic extension contracts and a specification for the classes of the component. The correctness of component contracts was defined in terms of durable correctness relative to $GCt$. So the last Lemma 10.2 provided us with the proof obligations to check for the correctness of components.

**Lemma 10.3.** A component is correct w.r.t. a component contract $(GCt, S)$ if the conditions of Lemma 10.2 are established.

*Proof.* Follows directly from Lemma 10.2 and Def. 5.7. □

**Example 10.6.** Consider again Ex. 1.1 (*without* `final` modifiers at the methods `earlierOrEqual(Date)` and `copy()`). As in Ex. 5.9, let $P$ be the component consisting only of `Period` and $cct = (GCt, S)$ consisting of the specification $S$ given by the annotations in Fig. 1.1 and

$$GCt := \{gct_{\texttt{earlierOrEqual(Date)}}, gct_{\texttt{copy()}}\}$$

with $gct_{\texttt{earlierOrEqual(Date)}}$ and $gct_{\texttt{copy()}}$ as defined in Ex. 10.2.

To prove the correctness of `Period` as a component w.r.t. the sketched component contract we have to prove the same proof obligations as in Ex. 5.9. Thus the component {`Period`} is a correct component w.r.t. *cct*. *

**Example 10.7.** Consider now the modified version from Ex. 1.2 in which `start` and `end` are insufficiently encapsulated. Everything is as in the last example except that we cannot ensure

$$\models_P^{GCt} IsGuard(D_1, \{\texttt{Period}\})$$

So we have to impose more restrictions on the context, which is allowed by the definition of component correctness. As in Ex. 10.3, we add the generic contract $gct_{\varphi_{\texttt{Period}}}$

```
generic contract {
  T unconstrained;
  (∅, {φPeriod})
}
```

to $GCt$ such that

$$GCt := \{gct_{\varphi_{\texttt{Period}}}, gct_{\texttt{earlierOrEqual(Date)}}, gct_{\texttt{copy()}}\}$$

Altogether, we have proven that the component {`Period`} is correct w.r.t. $(GCt, S)$. *

## 10.6 Design Implications

We have seen how open programs can be guaranteed to work in a partially or completely unknown context. We have also observed that it is in some situations quite complex to take sufficient care of invariants. We would thus like to briefly investigate the question how component design and specification should be, such that verification becomes easier.

First of all we can observe a trade-off between the *extensibility* of a system and the possibility of strict *modular verification*. An extensible program typically contains non-final dynamically bound methods and provides only little encapsulation. A program suited to modular verification offers only few possibilities to adapt functionality: methods are favoured to be not overridable or statically bound and there is much encapsulation. A program is less extensible, the more it is suited to modular verification with the goal of *strict* modular correctness, and vice versa. It is our contribution to have made a 'third way' viable. With generic extension contracts it is possible to have a user defined degree of encapsulation. So each developer can decide how much his program should be extensible, what the requirements on extensions are, and which parts should be entirely hidden from clients.

Another observation is that the use of components of a more common nature hampers modular verification. Keep the `Entry` class of our `null`-free linked list example in mind. This class was not designed to be used only in this particular `null`-free linked list but in any other, for instance unconstrained, linked list. Thus the invariant for `null`-freeness was attached to the list class and the methods of `Entry` were not specific enough to prevent `null` elements. If we however had had a class `NullFreeEntry` with an invariant attached to this class, invariant protection would have been much easier: Instead of employing a guard, we would have used simply the self-guard `Entry`. Thus more specific classes with more specific invariants are preferable for modular verification. One could equally state that it is difficult to protect invariants with a wide scope, such as making statements over a list and all its reachable elements. On the other hand, it is the goal of object-orientation to foster reuse, so verification must get along with the reuse of components of a more general nature. We have shown that we can cope with this demand on the verification side, but with considerable effort, and in some cases only by constraining the reuse context. It will often be a question of the application domain if more guarantees or more extensibility is desired. In safety critical areas probably the former is more appreciated while there might be other domains which require more extensibility and adaptability at the cost of guarantees.

## 10.7 Summary

In this section we have taken the final step to the verification with the goal of durable correctness of open programs and of component correctness. We have presented two proof obligation systems. Thee first allowed for strict proofs of durable correctness of open programs. The second liberalised this by imposing extension contracts on the context in which the program is used. This is needed if some properties cannot or are not intended to be protected by encapsulation. For protection by encapsulation, the techniques for modular verification of invariants from the last chapter have been transfered to open programs. We have seen at 'benchmark' examples that our approach works in practice and have stated that, in practice, an appropriate compromise between the possibility for modular verification and extensibility of programs must be found. Finally we have discussed how to extend the technique to abstract specifications using queries, to the verification of component contracts and we sketched some implications on how to specify and design verifiable components.

This concludes Part II on modular verification. Conclusions of the whole work follow.

# 11 Conclusions

Nil actum reputa si quid
superest agendum.

*(Lucan)*

The conclusions of this thesis contain a review of related work, an outlook to possible future activities improving or complementing our approach, and a summary of the work.

## 11.1 Related Work

In the following we compare related work with ours. The first area to review are general approaches to software specification and verification, both in theory and as tools. Then we look at notions of correctness of whole programs. Next are the two 'wings' of our approach: specifications of encapsulation and context. The final part contains approaches which fully aim at modular verification.

### 11.1.1 Program Specification and Verification

The idea of formally specifying programs with the intend to verify them is old and can at least be dated back to Hoare [1969] such as the idea of assigning pre- and postcondition pairs to pieces of programs. Meyer [1992] made specifications of programs in the context of object-oriented programs widely popular by referring to them as *contracts*. Formal specifications were becoming a first class citizen of programs, here in Meyer's Eiffel language. On the academic side interface specification languages emerged, like the *Larch* family of specification languages. An important offspring is the Java Modeling Language (JML) as discussed in Sect. 3.3.2. Several other similar contract-based languages are targeting Java, but are not as elaborated as JML. Examples are described in Kramer [1998], Bartetzko et al. [2001], Karaorman et al. [1999], Duncan and Hölzle [1998], and Findler and Felleisen [2001]. These developments have increased expressiveness of specifications over programs, for instance, Meyer's contract language did allow only boolean expressions of Eiffel, while JML allows for quantifications and convenient abbreviations for all kinds of purposes. All the above mentioned languages were primarily intended for runtime checking, not for formal verification.

Another direction of impact were specifications languages more on the design level, like Z [Spivey, 1992] and B [Abrial, 1996], and object-oriented derivations like Object-Z [Duke et al., 1991]. Even less formal approaches like the Unified Modeling Language (UML) [OMG] were pushed in the direction of formal specification languages with its integral part Object Constraint Language (OCL) [Warmer and Kleppe, 1999]. The application of such design-oriented specification languages for the specification and verification of programs requires a mapping from the more abstract domain to program code.

We have captured the common logical core of formal specification languages for object-oriented programs in the definition of specifications in Chapter 3. This is not a big deal, but progress is obtained in small steps: We have for instance defined a unified representation of exceptional behaviour, which is much simpler than in JML for instance. Another example is the uniform representation of class invariants simply as closed first order formulae, while for instance in JML there are two notions, static and instance invariants, to be dragged along. While the above mentioned specification languages tend to be quite verbose in order to make it specifiers easier to do their job, we just aimed at a condensed representation. This still allows for translations from specification languages into our representation.

A number of verification systems for Java-like languages have been developed in recent years. We have discussed the KeY system [Ahrendt et al., 2005a] which our work is based on in Sect. 1.1. There are other program verification tools, for instance *Jack* [Burdy et al., 2003], *Krakatoa* [Marché et al., 2004] and the *Loop* system [Jacobs and Poll, 2004]. To our knowledge they do not allow for the verification of assignable clauses. These systems work on single methods only and do not establish a property comparable to durable correctness. *ESC/Java2* [Cok and Kiniry, 2004] is an automatic extended static checker which is not sound. The *Jive* tool [Meyer et al., 2000] is not yet available. Jive's technique to modularly ensure invariants is the *Universe* type system as discussed below. The extended static checker *Boogie* [Barnett et al., 2005] built for the specification language *Spec#* for the programming language C# is an approach similar to ESC/Java2. Its technique for invariants is discussed below.

### 11.1.2 Notions of Correctness of Programs

One would expect that formal specification languages come with a precise semantics of under which conditions a program is correct with respect to a word of the specification language. This is however not the case. Yet the most precise semantics is the one of JML. JML is however still work in progress and even some details of the relatively stable core are not yet captured precisely.

The semantics of *preconditions* and *postconditions* is mostly common sense. However from time to time languages *require* preconditions to hold and enter into error handling otherwise, as Eiffel or the semantics induced by various runtime assertion checkers advocate.

*Assignable clauses* are in general regarded as the only way out of what is commonly known as the frame problem [Borgida et al., 1995]. A precise semantics of assignable clauses is defined in Beckert and Schmitt [2003]. We have followed this under the consideration of more complex modifier sets which can capture reachable objects and array ranges. JML defines the (roughly, see Sect. 3.3.2) same semantics informally. It however also allows for abstractly describing locations by *data groups* [Leino and Nelson, 2002]. This allows to specify locations which do not yet exist, which is necessary when contracts are inherited. We can solve this problem with the help of extension contracts. Müller et al. [2003] deal with the issue of assignable clauses containing abstract fields. Their semantics is based on the Universe model. Other languages ignore the problem or refer, as OCL, to an implicit assignable clause, which is in general insufficient [Roth and Schmitt, 2006].

Concerning the question of when *invariants* are supposed to hold, some approaches follow the naive approach of Meyer [1997] that invariants defined in a class must be established by operations of that class, which is too weak.

The most popular semantics refers to visible states [Poetzsch-Heffter, 1997, Leavens et al., 2005, Huizing and Kuiper, 2000] as already discussed in Sect. 3.2.10. In contrast to it, our observed-state semantics is not interested in intermediate states of the specified program, which is weaker but as we have explained more adequate.

Müller et al. [2004] (see below for a thorough discussion of this work) weaken the visible state semantics to a *relevant invariant semantics*. It is based on the Universe type system [Müller, 2002]. Thus a hierarchical partition of objects in *contexts* with a unique *owner* object is available. An object $e$ is *relevant* to the execution of a method if $e$ is in the context (or in one up the context hierarchy) of the current receiver object. If this is the case then $e$'s invariant must be satisfied in the visible states of that method execution. This semantics still considers internal states, it is coupled to the universe technique, and it is, in our opinion, highly complicated to explain to a software developer with mediocre formal background. Müller [2002] follows a similar approach but considers invariants simply as boolean model fields, that is fields for specification-only purposes, with an appropriate definition corresponding to the invariant.

The *Boogie methodology* is more extensively described below. It defines the following special semantics of when invariants must hold: they must hold whenever a specification-only `inv` field of an object explicitely requires this. $o$.`inv` is set to a type name which is either the dynamic type of $o$ or a supertype. The invariants of all supertypes of $o$.`inv` must hold in any state. The Boogie technique requires lots of new annotations with highly complicated semantics to be done by the programmer. Moreover again, and even more than with the visible state semantics, internal states are taken into consideration.

### 11.1.3 Constraining Context

It is quite obvious that in languages where aliasing effects can occur, but especially if dynamic binding takes place, it can never be excluded that correctness of a program is violated by malicious extensions of a system. In general only restrictions on the program context can help. The concept that context must adhere to certain conditions is, as far as we know, made explicit as *formal* constraints in our work for the first time.

Of course informal descriptions are around, as can be seen in the example in Sect. 1.2 from the Java API. But they do not suffice when the rigour of formal methods should be applied.

Some specification languages impose *implicit* requirements on the context: JML requires a behavioural subtyping discipline. All contracts are inherited to operations which override the specified operation. This makes all subtypes, even those which are not known when specifying the type, conform to their supertypes. This is however quite a strict policy, since programs which do not follow these guidelines are excluded, though they might be functionally correct. With generic contracts we can specify more precisely, *which* overriding methods must fulfil *which* conditions.

The *Contracts* technique by Helm et al. [1990] suggests, like our generic contracts, to generalise the contract concept to include other unknown participants of a contract than just the caller of a method. Moreover the idea that instantiations of contracts might prove necessary is introduced there. However the specification expressions used there are temporal properties and thus completely different to ours. Finally instantiations occur on the object level instead of on the type level.

Methodological similarities with the approach to constrain context instead of the program itself can be found in *assume-guarantee* reasoning [Henzinger et al., 1998]. As in our approach, reasoning about one module is done by assuming properties of the other modules, which are later verified. However the problem to be solved differs in many ways from ours and leads to other technical consequences. Also approaches in the verification of concurrent programs follow a similar approach by assuming conditions of allowed changes in the context a process is used. Only *if* these conditions are met a process is obliged to guarantee a behaviour. This is referred to as *rely-guarantee* conditions [Jones, 1983]. Our work can thus be considered as transferring these approaches to the verification of sequential object-oriented components.

### 11.1.4 Specification and Verification of Encapsulation

Several approaches to specify and verify encapsulation properties have already been discussed in Sect. 4.1.2. They served as a basis to justify why encapsulation should be specified differently. We have shown that we can simulate all of them.

Very recently the Universe type system has been integrated in JML [Dietl and Müller, 2005]. This integration is however quite loose. The usual annotations of the Universe type system are available as JML-like annotations to be put next to field and variable declarations. Usual JML expressions are almost not affected by these special annotations, except that there is a specification-only `owner` field available. Functional and encapsulation specifications however appear as completely unrelated issues.

We are not aware of any tight integration of functional specification languages and facilities to specify encapsulation comparable to ours.

There is also no work which tries to separate the issues of specifying encapsulation and checking it—a discipline which is conceived quite natural in the functional verification world. We have achieved this distinction, which opens up the advantage to employ the checking techniques for those problems which can be covered by them. For the verification of certain encapsulation properties we have made use of the Universe type system by Müller [2002].

A very recent approach to check encapsulation with a static analysis different from type systems is Burrows [2005]. The analysis is currently only for Featherweight Java. It seems possible to use this technique to prove certain encapsulation predicates.

### 11.1.5 Verification of Operation Contracts

All the verification systems described in Sect. 11.1.1 can prove satisfaction of pre-/post condition pairs, though ESC/Java2 does this in an unsound way. Most systems use Hoare logic or weakest precondition calculi, with the exception of KeY which uses a dynamic logic.

Proof obligations in a dynamic logic like JavaDL for the assurance of postconditions under the assumption of preconditions are quite standard. The idea of encoding thrown exceptions as we did has been discussed for instance in Beckert and Sasse [2001], Roth [2002].

Running systems which check assignable clauses are rare though. A more intricate JavaDL proof obligation than ours for assignable clauses has been presented by Sasse [2004]. The employed proof obligation potentially refers to all possible locations of the program, which makes it change un-modularly whenever the model changes. Spoto and Poll [2003] have designed an algorithm which uses abstract interpretation to prove assignable clauses. That work has not been implemented. Cataño and Huisman [2003] have implemented the static checker *Chase* which checks assignable clauses, but lacks soundness. Müller [2002] presents a technique to modularly verify assignable clauses, but it is difficult to compare this approach since the semantics of assignable clauses differs.

### 11.1.6 Analysis of Dependencies

Analyses of dependencies in specifications, like the use of our depends clauses (see Sect. 9.1), have been performed in earlier work as for instance in Leino and Nelson [2002]. Müller et al. [2004] informally introduce notions of dependees and dependencies but do not use them formally during reasoning. Instead they define admissible invariants on allowed access chains which makes it impossible to treat invariants which have an unpolished shape like $\forall x.\ (x \doteq a.b \rightarrow x.c \doteq 0)$ for which we would like to have $\mathrm{Exp}(a.b.c)$ as depends clause, not $\{a.b, *.c\}$.

Both approaches do not cover advanced description of locations, like dependencies from all slots of an array.

### 11.1.7 Modular Verification of Invariants

We are now reviewing complete approaches for the modular verification and its main problem, the verification of invariants. The two main competing approaches are techniques around the Universe type system [Müller et al., 2004] and the Boogie methodology developed at the Microsoft Research group [Barnett et al., 2004].

Both approaches provide invariant protection by means of two principles:

**Ownership.** Objects are assigned owners. An owner is responsible for modifications of an owned object. Ownership is integrated as an extension of the programming language by extending its type system.

**Visibility.** Invariants are visible for more objects than one. An invariant must thus in general be proven for more than the class which declares the invariant or for several objects of the same class.

A closer look reveals a relationship to our system of ensuring invariants modularly with the help of depends clauses and guarded invariants. The ownership technique corresponds to using guards, providing encapsulated objects which do not escape from entities responsible for maintaining invariants. The visibility technique corresponds in a sense to the use of self-guards (see below).

#### Modular Verification Based on Universes

The most advanced approach aiming at modular verification with the help of ownership types is Müller et al. [2004]. It is a variation of Müller [2002]. The focus in this work is on *layered* object structures. This results in restrictions on *admissible* invariants. Invariants are admissible if they are protected from uncontrolled violations via *ownership* and via *visibility*. The agglutination of these two concepts makes the approach quite bulky. Our technique does in principal not sort out invariants *a priori*, though there are syntactic restrictions as well, when guardedness must be proven.

The ownership technique in Müller et al. [2004] is based on Müller's Universe type system [Müller, 2002] (see above). For the ownership technique the invariants containing only the following *access expressions* $a_1 \cdots a_n$ ($a_i$ are field names or array accesses) are admissible: (a) single field name, (b) access expression with admissible prefixes followed by a constant field access, (c) sequence of field accesses with admissible prefixes and the first element is annotated with `rep` and all other (except for the last) are annotated with `rep` or `peer`. The proof obligations for the ownership technique aim at the *relevant invariant semantics* (see above). They require for every call in a method which is being verified that, before a method call, the current receiver object's invariant holds if the called method is in the same context. One may in turn *assume* that the invariants of all relevant objects hold before and after a method call.

The visibility based part additionally allows for access expressions which consist of field chains with `peer` annotated fields. The invariant containing such a chain must be *visible* for each class which declares a field of such a chain. Then one must show that the invariants of all visible classes in the current receiver's context hold after method execution and that the same holds before a call to another method in the current receiver's context is performed.

The ownership approach relies, as our guards, on *encapsulation*. However our encapsulation is more liberal: In the ownership jargon we allow for several owners, if they all adhere to invariants. This makes instruments like readonly references obsolete. For example the Producer-Consumer example (Sect. 10.3.1) which serves in that work as an example for the expressiveness of the technique could as well be solved by our technique (see Sect. 10.3.1). Moreover we can even allow `Consumer` to update the common buffer, which is not possible with the other approach.

Our technique does not have a direct visibility based part. Our self-guards may take over the role of visibility based invariants, however. For instance, a typical running example of Müller et al. [2004] for visibility based invariants, as depicted in Fig. 11.1, is treated by our technique as an invariant which is protected by a depends clause {∗.`spouse`.`spouse`, ∗.`spouse`}. `Person` is a self-guard of it. An important difference can be seen at this example: our guards are class based, not object based. This fits perfectly well to the fact that static verification aims at classes, not objects. In the example, neither

```
class Person {
  private /*@spec_public@*/ Person spouse;
  /*@ public invariant spouse==null || spouse.spouse==this @*/
  public void marry(Person p) {
    spouse=p;
    p.spouse=this;
  }
}
```

**Figure 11.1:** Example from Müller et al. [2004] as application of the visibility technique

a particular `Person` instance $p$ nor $p$'s spouse is responsible to protect the invariant but the class `Person` itself.

Another paper about exploiting the Universe approach to modularly ensure invariants is van den Berg et al. [2001]. They discuss under which conditions invariants can be assumed and which invariants must be proven. They define a conservative approach which essentially corresponds to the non-modular approach to preserve *all* invariants, but here with the restriction that these objects are *relevant*, in *all* operations. Relevance is not further specified. Moreover a more liberal approach is defined which relies on a technique like Universes.

Another major difference between ours and Universe based approaches is that, when a component is verified based on Universes, all reuse contexts must be be specified with Universe annotations, too. With our approach there are no such obligations to the context, except from generic contracts which must be obeyed by the context.

### The Boogie Methodology

The Spec# system [Barnett et al., 2005] supports an approach described in Barnett et al. [2004] (also called *Boogie Methodology* in some places) which makes explicit when invariants must hold. Classes contain always the field `inv` which is only allowed in specifications and the special methods `pack` and `unpack`. It is assigned the name of a supertype of its receiver object. Calling $o$.`pack(`$T$`)` on an object $o$ with a supertype of $T$ requires that the invariant of $o$ holds and sets $o$.`inv` to $T$. $o$.`unpack(`$T$`)` sets $o$.`inv` to the direct superclass of $T$. Moreover there is a specification-only boolean field `committed`, with the intention that $o$.`committed` is set to true only if $o$.`inv` equals the dynamic type of $o$. Furthermore a notion of ownership is introduced: fields may be declared with a `rep` modifier. Then $o$.`pack(`$T$`)` performs the following additional tasks: it requires that `inv` is already set to the direct supertype of $T$ and that all object references through a `rep` field have set `inv` to their dynamic type. It then commits these `rep` objects, and as already described, sets $o$.`inv` to $T$. $o$.`unpack(`$T$`)` in turn sets all `rep` objects' `committed` fields to `false`.

Field updates to $o$.`a` are now only possible if $o$.`inv` is set to a strict superclass of the class which $a$ is declared in. With this, in every program state and for every object $o$, if $o$.`inv` is set to $T$ then all (instance) invariants of $T$ hold for $o$.

This approach is extended by the work of Leino and Müller [2004] and of Barnett and Naumann [2004] which add more visibility based techniques, but maintain the general idea.

The Boogie methodology needs lots of new specification constructs which the developer must in detail know about. They are of an imperative nature (`pack`, `unpack`) and thus do not fit well into what we usually consider as functional declarative specification. The whole approach resembles more an extension of a programming model, that is programmers must conform to a certain protocol when assigning to locations. Moreover these annotation are not on a per-method basis (like operation contracts), but are assertions to be written inbetween of regular statements. All this clutters the usual design by contract based approach of specifying object-oriented programs. Invariants are furthermore treated as belonging to a particular object. We have seen that this is not necessarily the case. Finally, we believe that the classical view that invariants *must* hold at some places—according to durable observed-state correctness in the observer—is still what ordinary programmers expect. In general, they do not want to care about explicit markers that tell when an object is in a valid state. But the latter is definitely a remark which must be validated by practical experience with both approaches.

## 11.2 Future Work

We have shown the correctness of our approach and found it useful in our practical experiments. We have however not yet formally explored *complete-*

*ness* issues, such as an answer to the question if our technique classifies all durable correct programs as correct, relative to the classical completeness results for the used logic. Probably such a result will be difficult to achieve since it requires to consider, in the definition of observed-state correctness, *reachable* states which we would need to characterise *completely* by expressions of our, or an extended, specification language.

Though we have provided a treatment of assignable clauses, assignable clauses which refer to *abstract fields* or *data groups* are not covered. Abstract fields in assignable clauses allow to specify which set of locations may be modified also by extensions [Müller et al., 2003, Leino and Nelson, 2002]. Extending classes may associate concrete fields with these abstract fields. This allows also for better information hiding since fields declared as private are not necessarily exposed to the outside. We currently treat this issue by assigning assignable clauses to method *declarations*. That is, operation contracts are not inherited and thus, in principal, overriding methods may declare completely new assignable clauses. Extension contracts may then restrict allowed overridings in the sense that assignable clauses may only contain locations newly introduced by the subclass—in addition to the original assignable clause. However this approach does not solve issues with information hiding. This could be tackled by extending our approach to abstract fields. This however would imply to change a number of other artifacts like updates.

Generic extension contracts have only been elaborated as much as was needed in our work. It is well possible that there are more useful instantiation constraints than those we have presented. Here further practical experiences would be valuable.

Though our examples presented in Sect. 10.3 showed that our approach is viable, we consider it desirable to apply our approach to larger case studies.

## 11.3 Summary of This Work

Our work was concerned with the question how specification and verification can be efficiently applied to object-oriented components which are composed in an arbitrary manner.

Object-oriented programming languages like Java make it relatively easy to re-use and adapt parts of a component. Because of this, verification of components written in these languages is difficult. The main facility to adapt behaviour to new contexts, which is overriding methods and exploiting dynamic binding, is one of the problems which we are facing with the verification of components. The other problem is unrestricted aliasing of mutable objects. The latter makes objects which depend on a number of other objects prone to be transferred into an invalid state.

Unlike other approaches we rely on the abilities of a programmer to master the occurring problems by means of existing programming languages like Java. We do not extend the programming language. What we do instead is to extend the capabilities of specification languages to capture formally what a programmer has in mind in order to make the component *correct*.

There are two principal ways to go to make a component correct from a developer's point of view, which can be combined in many ways. A component can be constructed either (a) 'strong enough' to ensure a certain behaviour in *every* possible context or (b) the allowed context is constrained such that the component can ensure this behaviour. In its pure form, a decision for (a) requires (i) data encapsulation and (ii) absence of dynamic binding by using restrictive programming language accessibility modifiers. This—and especially the second item—makes systems, often undesirably, inextensible. The application domain will determine whether this is acceptable or not, for instance in safety critical domains it will likely be acceptable. If it is not, then it may be better to impose obligations on the context, for instance by requiring that subclasses must be behavioural subtypes.

We have provided formal techniques to capture both, encapsulation and restrictions on the context. *Encapsulation predicates* aim at the former, *generic extension contracts* at the latter. Both appear to the developer as natural extensions of existing specification languages.

With these two techniques, deductive verification can be applied to components. We first needed to clarify what the goal of verification, namely the *correctness* of components should be. We have defined several notions of correctness:

(1) *naive* correctness,
(2) *observed-state call* correctness,
(3) *observed-state durable* correctness, and
(4) *observed-state relative-durable* correctness.

Items (1) and (2) were rather easily establishable and left assumptions to the client of a component, as for instance to establish invariants. With (3) most tasks, such as the maintenance of invariants, were adopted by the component itself. (4) liberalised this again by allowing to impose extension contracts on the context. Only the two latter turned out to be useful for components.

Deductive verification includes two major parts: (a) a *calculus* which allows to discharge statements about programs, (b) the generation of *proof obligations* which are the input statements to be deduced by the calculus. Both parts needed to be addressed when dealing with components.

For (a) we have investigated the non-modular JavaDL calculus for Java and adapted it such that *relative validity* of formulae can be achieved. Mainly the rule to resolve dynamic method dispatching was affected.

For (b) we have defined proof obligations which served to establish single properties of operations including the correctness of assignable clauses, call correctness, durable correctness, and relative durable correctness. The main problem to adequately establish (relative) durable correctness is unrestricted aliasing of mutable objects which class invariants depend on. Our technique first extracts relevant locations of class invariants resulting in *depends clauses*. This makes only the really necessary data being encapsulated. Then *guard* or *self-guard* classes are identified which are in full control over modifications to objects relevant to these locations. Guardedness is a property which can be expressed by means of encapsulation predicates and which can be proven. Finally only these classes need to be verified with respect to the considered invariant. This makes verification modular.

Applying formal specification and verification to components considerably increases trust in the work of components. In fact, the made guarantees are the most rigid we can imagine. We have shown that, with our technique, there is no obstacle to specify and verify object-oriented components written in Java-like languages such that they work as promised wherever they are employed.

# Bibliography


Jean-Raymond Abrial. *The B Book: Assigning Programs to Meanings.* Cambridge University Press, August 1996.

Wolfgang Ahrendt, Thomas Baar, Bernhard Beckert, Richard Bubel, Martin Giese, Reiner Hähnle, Wolfram Menzel, Wojciech Mostowski, Andreas Roth, Steffen Schlager, and Peter H. Schmitt. The KeY Tool. *Software and System Modeling*, 4(1):32–54, 2005a.

Wolfgang Ahrendt, Andreas Roth, and Ralf Sasse. Automatic validation of transformation rules for Java verification against a rewriting semantics. In Geoff Sutcliffe and Andrei Voronkov, editors, *LPAR*, volume 3835 of *Lecture Notes in Computer Science*, pages 412–426. Springer, 2005b. ISBN 3-540-30553-X.

Paulo Sergio Almeida. Controlling sharing of state in data types. In M. Aksit and S. Matsuoka, editors, *ECOOP '97–Object-Oriented Programming*, volume 1241 of *Lecture Notes in Computer Science*, pages 32–59. Springer, 1997.

Uwe Aßmann. *Invasive Software Composition.* Springer-Verlag, 2003. ISBN 3-540-44385-1.

Thomas Baar. The definition of transitive closure with OCL—limitations and applications. In *Proceedings, Fifth Andrei Ershov International Conference, Perspectives of System Informatics, Novosibirsk, Russia*, volume 2890 of *Lecture Notes in Computer Science*, pages 358–365. Springer, July 2003.

Thomas Baar, Bernhard Beckert, and Peter H. Schmitt. An extension of Dynamic Logic for modelling OCL's *@pre* operator. In *Proceedings, Fourth Andrei Ershov International Conference, Perspectives of System Informatics, Novosibirsk, Russia*, volume 2244 of *LNCS*, pages 47–54. Springer, 2001.

Anindya Banerjee and David A. Naumann. State based ownership, reentrance, and encapsulation. In Andrew P. Black, editor, *ECOOP*, volume 3586 of *Lecture Notes in Computer Science*, pages 387–411. Springer, 2005. ISBN 3-540-27992-X.

Michael Barnett and David A. Naumann. Friends need a bit more: Maintaining invariants over shared state. In Dexter Kozen and Carron Shankland, editors, *MPC*, volume 3125 of *Lecture Notes in Computer Science*, pages 54–84. Springer, 2004. ISBN 3-540-22380-0.

Michael Barnett, Robert DeLine, Manuel Fähndrich, K. Rustan M. Leino, and Wolfram Schulte. Verification of object-oriented programs with invariants. *Journal of Object Technology*, 3(6):27–56, 2004.

Mike Barnett, K. Rustan M. Leino, and Wolfram Schulte. The Spec# programming system: An overview. In *CASSIS 2005 Post Conference Proceedings*. Springer, 2005.

Detlef Bartetzko, Clemens Fischer, Michael Möller, and Heike Wehrheim. Jass - Java with assertions. *Electr. Notes Theor. Comput. Sci.*, 55(2), 2001.

Bernhard Beckert. A dynamic logic for the formal verification of Java Card programs. In Isabelle Attali and Thomas P. Jensen, editors, *Java Card Workshop*, volume 2041 of *Lecture Notes in Computer Science*, pages 6–24. Springer, 2000. ISBN 3-540-42167-X.

Bernhard Beckert and Bettina Sasse. Handling Java's abrupt termination in a sequent calculus for Dynamic Logic. In B. Beckert, R. France, R. Hähnle, and B. Jacobs, editors, *Proceedings, IJCAR Workshop on Precise Modelling and Deduction for Object-oriented Software Development, Siena, Italy*, pages 5–14. Technical Report DII 07/01, Dipartimento di Ingegneria dell'Informazione, Università degli Studi di Siena, 2001.

Bernhard Beckert and Peter H. Schmitt. Program verification using change information. In *Proceedings, Software Engineering and Formal Methods (SEFM), Brisbane, Australia*, pages 91–99. IEEE Press, 2003.

Bernhard Beckert, Uwe Keller, and Peter H. Schmitt. Translating the Object Constraint Language into first-order predicate logic. In *Proceedings,*

*VERIFY, Workshop at Federated Logic Conferences (FLoC), Copenhagen, Denmark*, 2002.

Bernhard Beckert, Martin Giese, Elmar Habermalz, Reiner Hähnle, Andreas Roth, Philipp Rümmer, and Steffen Schlager. Taclets: A new paradigm for constructing interactive theorem provers. *Revista de la Real Academia de Ciencias Exactas, Físicas y Naturales, Serie A: Matemáticas (RACSAM)*, 98(1), 2004. Special Issue on Symbolic Computation in Logic and Artificial Intelligence.

Bernhard Beckert, Reiner Hähnle, and Peter H. Schmitt, editors. *The KeY Book*. Springer, 2006a.

Bernhard Beckert, Vladimir Klebanov, and Steffen Schlager. Dynamic logic. In Bernhard Beckert, Reiner Hähnle, and Peter H. Schmitt, editors, *The KeY Book*. Springer, 2006b.

Joshua Bloch. *Effective Java: Programming Language Guide*. The Java Series. Addison-Wesley, 2001.

Alexander Borgida, John Mylopoulos, and Raymond Reiter. On the frame problem in procedure specifications. *IEEE Trans. Software Eng.*, 21(10): 785–798, 1995.

Chandrasekhar Boyapati, Barbara Liskov, and Liuba Shrira. Ownership types for object encapsulation. In *ACM Symposium on Principles of Programming Languages (POPL)*, New Orleans, Louisiana, January 2003.

John Boyland. Alias burying: Unique variables without destructive reads. *Software—Practice and Experience*, 31(6):533–553, May 2001.

Manfred Broy and Johannes Siedersleben. Objektorientierte Programmierung und Softwareentwicklung - Eine kritische Einschätzung. *Informatik Spektrum*, 25(1):3–11, 2002. (in German).

Richard Bubel. Behandlung der Initialisierung von Klassen und Objekten in einer dynamischen Logik für JavaCard. Studienarbeit, Fakultät für Informatik, Universität Karlsruhe, 2001. (in German).

Richard Bubel and Reiner Hähnle. Formal specification of security-critical railway software with the KeY system. *Software Tools for Technology Transfer*, 7(3):197–211, June 2005.

Richard Bubel, Andreas Roth, and Philipp Rümmer. Ensuring correctness of lightweight tactics for Java Card Dynamic Logic. In *Proceedings of Workshop on Logical Frameworks and Meta-Languages (LFM) at Second International Joint Conference on Automated Reasoning 2004*, pages 84–105, 2004.

L. Burdy, A. Requet, and J.-L. Lanet. Java applet correctness: A developer-oriented approach. In K. Araki, S. Gnesi, and D. Mandrioli, editors, *FME 2003: Formal Methods: International Symposium of Formal Methods Europe*, volume 2805 of *Lecture Notes in Computer Science*, pages 422–439. Springer-Verlag, 2003.

Daniel Burrows. Static encapsulation analysis of Featherweight Java. Master's thesis, Graduate School of Pennsylvania State University, 2005.

F. Buschmann, R. Meunier, H. Rohnert, P. Sommerlad, and M. Stal. *Pattern-Oriented Software Architecture — A System of Patterns.* John-Wiley and Sons, 1996.

N. Cataño and M. Huisman. Chase: A static checker for JML's assignable clause. In Lenore D. Zuck, Paul C. Attie, Agostino Cortesi, and Supratik Mukhopadhyay, editors, *VMCAI: Verification, Model Checking and Abstract Interpretation*, volume 2575 of *Lecture Notes in Computer Science*, pages 26–40, New York, NY, USA, January 9-11 2003. Springer.

Dave Clarke, John Potter, and James Noble. Ownership types for flexible alias protection. In *ACM Conference on Object-Oriented Programming Systems, Languages and Applications (OOPSLA'98)*, Vancouver, Canada, October 1998.

Dave Clarke, James Noble, and John Potter. Who's afraid of ownership types? Technical report, Microsoft Research Institute, 1999.

David R. Cok and Joseph Kiniry. ESC/Java2: Uniting ESC/Java and JML. In Gilles Barthe, Lilian Burdy, Marieke Huisman, Jean-Louis Lanet, and Traian Muntean, editors, *CASSIS*, volume 3362 of *Lecture Notes in Computer Science*, pages 108–128. Springer, 2004. ISBN 3-540-24287-2.

W. Dietl and P. Müller. Universes: Lightweight ownership for JML. *Journal of Object Technology (JOT)*, 2005. To appear.

R. Duke, P. King, G. A. Rose, and G. Smith. The Object-Z specification language. In T. Korson, V. Vaishnavi, and B. Meyer, editors, *Technology of Object-Oriented Languages and Systems: TOOLS 5*, pages 465–483. Prentice Hall, 1991.

Andrew Duncan and Urs Hölzle. Adding contracts to Java with handshake. Technical Report TRCS98-32, The University of California at Santa Barbara, December 1998.

Christian Engel. A Translation from JML to JavaDL. Studienarbeit, Fakultät für Informatik, Universität Karlsruhe, February 2005.

Robert Bruce Findler and Matthias Felleisen. Contract soundness for object-oriented languages. In *OOPSLA '01: Proceedings of the 16th ACM SIGPLAN conference on Object oriented programming, systems, languages, and applications*, pages 1–15, New York, NY, USA, 2001. ACM Press. ISBN 1-58113-335-9.

Erich Gamma, Richard Helm, Ralph Johnson, and John Vlissides. *Design Patterns: Elements of Reusable Object-Oriented Software.* Addison-Wesley, Reading/MA, 1995.

Martin Giese. First order logic. In Bernhard Beckert, Reiner Hähnle, and Peter H. Schmitt, editors, *The KeY Book.* Springer, 2006.

James Gosling, Bill Joy, Guy Steele, and Gilad Bracha. *The Java Language Specification Second Edition.* Addison-Wesley, Boston, Mass., 2000. ISBN 0-201-31008-2.

James Gosling, Bill Joy, Guy Steele, and Gilad Bracha. *The Java Language Specification Third Edition.* Addison-Wesley, Boston, Mass., 2005.

Mark Grand. *Patterns in Java, volume 1.* John Wiley & Sons, Inc., 1998. ISBN 0-471-25839-3.

Mark Grand. *Patterns in Java, volume 2.* John Wiley & Sons, Inc., 1999. ISBN 0-471-25841-5.

David Gries and Fred B. Schneider. Avoiding the undefined by underspecification. In Jan van Leeuwen, editor, *Computer Science Today*, volume

1000 of *Lecture Notes in Computer Science*, pages 366–373. Springer, 1995. ISBN 3-540-60105-8.

John V. Guttag and James J. Horning, editors. *Larch: Languages and Tools for Formal Specification.* Texts and Monographs in Computer Science. Springer-Verlag, 1993. With Stephen J. Garland, Kevin D. Jones, Andrés Modet, and Jeannette M. Wing.

Richard Helm, Ian M. Holland, and Dipayan Gangopadhyay. Contracts: Specifying behavioural compositions in object-oriented systems. In *OOPSLA/ECOOP*, pages 169–180, 1990.

Thomas A. Henzinger, Shaz Qadeer, and Sriram K. Rajamani. You assume, we guarantee: Methodology and case studies. In Alan J. Hu and Moshe Y. Vardi, editors, *CAV*, volume 1427 of *Lecture Notes in Computer Science*, pages 440–451. Springer, 1998. ISBN 3-540-64608-6.

C. A. R. Hoare. An axiomatic basis for computer programming. *Commun. ACM*, 12(10):576–580, 1969. ISSN 0001-0782.

John Hogg. Islands: Aliasing protection in object-oriented languages. In *OOPSLA*, pages 271–285, 1991.

Kees Huizing and Ruurd Kuiper. Verification of object oriented programs using class invariants. In T. S. E. Maibaum, editor, *FASE*, volume 1783 of *Lecture Notes in Computer Science*, pages 208–221. Springer, 2000. ISBN 3-540-67261-3.

B. Jacobs and E. Poll. Java program verification at Nijmegen: Developments and perspective. In *Software Security - Theories and Systems: Second Mext-NSF-JSPS International Symposium, ISSS 2003, Tokyo, Japan, November 4-6, 2003*, volume 3233 of *LNCS*, pages 134 – 153. Springer, 2004. An earlier version appears as Technical Report NIII-R0316, Radboud University Nijmegen.

C. B. Jones. Tentative steps toward a development method for interfering programs. *ACM Trans. Program. Lang. Syst.*, 5(4):596–619, 1983. ISSN 0164-0925.

Murat Karaorman, Urs Hölzle, and John Bruno. jContractor: A reflective Java library to support design by contract. In *Proceedings of Meta-Level Architectures and Reflection*, volume 1616 of *LNCS*, July 1999.

Bastian Katz. Eine Modifies Klausel in KeY. Studienarbeit, Fakultät für Informatik, Universität Karlsruhe, 2003. (in German).

Reto Kramer. iContract—the Java Designs by Contract tool. In *Proc. Technology of Object-Oriented Languages and Systems, TOOLS 26, Santa Barbara/CA, USA*. IEEE CS Press, Los Alamitos, 1998.

Gary T. Leavens, Erik Poll, Curtis Clifton, Yoonsik Cheon, Clyde Ruby, David R. Cok, Peter Müller, and Joseph Kiniry. JML reference manual. Department of Computer Science, Iowa State University. Available from `http://www.jmlspecs.org`, July 2005.

Gary T. Leavens, Albert L. Baker, and Clyde Ruby. Preliminary design of JML: A behavioral interface specification language for Java. Technical Report 98-06-rev29, Iowa State University, Department of Computer Science, January 2006. URL `ftp://ftp.cs.iastate.edu/pub/techreports/TR98-06/TR.pdf`. To appear in *ACM SIGSOFT Software Engineering Notes*.

K. Rustan M. Leino and Peter Müller. Object invariants in dynamic contexts. In Martin Odersky, editor, *ECOOP*, volume 3086 of *Lecture Notes in Computer Science*, pages 491–516. Springer, 2004. ISBN 3-540-22159-X.

K. Rustan M. Leino and Greg Nelson. Data abstraction and information hiding. *ACM Trans. Program. Lang. Syst.*, 24(5):491–553, 2002. ISSN 0164-0925.

Claude Marché, Christine Paulin-Mohring, and Xavier Urbain. The Krakatoa tool for certification of Java/JavaCard programs annotated in JML. *J. Log. Algebr. Program.*, 58(1-2):89–106, 2004.

Bertrand Meyer. Applying Design by Contract. *IEEE Computer*, 25(10): 40–51, October 1992. ISSN 0018-9162.

Bertrand Meyer. *Object-oriented software construction (2nd ed.)*. Prentice-Hall, Inc., Upper Saddle River, NJ, USA, 1997. ISBN 0-13-629155-4.

J. Meyer, P. Müller, and A. Poetzsch-Heffter. The JIVE system — implementation description. Available from `sct.inf.ethz.ch`, 2000.

Wojciech Mostowski. *Formal Development of Safe and Secure Java Card Applets.* PhD thesis, Chalmers University of Technology, Department of Computer Science and Engineering, Göteborg, Sweden, February 2005.

P. Müller and A. Poetzsch-Heffter. Universes: A type system for alias and dependency control. Technical Report 279, Fernuniversität Hagen, 2001.

P. Müller, A. Poetzsch-Heffter, and G. T. Leavens. Modular specification of frame properties in JML. *Concurrency and Computation: Practice and Experience*, 15:117–154, 2003.

P. Müller, A. Poetzsch-Heffter, and G. T. Leavens. Modular invariants for layered object structures. Technical Report 424, Department of Computer Science, ETH Zurich, 2004.

Peter Müller. *Modular specification and verification of object-oriented programs.* Springer-Verlag New York, Inc., 2002. ISBN 3-540-43167-5.

Greg Nelson. Verifying reachability invariants of linked structures. In *Proceedings of the 10th ACM SIGACT-SIGPLAN symposium on Principles of programming languages*, pages 38–47. ACM Press, 1983. ISBN 0-89791-090-7.

James Noble, Robert Biddle, Ewan Tempero, Alex Potanin, and Dave Clarke. Towards a model of encapsulation. In *International Workshop on Aliasing, Confinement, and Ownership (IWACO)*, Darmstadt, Germany, July 2003.

OMG. *UML 2.0 Specification.* Object Management Group, 2003.

Object Modeling Group. UML 2.0 OCL specification, Nov 2003. OMG document ad/2003-10-14.

A. Poetzsch-Heffter. Specification and verification of object-oriented programs. Habilitation thesis, Technical University of Munich, January 1997.

Andreas Roth. Deduktiver Softwareentwurf am Beispiel des Java Collections Frameworks. Diplomarbeit, Fakultät für Informatik, Universität Karlsruhe, June 2002. (in German).

Andreas Roth. Specification and verification of encapsulation in Java programs. In Martin Steffen and Gianluigi Zavattaro, editors, *FMOODS*, volume 3535 of *Lecture Notes in Computer Science*, pages 195–210. Springer, 2005. ISBN 3-540-26181-8.

Andreas Roth. Proof obligations. In Bernhard Beckert, Reiner Hähnle, and Peter H. Schmitt, editors, *The KeY Book*. Springer, 2006.

Andreas Roth and Peter H. Schmitt. Ensuring invariant contracts for modules in java. In *Proceedings of the ECOOP Workshop FTfJP 2004 Formal Techniques for Java-like Programs*, number NIII-R0426 in Technical Report, University of Nijmegen, pages 93–102, June 2004.

Andreas Roth and Peter H. Schmitt. Specifications. In Bernhard Beckert, Reiner Hähnle, and Peter H. Schmitt, editors, *The KeY Book*. Springer, 2006. to appear.

Philipp Rümmer. Ensuring the soundness of Taclets—construction of proof obligations for JavaCardDL Taclets. Studienarbeit, Fakultät für Informatik, Universität Karlsruhe, Dec 2003.

Philipp Rümmer. A language for sequential, parallel, and quantified updates of first-order structures, Mar 2005. forthcoming.

Ralf Sasse. Proof obligations for correctness of modifies clauses. Studienarbeit, Fakultät für Informatik, Universität Karlsruhe, October 2004.

Ralf Sasse. Taclets vs. rewriting logic—relating semantics of Java. Technical Report in Computing Science No. 2005-16, Fakultät für Informatik, Universität Karlsruhe, Germany, May 2005.

J. M. Spivey. *The Z Notation: A Reference Manual.* Prentice Hall International Series in Computer Science, 2nd edition, 1992.

Fausto Spoto and Erik Poll. Static analysis for JML's assignable clauses. In *Foundations of Object-Oriented Languages (FOOL10)*, 2003.

Sun Microsystems, Inc. Java 2 Platform, Standard Edition, v 1.4.2 API Specification, 2003a. URL `http://java.sun.com/j2se/1.4.2/docs/api/`.

Sun Microsystems, Inc. *Java Card 2.2 Platform Specification*. Sun Microsystems, Inc., Palo Alto/CA, USA, September 2002b. URL `java.sun.com/products/javacard/specs.html`.

Clemens Szyperski. *Component Software*. Addison-Wesley, 1998.

Kerry Trentelman. Proving correctness of JavaCardDL Taclets using Bali. In Bernhard K. Aichernig and Bernhard Beckert, editors, *SEFM*, pages 160–169. IEEE Computer Society, 2005. ISBN 0-7695-2435-4.

J. van den Berg, C.-B. Breunesse, B. Jacobs, and E. Poll. On the role of invariants in reasoning about object-oriented languages. In *Formal Techniques for Java Programs. Proceedings of the ECOOP'2001 Workshop*, 2001.

Jan Vitek and Boris Bokowski. Confined types in Java. *Software—Practice and Experience*, 31(6):507–532, 2001.

Jos Warmer and Anneke Kleppe. *The Object Constraint Language: Precise Modelling with UML*. Object Technology Series. Addison-Wesley, Reading/MA, 1999.

Benjamin Weiß. Proving encapsulation in KeY with the Universe type system. Studienarbeit, Fakultät für Informatik, Universität Karlsruhe, 2006.

Printed in Dunstable, United Kingdom

91343791R00151